RENAISSANCE DRAMA
New Series III ❧ *1970*

Renaissance Drama

New Series III

*Essays Principally
on Drama in Its
Intellectual Context*

Edited by S. Schoenbaum

Northwestern University Press

EVANSTON 1970

THE ILLUSTRATION on the front cover is a reproduction of an anonymous woodcut of Machiavelli taken from Orestes Ferrara, *Machiavel* (Paris, 1928). The original is in the print room of the Bibliothèque Nationale. The illustration on the back cover is from Francis Kirkman, *The Wits, or Sport Upon Sport* (London, 1662).

Editorial Note

RENAISSANCE DRAMA, an annual publication, provides a forum for scholars in various parts of the globe: wherever the drama of the Renaissance is studied. Coverage, so far as subject matter is concerned, is not restricted to any single national theater. The chronological limits of the Renaissance are interpreted liberally, and space is available for essays on precursors, as well as on the utilization of Renaissance themes by later writers. Editorial policy favors articles of some scope. Essays that are exploratory in nature, that are concerned with critical or scholarly methodology, that raise new questions or embody fresh approaches to perennial problems are particularly appropriate for a publication which originated from the proceedings of the Modern Language Association Conference on Research Opportunities in Renaissance Drama.

Volume IV of this series will have as its focus the playwright in the playhouse. The editors would like to encourage contributions on such topics as Renaissance playhouses and players, the stage history of plays of the period, problems of staging both in original production and in modern revivals; also critical studies emphasizing theatrical considerations. Manuscripts, for which the deadline is 15 September 1971, should be addressed to the

Editor, RENAISSANCE DRAMA, Northwestern University, 617 Foster Street, Evanston, Illinois 60201. Prospective contributors are requested to follow the recommendations of the *MLA Style Sheet* (revised edition) in preparing manuscripts. For quotations from Shakespeare the Alexander edition is used.

Contents

RENAISSANCE DRAMA

New Series III ❧ *1970*

Machiavelli and Marlowe's
The Jew of Malta

N. W. BAWCUTT

M ARLOWE's *The Jew of Malta* opens with a prologue put into the
mouth of Machiavelli. This prologue has provoked a good deal
of discussion, but there seems to be no consensus on how we should
respond to it. For some scholars Machiavelli is the presiding genius of the
play; for others it is obvious, in view of the opinions Marlowe attributed
to Machiavelli, that he possessed little accurate knowledge of him. It has
also been debated whether the prologue has a genuine relationship to the
rest of the play or is simply an extraneous piece of sensationalism which
may even have been added after the play itself was written. I should
make it clear immediately that I have not discovered any fresh evidence
that proves beyond doubt that Marlowe either had or had not read
Machiavelli's own writings, though it would surely be surprising if a

I should like to thank those who helped me to get hold of otherwise inaccessible
material during the preparation of this essay: Professor Clifford Leech; Professor
Giorgio Melchiori; Miss Eda Whelan, formerly of the Harold Cohen Library,
The University of Liverpool; and Miss Phyllis Downie of Edinburgh University
Library. Professor Leech, Professor Harold Jenkins, and Mr. B. F. Nellist read the
typescript and made helpful suggestions for improvements.

3

man of Marlowe's temperament had had no firsthand contact with the work of such a notorious figure. My intention is to set Marlowe's play in the context of the sixteenth-century response to Machiavelli, or rather, since this is a very large and complicated topic, of those aspects of the sixteenth-century response which seem to me to throw most light on Marlowe. When *The Jew of Malta* is seen in this context, I would argue, some of the difficulties of interpreting its Machiavellian element are much more easily resolved.

Marlowe's play is generally thought to have been written in 1589 or 1590, and I have therefore tried to choose the greater part of the illustrative material from books published before 1589. A quotation from an individual work is not intended to imply that Marlowe himself must necessarily have read that particular book; it simply indicates that certain ideas were current in Marlowe's day and easily accessible to him. In discussing Machiavelli himself, I have taken into account only those writings by him which were in print by 1589 and have ignored manuscripts, letters, and diplomatic documents which were not printed until long after the sixteenth century.

I

The first necessity, however, is to clear out of the way a harmful oversimplification which has proved remarkably persistent. I think it very unlikely that Marlowe simply took over his prologue ready-made from a single source. Ever since Meyer came across a Latin poem by Gabriel Harvey published in 1577 and argued that Marlowe's prologue was indebted to it, scholars have repeated the assertion, sometimes in a wildly exaggerated form.[1] In fact, all the two passages have in common is that they are both put into the mouth of Machiavelli, and there are no detailed resemblances between them. The only specific comparison made by Meyer was between Harvey's

Aut nihil, aut Caesar; noster Alumnus erat[2]

1. Edward Meyer, *Machiavelli and the Elizabethan Drama* (Weimar, 1897), pp. 22–23.

2. Gabriel Harvey, "Epigramma in effigiem Machiavelli: Machiavellus ipse loquitur," *Gratulationum valdinensium libri quattuor* (London, 1577), II, 9.

and Marlowe's

> What right had Caesar to the empery? [3]

As the two Caesars are different individuals, the similarity is illusory. "Aut Caesar, aut nihil" was the personal motto of Cesare Borgia, and "noster Alumnus erat" (which some scholars have found puzzling) means that Harvey's version of Machiavelli claims Borgia as his pupil. Marlowe's line makes full sense only in connection with the line before ("Many will talk of title to a crown"); the reference is to Julius Caesar, and in particular to the controversy, which continued for many centuries, whether Caesar, who had no legal right to his power, ought to be regarded as a tyrant or not, since the absence of a legal title to power was one of the stock characteristics of a tyrant.[4]

Harvey and Marlowe also differ considerably in the tone of their writing. Harvey is vague and bombastic; his Machiavelli is a literally bloodthirsty monster with a sword in one hand, a stone in the other, and poisons lurking in his mouth. Marlowe's Machiavelli is self-confident, scornful, and sarcastic, and his list of precepts, whatever its relationship may be to Machiavelli's own opinions, does have some affinity with Machiavelli's manner of writing, his concise and sometimes ironic expression of a rapid sequence of ideas. It seems unnecessary, therefore, to argue that Marlowe borrowed anything more from Harvey than a very general hint or outline. I should also make it clear that Marlowe's prologue has little in common with Gentillet's famous attack on Machiavelli, first published anonymously in 1576.[5] There are indeed one or two parallels, which will be discussed later, but certainly not the succession of reasonably close resemblances we should expect if Marlowe were writing with Gentillet open in front of him. In addition, the two writers coincide chiefly at

3. Prologue, l. 19. All references are to *The Jew of Malta and The Massacre at Paris,* ed. H. S. Bennett (London, 1931).

4. For a Renaissance discussion see Coluccio Salutati, *De tyranno,* chap. III (trans. E. Emerton in *Humanism and Tyranny* [Cambridge, Mass., 1925], pp. 93 ff.). The political significance of the controversy over Caesar is stressed by Hans Baron, *The Crisis of the Early Italian Renaissance,* 2d ed. (Princeton, N. J., 1966), pp. 48 ff.

5. *Discours sur les moyens de bien gouverner et maintenir en bonne paix un royaume ou autre principaute . . . contre Nicholas Machiavel Florentin* (n. p., 1576); Latin trans. (n. p., 1577); English trans. (London, 1602).

points where Gentillet expresses fairly commonplace sentiments that Marlowe could easily have acquired elsewhere. But it seems quite likely that Marlowe read Gentillet, and a number of the ideas contained in Gentillet can help us to a better understanding of Marlowe.

II

Before we can generalize confidently about the English reaction to Machiavelli in the sixteenth century, we need to assemble as wide a range of material as possible. If we compare Meyer's pioneering study with the work of Mario Praz, and with Felix Raab's brilliant *The English Face of Machiavelli*,[6] one obvious reason for the superiority of the later scholars is that they drew upon a strikingly larger range of material than was available to Meyer. But though much has already been done, there are still gleanings to be made,[7] and Raab did not sufficiently emphasize the foreign influence in the English response to Machiavelli. No doubt there were important national differences, which should not be minimized, in sixteenth-century attitudes to Machiavelli, but there were also trends and influences which were international. The major writings on Machiavelli were frequently carried across national boundaries, sometimes regardless of political and religious oppositions. One of the earliest attacks on Machiavelli, the *De nobilitate Christiana* of the Portuguese bishop Osorio, was first published in Lisbon in 1542, then in Florence in 1552, and then in London, first in translation in 1576 and then in Latin in 1580; it was well known to Roger Ascham[8] and was praised by Laurence Humphrey.[9] Admittedly the book has only a little to say about Machiavelli, but many Englishmen must have come into contact with it.

The major foreign influence undoubtedly came from France. It would

6. Mario Praz, "The Politic Brain: Machiavelli and the Elizabethans," in *The Flaming Heart* (New York, 1958), pp. 90–145. (This essay was first published in 1928.) Felix Raab, *The English Face of Machiavelli* (London, 1964).

7. Several of the allusions quoted in this paper are not mentioned by Raab. See also "Some Elizabethan Allusions to Machiavelli," *English Miscellany*, XX (1969), 53–74.

8. See L. V. Ryan, *Roger Ascham* (Stanford, Calif., 1963), p. 208.

9. *The Nobles, or of Nobilitye* (London, 1563), fol. Biiiᵛ.

be a gross mistake to assume that the French reaction can be equated simply with Gentillet; there were numerous French discussions of Machiavelli before and after Gentillet, who added little of real significance to what his predecessors had said, and my impression is that no study of this subject has yet been published which is adequate to the full complexity of the material and does for France what Raab has done for England. All Machiavelli's major writings were translated into French by 1577, and some much earlier than that; the translations of *The Prince* and *Discourses* were frequently reprinted and contain prefaces and dedications of great interest.[10] The extent to which this varied material was known in England is not sufficiently realized. In a manuscript letter which has often been quoted, Gabriel Harvey surveyed the books in vogue in the Cambridge of his day and mentioned two which were especially popular:

You can not stepp into a schollars studye but (ten to on) you shall litely finde open ether Bodin de Republica or Le Royes Exposition uppon Aristotles Politiques or sum other like Frenche or Italian Politique Discourses.[11]

The preface to the French edition of Bodin's *Republic,* first published in 1576, contained a sharp attack on Machiavelli, who is also referred to several times in the second work Harvey mentions, Louis Le Roy's translation of Aristotle's *Politics* with a commentary, first published in 1568, and translated into English in 1598.[12] An earlier work by Bodin, his *Methodus ad facilem historiarum cognitionem* (1566), contains several references to Machiavelli and was well known in England.[13] The French civil wars provoked a large number of controversial pamphlets, many of which contain allusions to Machiavelli, and they were known to English-

10. See W. H. Bowen, "Sixteenth Century French Translations of Machiavelli," *Italica,* XXVII (1950), 313–320; and Anna Maria Battista, "La Penetrazione del Machiavelli in Francia nel secolo XVI," *Rassegna di politica e di storia,* no. 67 (1960), 18–32; no. 68 (1960), 31–32.

11. *Letter-Book of Gabriel Harvey,* ed. E. J. L. Scott (London, 1884), p. 79.

12. *Les Politiques d'Aristote* (Paris, 1568; repr. 1576). There also exists a manuscript translation into English which apparently differs from the published translation of 1598; see *RN,* XIII (1960), 348.

13. L. F. Dean, "Bodin's *Methodus* in England before 1625," *SP,* XXXIX (1942), 160–166.

men both in the original and in translation.[14] I think it legitimate, there-
fore, to quote from Continental as well as from English works; when the
Continental works were translated into English, references will be to the
English translation.[15]

We must not underestimate the range and complexity of the sixteenth-
century response to Machiavelli. Marlowe may have exaggerated when he
makes Machiavelli say:

> Admir'd I am of those that hate me most:
> Though some speak openly against my books,
> Yet will they read me . . .
>
> (*The Jew of Malta, Prol.*, ll.9–11)

But there is some truth in it. Machiavelli's writings, especially *The Prince*
and *Discourses,* often seem to have had for sixteenth-century readers the
lure of a kind of forbidden knowledge, irresistible to the intellect but condemned by the moral sense. The response could therefore be one of strong
admiration, or intense hatred, or a whole range of mixed feelings in between these two extremes. There is perhaps no need to document the
hatred; the admiration sometimes took surprisingly extreme forms.
Jacques Gohory described Machiavelli as "le plus gentil esprit qui soit
apparu au monde depuis les derniers siecles," [16] and for the Swiss physician J. N. Stupanus Machiavelli was the only man to understand properly
the use of history:

In consilijs capiendis ac rerum suscipiendarum deliberatione, solus videtur
Historiae vsum intellexisse: tanta scilicet fuit eius solertia & industria in con-
ferendo praesentia exempla cum praeteritis, domestica cum peregrinis, similia
similibus, vt ex praeteritis rerum futurarum euentus prouidere persaepe po-
tuerit.[17]

14. See the valuable bibliography in Appendix A of J. M. H. Salmon's *The
French Religious Wars in English Political Thought* (Oxford, 1959).

15. In some cases the translations were published after Marlowe's death; I have
checked these to make sure that they translate with reasonable fidelity an original
that was available to Marlowe.

16. *Les Discours de Nicolas Macchiavel* (Paris, 1571), Dedication, fol. aii[v].
Gohory also described Machiavelli as "le plus cler & subtil esprit politic de ce
siecle," and worthy to be ranked with the great classical historians (*ibid.*, p. 178[v]).

17. *Nicolai Machiavelli Princeps . . . Adiecta sunt eiusdem argumenti, Aliorum
quorundam contra Machiauellum scripta de potestate & officio Principum, & contra
tyrannos* (Basel, 1580), Epistola Dedicatoria, fol. a2[v]–a3. For the background to

Machiavelli was the only one of his immediate predecessors for whom Justus Lipsius, writing as a political philosopher, felt any respect, but he included a moral reproof which may or may not be written with much conviction:

. . . unius tamen Machiavelli ingenium non contemno, acre, subtile, igneum: et qui utinam Principem suum recta duxisset ad templum illud Virtutis et Honoris! Sed nimis saepe deflexit, et dum commodi illas semitas intente sequitur, aberravit a regia hac via.[18]

Claude Mignault probably spoke for many in his account of Machiavelli, whom he described as

. . . auctor Italus (de quo quid ego cum aliis multis in totum sentiam, nihil habeo dicere, nisi quod existimem eum in ciuilibus negotiis admodum perspicacem, & magni certe ingenij virum, sed in quo tamen parum fidei esset & verae religionis, vt eius scripta declarant).[19]

Attitudes similar to these could be expressed in England; in his dedication to Sir Christopher Hatton of his translation of *The History of Florence* Thomas Bedingfield remarked, among other compliments to Machiavelli:

Yet do I thinke (and so do others of more judgement) that this Historie doth equall or excell the most part that have bin written: not so much for the order and argument of the matter, as the juditiall discourses and observations of the Authour.[20]

Alberico Gentili, the famous Italian jurist who came to live in England, wrote his *De legationibus,* published in London in 1585, for the benefit of those who were to represent their countries abroad. Such men needed a knowledge of the writings of historians, especially those historians who explained the causes and significance of events, and Gentili did not hesi-

---

Stupanus see Werner Kaegi, "Machiavelli a Basilea," *Meditazioni Storiche,* ed. D. Cantimori (Bari, 1960), pp. 155–215.

18. *Politicorum sive civilis doctrinae libri sex* (Leyden, 1589), fol. **I^v. The section containing this allusion was omitted from the English translation of 1594.

19. *Omnia Andreae Alciati V. C. emblemata: Cum commentariis . . . per Claudium Minoem* (Antwerp, 1577), p. 487. In the Antwerp edition of 1581, p. 522, Mignault strengthened the condemnation by adding "aut nihil plane" after "parum."

20. Machiavelli, *The Florentine Historie,* trans. Thomas Bedingfield (London, 1595); Tudor Translations (London, 1905), A2.

tate to recommend Machiavelli in this connection and to defend him
against his enemies:

Nec vero in negotio isto verebor omnium praestantissimum dicere, et ad imi-
tandum proponere Machiauellum, eiusque plane aureas in Liuium Obserua-
tiones. Quod namque hominem indoctissimum esse volunt, et scaelestissi-
mum; id nihil ad me, qui prudentiam eius singularem laudo, nec impietatem,
aut improbitatem, si qua est, tueor. Quamquam si librum editum adversus
illum considero, si Machiauelli condicionem respicio, si propositum scribendi
suum recte censeo, si etiam meliori interpretatione volo dicta ipsius adiuuare,
non equidem video, cur et iis criminibus, mortui hominis fama liberari non
possit. Qui in illum scripsit, illum nec intellexit, nec non in multis calumnia-
tus est.[21]

Several of these quotations illustrate that the aspect of Machiavelli that
most impressed his sixteenth-century admirers was his gift for interpreting history, not merely recording it, and for drawing lessons from the past
which would be useful for the future.

It is particularly important to put ourselves into a sixteenth-century
frame of mind when considering those writers whose reaction to Machiavelli was one of implacable hostility, especially as they were more numerous, or at least expressed their opinions more openly, than his admirers
and are on the whole more relevant to the study of Marlowe. Some modern scholars almost seem to regard Machiavelli as the victim of a mysterious and inexplicable legend that grew round his name and turned it into
a symbol of repulsion and horror. There is more logic to the matter than
this, and as Raab has forcefully argued, the root cause of anti-Machiavellianism was a genuine moral repulsion at some of Machiavelli's doctrines.[22] This reaction was based, no doubt, mainly on *The Prince* and a
few sections of the *Discourses,* and its effect was to limit and distort the
ideas of Machiavelli to such an extent that modern admirers of Machiavelli can hardly be blamed for regarding it as irrelevant to a scholarly assessment of him. It is also true that anti-Machiavellianism continued to
grow for reasons which have little direct connection with Machiavelli
himself, such as the massacre of St. Bartholomew in 1572. But the original

21. Alberico Gentili, *De legationibus libri tres* (London, 1585), p. 109. Presumably the "librum . . . adversus illum" is Gentillet.
22. Raab, *English Face of Machiavelli,* pp. 30–34.

antipathy was at first hand, as is shown by one of the earliest attacks on Machiavelli to be published, part of a short treatise *De libris Christiano detestandis, & a Christianismo penitus eliminandis* printed by Lancelotto Politi as an appendix to his *Enarrationes* in 1552.[23] He began by expressing surprise that a Christian country should allow the sale and diffusion of books by someone he called "hominem omnis prorsus religionis expertem & contemptorem." *The Prince* and *Discourses* were mentioned by name and, according to Politi, showed clearly that Machiavelli was "impium & atheon." He then listed some of the beliefs of this "filius perditionis," paying particular attention to his hypocritical attitude to religion. To prove his argument he gave a reasonably accurate account of chapter xviii of *The Prince,* partly by direct translation from Italian into Latin and partly by summary. The rest of the treatise was mainly an expression of pious horror, but there can be no doubt of the genuineness of Politi's indignation.

It was also possible at this time for commentators on Machiavelli to combine attitudes which to modern readers seem contradictory. The most elaborate discussion of Machiavelli by an Englishman in the reign of Elizabeth is John Case's *Sphaera civitatis* (1588), written in Latin.[24] Case was a conventionally-minded moralist for whom faith and justice were the foundations of society, and he attacked Machiavelli both at the beginning and at the conclusion of his book. It is quite clear that Case had first-hand knowledge of *The Prince* and *Discourses,* and at various points in his rather long-winded book he gave precise marginal references to Machiavelli's writings. Though most of them are in a context of hostility, some are to all appearance completely without hostility or animus; Machiavelli is simply treated as a respectable authority on the issue under discussion.[25] Even while attacking Machiavelli Case was forced to acknowledge his specious attractiveness:

23. *Enarrationes . . . Ambrosii Catharini Politi . . . in quinque priora capita libri Geneseos* (Rome, 1552), cols. 339–342.

24. Attention was first drawn to this book by D. C. Allen, "An Unmentioned Elizabethan Opponent of Machiavelli," *Italica,* XIV (1937), 90–92. Unfortunately, Allen's brief discussion is inadequate and misleading; he says, for example, that Case made two specific allusions to Machiavelli's writings, whereas the true number is nearer to thirty. Raab does not mention the book.

25. Case, *Sphaera civitatis* (Oxford, 1588), pp. 278, 315, 340, 368, 486, 509.

Nam quamuis multa in illo speciem sapientiae habent, tamen qui plus fellis quam mellis, sceleris quam virtutis nobis propinat; non legendum, non audiendum censeo.[26]

He made the same point a few lines later:

. . . sua praecepta prima fronte docta, primoque auditu rara, at non sine pernicie civitatis venditat.

Case's basic attitude was hostility, but it was not strong enough to lead to a complete rejection of Machiavelli. At times this kind of approach could degenerate into downright hypocrisy; Giuliano Procacci has shown that Louis Le Roy, in the work already mentioned, was usually uncomplimentary to Machiavelli whenever he mentioned his name but in at least three places plagiarized fairly substantial passages from Machiavelli.[27]

The ability of sixteenth-century writers to combine apparently irreconcilable attitudes should be remembered in considering the long-debated question whether Elizabethan readers derived their knowledge of Machiavelli from the original or from Gentillet. Meyer argued from the evidence available to him that Gentillet was the main source.[28] Subsequent research, however, proved more and more conclusively that the Elizabethans did know Machiavelli's writings, in the original or in translation, and as a result of this Raab brushed aside what he called "the myth of Gentillet."[29] Ribner attempted to settle the problem by arguing that two separate traditions existed side by side, the one deriving from Machiavelli himself, the other from Gentillet and other opponents.[30]

Yet even this oversimplifies the problem. Possibly the cause of the difficulty has been an unquestioned assumption that Machiavelli and Gentillet are contradictory and mutually exclusive, that anyone with access to Machiavelli's own writings would despise the distortions of Gentillet. Certainly no modern scholar would regard Gentillet as an acceptable substitute for Machiavelli, or even as a reasonably intelligent commentary on him, but we must not assume that this was necessarily true in the six-

26. *Ibid.,* Prolegomena, p. 2.

27. Giuliano Procacci, *Studi sulla fortuna del Machiavelli* (Rome, 1965), pp. 51–52, 61–62, 117.

28. *Machiavelli and the Elizabethan Drama,* pp. ix–x.

29. Raab, *English Face of Machiavelli,* pp. 56–57.

30. Irving Ribner, "Marlowe and Machiavelli," *Comparative Literature,* VI (1954), 349–351.

teenth century. If the "librum editum adversus illum" mentioned above by Alberico Gentili is in fact a reference to Gentillet, this gives us a valuable indication that at least one contemporary reader thought Gentillet biased and unfair, but on other readers Gentillet may have had the effect of awakening them to evils in Machiavelli that they had not hitherto perceived; this at any rate is the impression given by Francois De la Noue, whose *Politic and Military Discourses* were translated into English in 1587:

I haue heretofore greatly delighted in reding Machauels *Discourses* & his *Prince,* because in the same he intreateth of high & goodly politike & martial affaires, which many Gentlemen are desirous to learne, as matters meete for their professions. And I must needs confesse that so long as I was content sleightly to runne them ouer, I was blinded with the glosse of his reasons. But after I did with more ripe iudgement throughly examine them, I found vnder the fayre shew many hidden errors, leading those that walke in them into the paths of dishonour and domage. But if any man doubt of my sayings, I would wish him to reade a booke intituled *Antimachiauellus,* the author whereof I know not, and there shall he see that I am not altogether deceiued.[31]

De la Noue's "the author whereof I know not" is a useful reminder that Gentillet was published anonymously; some contemporaries seem to have had difficulty in knowing how to refer to him, and we should not expect to come across citations of his name. John Case knew Gentillet's book and made six allusions to it; he called it simply *"Antimacch."* but gave book

31. *The Politicke and Militarie Discourses of the Lord De la Noue,* trans. E. A. (London, 1587), fol. G4. Meyer has shown (*Machiavelli and the Elizabethan Drama,* p. 53) that Richard Harvey referred favorably to Gentillet as "a religious french protestant" in *A Theological Discourse of the Lamb of God* (London, 1590), p. 97. Nadja Kempner has suggested, in *Raleghs staatstheoretische Schriften: Die Einführung des Machiavellismus in England* (Leipzig, 1928), p. 23, that there is a hostile allusion to Gentillet in the anonymous preface "Al Lettore" of Wolfe's edition of the *Discorsi* (London, 1584), fol. *3, where an unnamed opponent of Machiavelli is described as full of insults and lies and his writings are considered "degni di servire a questi venditori di salciccie, & di sardelle." There appear to be allusions, on the whole favorable, to Gentillet in Pasquier's letter to Chandon (*Les Lettres d'Estienne Pasquier* [Paris, 1586], pp. 274ᵛ–275) and in Lambert Daneau's *Politicorum aphorismorum silva* (Leyden, 1591), p. 9. The earliest use of Gentillet's name I have come across is in Georg Draud's *Bibliotheca classica* (Frankfurt, 1611), p. 843.

and maxim references which are unquestionably to Gentillet.[32] Evidently Case read Machiavelli partly for himself, from the originals, and partly through the distorting lens of Gentillet, but he does not seem to have felt that there was anything illogical in this procedure. (Perhaps it might be mentioned here that a rather later figure, William Drummond of Hawthornden, possessed copies of Machiavelli's writings, including *The Prince* and *Discourses,* in French and Italian, as well as Gentillet in French.)

The fact that Gentillet was not the only opponent of Machiavelli known to some Elizabethans is shown by William Covell's *Polimanteia,* published in 1595. Covell was interested in literature (he has numerous allusions to Elizabethan poets, including Shakespeare), and also in politics; he alluded to Bodin and Machiavelli in a way that suggests that he knew their writings, and on one page he gave a marginal list of writers who had exposed the errors of Machiavelli. This includes Ambrogio Catherino (i.e., Lancelotto Politi), Molanus, Giovanni Botero, "Anonymos" (presumably Gentillet), Petrus Coretus, Antonio Possevino, and "learned Puritans." [33] Several of these names will be familiar to those who have studied the history of Machiavelli's reputation in the sixteenth century, and I think it is safe to assume that their works circulated in England together with the writings of Machiavelli. It is clear, in other words, that we are not forced to choose between Machiavelli on the one side and his opponents on the other as sources for Elizabethan knowledge; some Elizabethans read both simultaneously.

An important factor in the way we respond to Machiavelli is the context in which we view his writings. The chief tendency of modern scholarship is to see Machiavelli against a background of the history and politics of his own day, with particular emphasis on the disastrous and humiliating Italian wars of the late fifteenth and early sixteenth centuries, which led in the end to an almost complete loss of Italian independence. Our sympathies readily go out to a man whose overriding preoccupation was a wish to redeem Italy from decadence, and even his more "Machiavellian" elements, such as his allowance of ethically dubious means, can be

32. Case, *Sphaera civitatis,* pp. 439, 490, 500, 501, 502, 506. Allen argues that Case borrowed his ideas from Gentillet but says nothing about these specific allusions.

33. Covell, *Polimanteia* (London, 1595), fol. Bb3ᵛ.

seen as a desperate response to a desperate situation. Machiavelli's dislike of moderation and the middle way was partly inspired by the indecisiveness of the Florentine Republic, which sometimes vacillated between two policies or factions in such a way as to incur the enmity of both sides. His striking use of Cesare Borgia as an example for imitation in *The Prince* resulted from his perception of a historical parallel; history was repeating itself, and what had been achieved in the past by the joint power of a Borgia prince and pope could be repeated and improved upon by a Medici prince and pope.

Little of this counted in the sixteenth century, when Machiavelli's writings were usually read as general treatises on the administration of society. His allowance of evil means, for example, was seen by some writers as clear proof of his viciousness. For Case the logic was simple: if Machiavelli was anxious, as he claimed to be, to help men and do good to society (and it is perhaps significant that Case was willing to concede this much), why did he not advocate honest means for this honest purpose?

. . . is enim non ad malum sed ad bonum, non ad perniciem sed ad salutem, non ad ignominiam sed ad dignitatem & honorem omnem suum de republica sermonem se retulisse scribit: si ad bonum, cur medijs honestis non vtitur? Sed astute ille sub specie pietatis iugulum virtutis fodit.[34]

Machiavelli's contempt for compromise was seen as a willingness to endorse unlimited extremes of wickedness, and his use of Cesare Borgia as an example aroused repeated condemnation. Gentillet codified it into one of the maxims he attributed to Machiavelli, that "A Prince ought to propound unto himselfe, to imitate Cesare Borgia the sonne of Pope Alexander the Sixt," [35] and De la Noue, in a discussion of tyranny, singled out Cesare Borgia as an evil example:

I will content my selfe with the alleadging of one onely, which is of *Caesar Borgia, Pope Alexander the 6. his bastard sonne,* who in horrible wickednesse was equall with the tyrants of olde time, who also is the goodly patterne that *Machiauel* propoundeth to teach Princes how to rule. This man replenished all Italy with bloud and vice, & found but ouer many defenders and adherents

34. Case, *Sphaera civitatis,* Prolegomena, p. 5. Case gives a marginal reference to the Proemes of Books I and II of the *Discorsi.*

35. *A Discourse Upon the Meanes of Well Gouerning . . . a Kingdom,* trans. Simon Patericke (London, 1602), Book III, Maxim 7, p. 184.

to assist him. Truly that man had but a slender discretion and lesse vertue, that coulde have sought to liue in such a tyrannous concord.[36]

Some of these writers may have known Guicciardini's hostile portrayal of the Borgias; this is certainly true of a writer too late for Marlowe to have seen, Thomas Fitzherbert, who repeatedly used knowledge of Cesare Borgia gained from Guicciardini's *History of Italy* as a stick to beat Machiavelli.[37] Gentillet knew the unfavorable portrait of Cesare Borgia in Sabellico's *Enneades,* and used it to attack both Borgia and Machiavelli.[38]

The context in which Machiavelli was most frequently set in the sixteenth century, especially by those who were hostile to him, was undoubtedly the literature of Greece and Rome, and some aspects of Machiavelli's early reputation bear witness to the strength and persistence of the classical tradition. There was, after all, a good deal of justification for this. Machiavelli had many classical affiliations; his chief work, the *Discourses,* was a series of meditations inspired by the early books of Livy, and he borrowed a number of ideas and illustrations from the classics, though he did not pepper his pages with names and quotations in the manner of his more pedantic contemporaries and successors. (The precise extent of Machiavelli's firsthand knowledge of the classics is a matter of debate among modern scholars, but this does not affect the argument.) An Elizabethan writer who used the lion and the fox as symbols of force and fraud need not necessarily have read chapter xviii of *The Prince,* since the idea derives from Cicero's *De officiis* and Plutarch's *Life of Lysander.* (In fact Cicero condemned both force and fraud as unworthy of man, and Politi used Cicero's arguments to attack Machiavelli.) [39] When a modern reader comes across a sixteenth-century opponent of Machiavelli who piles up classical citations and examples, he is likely to regard the technique as tedious and conventional, but he needs to remember that many men in the sixteenth century considered it as Ma-

36. De La Noue, *Politicke and Militarie Discourses,* fol. D6. Cf. Matthieu Coignet, *Politique Discourses vpon truth and lying,* trans. Sir E. Hoby (London, 1586), p. 120.

37. T. Fitzherbert, *The First Part of a Treatise concerning Policy and Religion* (Douay, 1606), pp. 26–27, 119–120, 337, 355.

38. Gentillet, *Discourse,* p. 187. See *Opera M. Antonii Coccii Sabellici* (Basel, 1538), II, 807–817.

39. Politi, *Enarrationes,* col. 342.

chiavelli's own technique. Raab dismissed Thomas Fitzherbert's attack on Machiavelli on the grounds that he failed to answer Machiavelli on his own terms. As Raab put it:

Machiavelli can only be refuted convincingly by thinkers of Guicciardini's type; that is, by those who can combat him on his own terms, and this proved impossible for men whose purpose in attacking him lay precisely in a refusal to admit that autonomy for the political sphere upon which his whole analytical complex was based.[40]

This is well argued, but we should remember that at one point Gentillet stated that he intended to fight Machiavelli with his own weapons; he could have confuted him with scriptural quotations, but this would have been almost too easy:

I have alreadie said in another place, that I will not imploy the sacred armour of the holy scripture, to fight against this profane and wicked Atheist, but I will still give him this advantage, to contend with his owne armes; namely, with profane authors, which were not Christians, and which heerein alone resemble him; for in other things hee holds nothing of them, and especially in the matter whereof wee speake, they have beene most farre from his detestable doctrine.[41]

Evidently for Gentillet one way to combat Machiavelli "on his own terms" was to produce classical examples from which conclusions could be drawn that contradicted Machiavelli's conclusions, and Gentillet frequently did this. Modern scholars tend to search for, and discuss, the basic principles underlying Machiavelli's writings, and are not, on the whole, very much concerned with the historical examples, frequently from classical sources, from which he drew his principles. In the sixteenth century this would probably have been regarded as a rather odd and one-sided approach.

Sixteenth-century writers placed Machiavelli in a variety of classical contexts, but perhaps the most common and most important was provided by Aristotle's *Politics*.[42] In Book V, chapter xi, Aristotle discussed the vari-

40. Raab, *English Face of Machiavelli*, p. 81.

41. Gentillet, *Discourse*, p. 229.

42. Some of the points made in this section have been anticipated by Giuliano Procacci in chap. III ("Machiavelli Aristotelico") of his *Studi sulla fortuna del Machiavelli*, pp. 45–75, which I did not see until I had completed a first draft of this essay. I have let my version stand, however, as our interests and citations only

ous means by which a tyrant can preserve his power and divided them into two major groups. If the tyrant rules by force, he should kill off the leading men of his kingdom, forbid social gatherings where discontent might spread, close down schools and academies, set spies on the people, maintain divisions and factions among his subjects, and so on. If, on the other hand, he wishes to use a more subtle method, he should make every attempt to appear good, devout, and conscientious, even though he is really nothing of the sort. It is hardly necessary to stress, in view of the popularity and authority of Aristotle, that these ideas were widely known, and the first group, in particular, was virtually codified into a stock pattern of tyrannical behavior. Bartolus of Sassoferrato discussed the list of characteristics in chapter viii of his *De tyrannia;* he gave his source as Plutarch's *De regimine principum,* but Emerton noted that there is no extant work by Plutarch with this title and suggested that a more probable source was Egidio Colonna's *De regimine principum,* Book III, part 2, chapter x.[43] A later discussion occurs in chapter vi of Bodin's *Methodus.*[44]

The earliest writer I have come across who virtually accuses Machiavelli of plagiarizing Aristotle is Louis Le Roy, in his translation of the *Politics.* In the commentary on Book V, chapter xi, Le Roy brought in Machiavelli:

Machiauel of Florence writing of a Prince, hath taken from this place the most part of his precepts, adding thereunto Romane and Italian examples.[45]

The same point was made a page later:

Aristotle seemeth to haue beene too curious in the setting downe of these Tyrannicall meanes, sith euill Princes are sufficiently inclined of themselues, to inuent what will serue for the maintaining of their high estate and safety, so as it is not needful to instruct them by bookes. Machiauel fashioning his

partially overlap. The connection between Machiavelli's *Prince* and the traditional account of the tyrant is briefly noted by Praz, *Flaming Heart,* pp. 96–97, without any illustrative evidence.

43. I have used the version of Bartolus in Emerton's *Humanism and Tyranny;* see esp. pp. 141–142.

44. *Methodus ad facilem historiarum cognitionem* (Paris, 1566), pp. 257–259.

45. Louis Le Roy, *Aristotles politiques, or Discovrses of Government* (London, 1598), p. 329. The same point, possibly borrowed from a French edition of Le Roy, is made by Francois Grimaudet, *Les Opuscules politiques* (Paris, 1580), pp. 74–74ᵛ.

Prince, hath fetched from hence (as I haue alleadged) the principall grounds of that institution, which must bee red with great discretion, because it is written by an Authour without conscience, and without religion, respecting onely worldly power and glorie, which deceiueth many men.[46]

Gentillet regarded Machiavelli's writings as a handbook for tyrants, or as he put it:

. . . his onely purpose was to instruct a prince to bee a true tyrant, and to teach him the art of tyrannie.[47]

He then related Machiavelli not directly to Aristotle but to the list of ten characteristics of a tyrant given by Bartolus, though it is typical of Gentillet's clumsy methods that he ignored the discussion of the list by Bartolus in which he put forward several reservations and qualifications. After briefly summarizing chapter viii of Bartolus, Gentillet commented:

. . . in all this doctrine of Bartolus can you find one onely point, that Machiavell would not have applied and taught to a Prince? All these tenne kinds of tyrannicall actions, set down by Bartolus, are they not so many Maximes of Machiavell his doctrine taught to a prince? [48]

A slightly later Huguenot pamphlet, the pseudonymous *Vindiciae contra tyrannos*, was obviously written with a full knowledge of the whole tradition. The preface to the *Vindiciae*, apparently by a second author, laid great emphasis on the work as an attack on Machiavelli, though he is never mentioned in the body of the text. But the third section of the *Vindiciae* gave an elaborate account of the nature of a tyrant, and here we find marginal references to several of the works already mentioned: Machiavelli's *The Prince*, Book V, chapter xi of Aristotle's *Politics*, Bartolus' *Tractatus de tyrannide*, and Aegidius Romanus' (i.e., Egidio Colonna's) *De regimine principum*, as well as to Plutarch, Suetonius, St. Augustine, and Thomas Aquinas.[49]

46. *Aristotles politiques*, p. 330. This and the preceding quotation accurately translate an original text first printed in 1568—four years before the massacre of St. Bartholomew and eight years before Gentillet.

47. Gentillet, *Discourse*, p. 142.

48. *Ibid.*, p. 143.

49. *Vindiciae contra tyrannos . . . Stephano Iunio Bruto Celta, auctore* (Edinburgh, 1579), pp. 170 ff. It is very unlikely that either this book or *Le Reveille-Matin des Francois* (see n. 75) was actually printed at Edinburgh; see R. Dickson and J. P. Edmond, *Annals of Scottish Printing* (Cambridge, Eng., 1890), p. 512.

The most elaborate treatment of the connection between Aristotle and Machiavelli appears to be that by the Englishman John Case.[50] Case's book followed, chapter by chapter, the subject matter of Aristotle's *Politics,* though at times in a very approximate fashion, and this meant that when Case arrived at Book V, chapter xi, of his own work he needed to discuss the means used by a tyrant to preserve his tyranny. But Case hesitated to do so, since it was from this source that Machiavelli drew his poisonous doctrines:

Anceps hic sum, vtrum melius sit de conseruatione tyrannidis plura nunc scribere quam de re tam vili & periculosa penitus tacere; si Arist. sequar dicendum est, at vereor ne Machiauellus sub sua larua & pallio rideat: Hinc enim suum venenum hausit, hinc sua principia & fundamenta petijt, hinc suum principem vel potius tyrannum didicit: quid agam igitur? [51]

He decided to continue, however, in the spirit of a doctor studying poisons. It occurred to him that the reader might wonder why Aristotle himself had gone into so much detail on the topic; Case's answer was that Aristotle was trying to put us on our guard against the tricks of the tyrant:

Si ergo hoc loco quaeras cur tam ample, solicite ac copiose de causis conseruandae tyrannidis disputet Philosophus: Respondeo hoc non fecisse quia fauet, sed vt tyrannorum sophismatis & arcanis ad viuum reseratis, nos illorum insidias citius fugiamus.[52]

Case then proceeded, in the manner of Aristotle, to give two lists of tyrannical devices, the first based on force, the second on fraud. To go through these lists in detail would be unnecessarily tedious; we may note, however, that at various points in both lists Case gave marginal references to Machiavelli and also to Gentillet. Case was at one time a fellow of St. John's College, Oxford, and the maxim he attacked with the greatest indignation was the injunction that the tyrant should close down colleges and academies. In view of the prologue to *The Jew of Malta,* in which the soul of Machiavelli delivers a series of precepts, we should perhaps

---

Case made two references to the *Vindiciae* and one to Bartolus (*Sphaera civitatis,* pp. 370, 426).

50. For a later brief example see Fitzherbert, *First Part of a Treatise,* pp. 384–385.

51. Case, *Sphaera civitatis,* p. 495.

52. *Ibid.*

also notice that for the first list, the maxims based on force, Case used a strikingly theatrical means of presentation, summoning up a lurid chorus of furies to pronounce the maxims in turn. The first fury appeared surrounded by flames and declared that the tyrant should kill off the learned men and nobility:

Istarum prima tota flammigera veluti ab inferis in theatrum prodiens, hanc legem tradit. Nobiles (inquit) & sapientes viri tanquam eminentiora papauerum capita obtruncentur; mortui enim non mordent, vires sepultae non laedunt, potentes oppressi non nocent; si ergo in altum accrescant cedri exscindantur, nam si diutius viuant nocebunt plurimum.[53]

Halfway through the list, however, Case tired of the device, and the remaining maxims were briefly summarized.

As is customary with Case, the chapter ended with a series of objections put by an imaginary opponent and then demolished by Case. If, for example, Machiavelli got his ideas from Aristotle, why should we blame him any more than we blame Aristotle? The answer is the stock one: Aristotle was exposing and attacking the tyrant's devices, while Machiavelli was recommending them:

Aliud Machiauellus, aliud Arist. sibi proposuit, ille enim ad monarchiam, hic ad tyrannidem has causas retulit; quippe Philosophus admodum sapienter arcana tyrannorum hoc modo retexit, at Machiauellus istas vitae & administrationis labes tanquam leges in regno & rege posuit.[54]

Another objection on the same page is rather more subtle. Case had admitted earlier (Book IV, chapter xiii) that at times a magistrate could legitimately use deception, and some of the devices he lists are occasionally practiced even by good kings; why, then, should he respond so violently to Machiavelli? Case's reply was that deceptions must be judged by their purpose, or as he puts it, "sophismata ex fine aestimanda sunt"; they can be permitted when used for the benefit of society as a whole. Obviously, it did not occur to him that a justification of this kind might be put forward for Machiavelli, and the final chapter of *The Prince* can have made little impact on him.

The fact that Machiavelli himself repeatedly attacked tyranny, most strikingly in the *Discourses*, Book I, chapter x, made little difference to

53. *Ibid.*, p. 497.
54. *Ibid.*, p. 504.

this way of placing him. A relevant factor was perhaps that by the sixteenth century, in Western Europe at least, monarchy had firmly established itself as the normal form of political organization, and in many of
the less original political thinkers the major issues of politics were resolved and simplified into a question of the way a king should behave;
the good king, pious, just, and concerned for his people, was contrasted
with the evil king or tyrant, faithless, cruel, and selfish. When it was
necessary to place the prince described by Machiavelli in one of these
two categories, there could be little hesitation; he possessed few of the
attributes traditionally assigned to the good prince, and several of those
assigned to the evil prince, and must therefore be classified as a tyrant.

The power of the traditional categories is shown even in some of the
defenders of Machiavelli. Gentili, for example, asserted that Machiavelli
supported democracy, and that his aim in writing *The Prince* was to educate the people in the evil ways of the tyrant:

Itaque tyranno non fauet: sui propositi non est, tyrannum instruere, sed
arcanis eius palam factis ipsum miseris populis nudum et conspicuum exhi-
bere.[55]

Fitzherbert, writing in 1606, recorded that "at this day" there were Floren-
tines who defended Machiavelli by arguing that he was secretly an enemy
to the Medici and wanted them to behave like tyrants in order to make
them odious to the people, who would rise up against them and restore
democracy.[56] (Fitzherbert, incidentally, was decidedly skeptical about the
matter.) This approach has sometimes been regarded as yet another of the
oddities of the sixteenth-century response to Machiavelli; I would prefer
to argue that it shows how difficult it was even for admirers of Machiavelli
to break away from traditional patterns of thought. Gentili did not think
to use the argument that Machiavelli was not attempting to describe a
tyrant, and all he could do to answer the charges of Le Roy and others
like him was to invert the proposition and assert that Machiavelli, like

55. Gentili, *De legationibus,* p. 109.
56. Fitzherbert, *First Part of a Treatise,* p. 412. This is curiously similar to what
Cardinal Pole had said earlier in his *Apologia . . . Ad Carolum V. Caesarem*
(see *Epistolarum Reginaldi Poli . . . Collectio* [Brescia, 1744], I, 151–152), but I
have not found any evidence that this work, apparently not printed until 1744,
would have been available to Fitzherbert.

Aristotle, was condemning rather than approving the behavior he described.

Aristotle was only one of several classical contexts in which Machiavelli was placed. Case, for example, said that another of his inspirations was the evil Roman emperors:

O monstrum hominum Machiauelle, qui ex ouis a Nerone, Caligula, Commodo & Seuero partis tot sis enixus scorpiones, tot Basiliscos, qui ita mordent, ita pungunt, ita inficiunt, vulnerantque animos multorum hodie vt ab omni vnitate, ordine, pace, religione distracti sine fide, sine Christo, sine Deo viuant.[57]

Henri Estienne described Machiavelli as the reincarnation of the wicked counselor Pothinus from Lucan's *Pharsalia,* Book VIII,[58] and modern scholars writing on Machiavelli's sixteenth-century reception have seen links with Seneca [59] and Tacitus.[60] This leads, I think, to the point that needs greatest emphasis. Sixteenth-century readers rarely saw Machiavelli in isolation; they tended to place him within existing traditions of thought, and what is more, to conflate and assimilate his ideas into those traditions. This was a common characteristic of the time; as C. S. Lewis comments, in discussing the critical traditions behind Sidney's *Apology for Poetry:*

The men of that age were such inveterate syncretists, so much more anxious to reconcile authorities than to draw out their differences, that the Aristotelian and neo-Platonic views are not clearly opposed and compared, but are rather contaminated by each other and by many more influences as well.[61]

This might be compared to what Kristeller says about Renaissance Platonism in general:

We must resign ourselves to the fact that in most cases the Platonist elements of thought are combined with doctrines of a different origin and character,

---

57. Case, *Sphaera civitatis,* p. 101.

58. Henri Estienne, *Principum monitrix musa* (Basel, 1590), p. 252.

59. W. A. Armstrong, "The Influence of Seneca and Machiavelli on the Elizabethan Tyrant," *RES,* XXIV (1948), 19–35.

60. See G. Toffanin, *Machiavelli e il Tacitismo* (Padua, 1921). Later scholars have argued that Toffanin exaggerates the influence of Tacitus on Machiavelli himself, but there can be no doubt that in the late sixteenth century Tacitus and Machiavelli were frequently read in conjunction.

61. C. S. Lewis, *English Literature in the Sixteenth Century* (Oxford, 1954), p. 321.

and that even the professed Platonists did not express the thought of Plato
in its purity, as modern scholars understand it, but combined it with more
or less similar notions that had accrued to it in late antiquity, the Middle
Ages, or more recent times.[62]

What was true for Plato was also true, broadly speaking, for Machiavelli.

The habit of blending and mingling rather than separating helps to explain why so often ideas were attributed to Machiavelli which he had not
expressed and the ideas he did express were distorted or ignored. This is
to some extent illustrated by Gentillet's treatment of Machiavelli's attitude to the use of fortresses. Maxim 33 of Book III of Gentillet stated that
"A Prince which feareth his subiects, ought to build fortresses in his
countrey, to hold them in obedience." [63] In itself this is reasonably faithful to part of Machiavelli's argument in chapter xx of *The Prince,* and
Gentillet also gave a summary of that chapter which included Machiavelli's assertion that the best fortress for a prince was not to be hated by
his subjects. Gentillet even included a marginal reference to *Discourses,*
Book II, chapter xxiv, though he gave no hint that in this chapter Machiavelli vigorously attacked the use of fortresses under any circumstances. But so strongly was Gentillet in the grip of the traditional view
of the tyrant that though in a sense he had read what Machiavelli actually wrote he could give only one meaning to it:

Although *Machiavell* have not dealt with the art of tyrannie in his writings
by a methode, yet hath hee not left behind, any part of that art: For first he
hath handled, How a tyrannie ought to be builded, that is, by crueltie, perfi-
die, craft, perjurie, impietie, revenges, contempt of counsell and friends, enter-
tainement of flatterers, tromperie, the hatred of vertue, covetousnesse, inconstancie, and other like vices, whereby hee hath demonstrated, that men must
ascend as by degrees to come unto a soveraigne wickednesse. Secondly, hee
hath shewed how one ought to bee maintained and conserved in that high
degree of wickednesse and tyrannie, namely, by maintaining amongst subiects
partialitie and seditions, and in holding them in povertie and necessitie. Now
he yet addeth another mean, namely, to build Fortresses against his subjects . . .[64]

62. P. O. Kristeller, *Renaissance Thought: The Classic, Scholastic, and Humanist
Strains* (New York, 1961), p. 69.
   63. Gentillet, *Discourse,* p. 347.
   64. *Ibid.,* p. 348.

Gentillet was perhaps an extreme example of the way in which Machiavelli could be distorted, but he was by no means untypical.

One final example of conflation can be given which brings us nearer to the drama. In Shakespeare's *3 Henry VI* Richard of Gloucester boasts of his skill in deception:

> I can add colours to the chameleon,
> Change shapes with Proteus for advantages,
> And set the murderous Machiavel to school.
>
> (III.ii.191–193)

In the version of the text known as *The True Tragedy of Richard Duke of York* the last line reads:

> And set the aspiring Cataline to school.

There is an interesting anticipation of this in the anonymous Catholic pamphlet of 1572, *A Treatise of Treasons against Q. Elizabeth*. In the preface the author bitterly attacked Machiavelli and argued that the government of England was falling into the hands of his disciples. But he also referred to his opponents as "Catilines," at one point even using the phrase "these Machiauel Catilines." [65] Scholars discussing the variant in Shakespeare have sometimes suggested that if "Machiavel" and "Catiline" were interchangeable as terms of abuse, neither word could have much real significance. [66] The Elizabethans did indeed stretch the word "Machiavel" so widely that at times it became virtually meaningless, but this particular parallel may have seemed perfectly logical to them; Sallust's account of Catiline, the cunning and unscrupulous power-seeker, could easily be seen as an illustration of the kind of behavior many of them believed Machiavelli to recommend in his *Prince*. It may possibly be relevant in this connection that in 1575 Hierosme de Chomedy (the earliest translator of Guicciardini into French) published in Paris his *Histoire de la coniuration de Catiline* and included in it a *Traicté des coniurations* translated from Book III, chapter vi, of the *Discourses*. Unfortunately I have

---

65. *A Treatise of Treasons* (n.p., 1572), p. 83. The interest of this work was first noticed by L. B. Campbell, *Shakespeare's Histories: Mirrors of Elizabethan Policy* (San Marino, Calif., 1947), pp. 321–323.

66. E. g., B. Spivack, *Shakespeare and the Allegory of Evil* (New York, 1958), pp. 377–378.

not been able to examine the book; [67] apparently Chomedy treated Machiavelli with great respect, according to a passage Miss Battista quotes from his preface:

J'ay adiusté à la presente traduction un Discours de Machiavel touchant les coniurations pourceque là dedans y a une fort bonne instruction, tant pour les Princes que pour les suiects accompagnée d'une infinité de beaulx exemples, entre les quels celuy de Catiline n'est pas oublié.

Indeed Machiavelli himself in that chapter mentioned Sallust as universally known ("Ciascuno ha letto la congiura di Catilina scritta da Sallustio"),[68] and there is nothing fundamentally incongruous in the way Chomedy associated Sallust and Machiavelli as authorities on conspiracy.

The blurring-together of Machiavelli and other writers may understandably be offensive to a modern scholar, whose training and instinct is to isolate and clarify, to see an author from the past as exactly as possible in his own individuality. But I have tried to indicate in earlier paragraphs of this section something of the sheer muddle of the sixteenth-century response, and I know of no sixteenth-century writer who shows in his approach to Machiavelli the rigorous concern for accuracy of the best modern scholarship. This may very well mean that a study of sixteenth-century attitudes is more valuable for the light it throws on the sixteenth century than for the light it casts on Machiavelli, though it might be suggested that if sixteenth-century writers laid too much stress on the "Machiavellian" elements of Machiavelli, some modern scholars do the opposite, and it seems to me that one of the chief difficulties in assessing Machiavelli is to strike the right balance between seeing him in his own age and seeing him as permanently relevant to the problems of politics. It is, therefore, pointless to rebuke the Elizabethans for not reading Machiavelli in a twentieth-century fashion. It could be said that we tend to draw from an author the ideas and attitudes we expect to find in him, and Elizabethan prejudices and preconceptions were very different from ours. Indeed, one or two recent studies (which are so superficial that I would prefer not to specify them) of Machiavelli's influence on certain Elizabethan writers seem to me to go astray simply because they juxtapose Machiavelli's own writings, seen in isolation in the light of

67. I owe the reference to Battista, "La Penetrazione del Machiavelli," pp. 29–30.
68. *Il Principe e Discorsi*, ed. Sergio Bertelli (Milan, 1960), p. 409.

modern scholarship, against the writings of the author he is supposed to have influenced, without paying any attention to the elaborate context in which Machiavelli was read.

III

We may now turn to some considerations more directly relevant to Marlowe. The artificiality of making a sharp distinction between a learned response based on Machiavelli's own writings and a popular response derived from Gentillet has, I hope, been clearly demonstrated. There may have been a few (I suspect a very few) Elizabethans who read Machiavelli in something like a modern fashion, and there were doubtless many Elizabethans who had no firsthand knowledge of Machiavelli and were prejudiced against him simply through hearsay or the distorting attacks of his opponents, but there was also a considerable range and variety of responses in between these two extremes. Some of the most violent attacks on Machiavelli, and some of the most ludicrous distortions of his ideas, came from men who were learned to a greater or lesser degree; they were writing on issues that seemed to them of deep significance and would, I feel, have resented any imputation that they were caricaturing Machiavelli for the sake of popular entertainment.

Nor should we generalize too sweepingly about the dramatists who made use of the Machiavellian villain in their plays. It is sometimes said that the Elizabethans learned what they knew of Machiavelli from the poets and dramatists who parodied his real opinions, but this can have only a limited validity. Possibly some Elizabethans picked up what little knowledge they had of Machiavelli from their visits to the theater, but there were many others for whom this would be quite untrue. What seems to me undeniable (though as so many of the plays written before 1590 have perished, it would be wise not to be too dogmatic) is that Machiavelli's reputation was firmly established in political and religious contexts long before the dramatists made use of him, and I would even argue, though this is more open to question, that no matter how absurd the dramatists' distortions may seem, they were simply pushing to an extreme approaches that had already become manifest in theological and political polemic. Many of the earlier writers had described the kind of evil behavior to be expected from followers of Machiavelli, and the dramatists illustrated this behavior as vividly and strikingly as they could.

Much of the material used by the dramatists could legitimately be described as "pseudo-Machiavellian," to use Ribner's phrase, but I would not go on with Ribner to say that it bears "no relation to anything Machiavelli ever wrote." [69] In the fifth act of *The Jew of Malta,* for example, Barabas invites the Turkish general Selim-Calymath and his followers to a banquet, with the intention of destroying them either by blowing them up or by making them fall into a cauldron of boiling water. For many critics the second half of *The Jew of Malta* represents a disastrous lapse into melodrama, and this is no doubt the kind of incident that provokes such a judgment. But Marlowe's plot-situation could also be regarded as an elaborate version of what might be termed the "treacherous banquet," a stock device that is mentioned frequently in the historians read by Marlowe and his contemporaries; Hanno the Carthaginian tried but failed to make use of it,[70] and if Marlowe knew the Book of Maccabees, as is suggested by *The Jew of Malta,* II.iii.155–156, he would have known that at the end of the first book of Maccabees Ptolemy used this trick to kill Simon Maccabee and two of his sons.

What is more important in this context is that the device also occurs in Machiavelli's writings, most strikingly in chapter viii of *The Prince,* where Machiavelli describes in some detail how Oliverotto da Fermo invited the leading citizens of Fermo, including the uncle who had helped to bring him up, to a banquet and then massacred them in order to secure control of the town. The trick is also mentioned in the *Vita di Castruccio Castracani,* where Neri della Faggiuola, on the advice of his father Uguccione, betrayed Castruccio himself in this way, but lacked the courage to carry through to the end by killing Castruccio. A slightly different kind of treachery, particularly striking for the apparently dispassionate way in which Machiavelli tells the story, is Castruccio's own treatment of Stefano di Poggio.

Modern scholars may argue that Machiavelli did not approve or even condone this kind of behavior; what is indisputable is that Machiavelli did not condemn it in the explicit fashion that most sixteenth-century

69. Ribner, "Marlowe and Machiavelli," p. 352.

70. Machiavelli mentioned this in *Discorsi,* III, 6 (Bertelli ed., p. 409); his source was Book XXI of Justin.

moralists would have thought appropriate. Gentillet, in his blunt, simple-minded way, had no doubt about the matter; in one chapter he gave a long list of model kings and emperors, beginning with Augustus, Vespasian, and Trajan, and then commented:

These bee they that a prince must propose to imitate, not such of no account, as deserves not a place amongst princes, such as *Agathocles* a potters sonne, and usurper of the Sicilian tyrannie; or *Oliver de Ferme,* a barbarous and most cruell souldiour, who massacred his owne parents & friends, to usurpe the tyrannie of the place of his nativitie; or that *Caesar Borgia* the Popes bastard, full of all disloyaltie, crueltie, inconstancie, and other vices, and farre from all Royall vertues, which *Machiavell* proposeth for patternes to bee imitated of princes.[71]

I do not propose to examine the whole of Machiavelli's writings in order to bring out the "Machiavellian" elements which are undoubtedly contained in them, but I would argue nonetheless that there are affinities, certainly tenuous at times, between the lurid stories of treachery and betrayal popular with the dramatists and certain anecdotes and ideas to be found in Machiavelli himself. Like many of the earlier writers on Machiavelli, the dramatists treated these aspects of him as though they were all he had to offer and conflated them with material from other sources.

It would be of great value to know the exact state of Machiavelli's reputation in 1589, how widely he was known and to what kinds of people. Anna Maria Battista has argued that in France in 1589 there occurred a sudden enlargement of knowledge of Machiavelli, though usually at a very superficial level; the treacherous assassination of the Duke of Guise at the end of 1588 infuriated the preachers and pamphleteers of the Catholic League, who in innumerable sermons and pamphlets brought the name of Machiavelli into the awareness of ordinary people in a way that, according to Miss Battista, had not been true of Huguenot writings inspired by horror at the Massacre of St. Bartholomew, which circulated only among the more intellectually minded. As she puts it:

È opportuno, infatti, osservare che mentre l'antimachiavellismo ugonotto, per quanto fazioso, rimane un fenomeno culturale, circoscritto ad una élite di intellettuali, con la *Ligue* Machiavelli scende nelle piazze, trascinato nel vivo dei tumulti dalle parole infuocate dei predicatori, diventa un personaggio

71. Gentillet, *Discourse,* p. 297.

popolare sinonimo di corruzione e di perfidia, che accende la fantasia del popolo in rivolta.[72]

I do not know whether or not this is completely true; as far as England is concerned, my impression is that references to Machiavelli in English plays, poems, and fiction are relatively rare up to 1589 but fairly common after that date, though the evidence is no doubt too scanty to have clear statistical significance. John Case, writing in 1588, was well aware that the most dangerous works of Machiavelli had not yet been translated into English and asserted that the people (meaning presumably those who knew no other language than English) had not yet been influenced by him:

Adhuc illum in vernaculum sermonem translatum populus non didicit, adhuc eius virus non sensit.[73]

(Case then stressed how wicked it would be if anyone did make Machiavelli easily available in the vernacular.) It may then, perhaps, be true that in the late 1580's Machiavelli's name began to percolate outwards from the learned controversialists in politics and religion to a wider section of the population that would be more likely to provide the audience at the public theaters, and that Marlowe, with the good dramatist's flair for what would be of interest to his audience, wrote *The Jew of Malta* partly to take advantage of this movement of opinion. It must be emphasized, however, that in the present state of knowledge all this must necessarily be very speculative.

Marlowe himself clearly knew something of the sixteenth-century material that has been drawn on for this paper. The prologue to *The Jew of Malta* alludes in its opening lines to the death of the Duke of Guise, and *The Massacre at Paris* is evidence of his interest in the French civil wars; indeed, if Kocher's conclusions are correct, Marlowe had a fairly extensive knowledge of the literature inspired by this crisis.[74] There may be some significance in the fact that in *The Jew of Malta* Marlowe used some of

---

72. A. M. Battista, "Sull' antimachiavellismo francese del sec. XVI," *Storia e politica*, I (1962), 419.

73. Case, *Sphaera civitatis*, Prolegomena, p. 4.

74. P. H. Kocher, "Francois Hotman and Marlowe's *The Massacre at Paris*," *PMLA*, LVI (1941), 349–368; "Contemporary Pamphlet Backgrounds for Marlowe's *The Massacre at Paris*," *MLQ*, VIII (1947), 151–173, 309–318.

the ideas and phrases that were constantly bandied about in theological and political polemic. Barabas, for example, tries to justify to Abigail his treacherous behavior towards Lodowick:

> It's no sin to deceive a Christian;
> For they themselves hold it a principle,
> Faith is not to be held with heretics . . .
>
> (II.iii.310–312)

Marlowe had already used the idea that faith need not be kept with heretics in the second part of *Tamburlaine*, II.i.33–41, in a scene in which Frederick and Baldwin persuade King Sigismund to break his oath to Orcanes and treacherously attack the Turks, which he does with disastrous results. The idea was found repeatedly in theological controversy of the French civil war period, and several writers argued that it originated at the Council of Constance in 1415 as a justification for the burning of John Huss despite the safe-conduct he had been given. As one anonymous author put it:

Souuenez vous que c'est vn article de foy resolu et arreste au concile de Constance, auquel Jean Hus fut brusle contre le sauf conduit de l'Empereur, qu'il ne faut point garder la foy aux heretiques.[75]

Thomas Lupton said the same thing:

For it is a maxime and a rule with the Pope and his partakers, that *Fides non est seruanda haereticis*, Faith (or promise) is not to be kept with Heretickes.[76]

A marginal note reads *"Consil. Constan. Session 19."* The idea is also found in Bodin, who immediately afterwards retold the story of the way in which Cardinal Saint Julian persuaded the King of Hungary to break his truce with the Turks—the precise story which suggested Marlowe's plot in part two of *Tamburlaine*, though Marlowe could obviously have come across it elsewhere.[77]

75. "Eusebe Philadelphe," *Le Reveille-Matin des Francois, et de leurs voisins* (Edinburgh, 1574), pt. I, p. 36.

76. T. Lupton, *A Persuasion from Papistrie* (London, 1581), p. 47. Molanus (see above, p. 14), who was Professor of Theology at Louvain, attempted to justify the way Huss had been treated in Book II of his *De fide haereticis servanda* (Cologne, 1584), which contains an attack on Machiavelli.

77. Jean Bodin, *The Six Bookes of a Commonweale*, trans. Richard Knolles (London, 1606), pp. 627–628. Marlowe's immediate source was probably Bonfinus,

In an early scene of *The Jew of Malta* Barabas remarks that

> . . . crowns come either by succession,
> Or urg'd by force; and nothing violent,
> Oft have I heard tell, can be permanent.

(I.i.129–131)

"Oft have I heard tell" is enough to remind us that "nothing violent can be permanent" is an extremely common proverb with a long history; [78] but Marlowe uses it in a political context, to refer to kingdoms established by force, in a way that parallels some of the political writings of the time. Gentillet used the proverb in connection with tyrants:

> . . . we seldome or never see, tyrants live long, because all tyrannie comprehendeth violence, and that by nature violent things cannot endure.[79]

Almost identical formulas can be found in Case:

> . . . quod violentum & contra naturam est diu constare non potest: sed probatum est tyrannidem esse violentam & contra naturam: ergo diu florere non potest.[80]

Examples of this kind may not carry much weight individually, but there are several others which will be discussed later, and their cumulative effect is such as to convince me that the parallels between *The Jew of Malta* and contemporary political writings cannot be merely accidental.

In view of the frequency with which Cesare Borgia is mentioned in connection with Machiavelli, it is interesting to observe that Marlowe knew something of the contemporary gossip about him. As Barabas stirs the poison into the porridge that is to kill his daughter Abigail, he comments:

> And with her let it work like Borgia's wine,
> Whereof his sire, the Pope, was poisoned!

(III.iv.94–95)

Rerum ungaricum decades quattuor (1543); see Ethel Seaton, "Marlowe and His Authorities," *TLS* (June 16, 1921), p. 388.

78. M. P. Tilley, *A Dictionary of the Proverbs in England in the Sixteenth and Seventeenth Centuries* (Ann Arbor, Mich., 1950), N321. The idea derives ultimately from Aristotle's *Physics*.

79. Gentillet, *Discourse,* p. 316. Similar observations occur on pp. 13 and 200.

80. Case, *Sphaera civitatis,* p. 491.

The reference is clearly to the legend, widely current in the sixteenth century, that Pope Alexander VI died accidentally through drinking poisoned wine that his son Cesare Borgia had prepared for other victims. Modern historians have long rejected the story, but it was believed by as responsible a historian as Guicciardini, and Marlowe could easily have picked it up from Fenton's translation of the *History of Italy*,[81] though there were numerous versions of it available at the time. Machiavelli himself, of course, never mentioned the story, and Gentillet, rather surprisingly, made no allusion to it.

Marlowe's use of the anecdote helps us to understand why poison is one of the standard tools of the Machiavellian stage villain. Machiavelli himself said little about the use of poison and stressed chiefly its unreliability.[82] But to many readers of the sixteenth century the logic of the matter would have been, I imagine, as follows: Machiavelli recommends Cesare Borgia as a model to imitate; Guicciardini shows us that Borgia was a poisoner (and much that was wicked besides; Guicciardini obviously had no love for the Borgias);[83] therefore Machiavelli recommends the use of poison. Any attempt to reply to this by saying that Machiavelli recommended Cesare Borgia for imitation only for certain limited aspects would have seemed an oversubtle evasion of the main issue.

There is little evidence in *The Jew of Malta* to indicate clearly that Marlowe had a firsthand knowledge of Machiavelli's writings, and where there are parallels we usually find that Marlowe could have derived the idea from one of Machiavelli's opponents. For example, Barabas twice asserts that he cannot easily forget the wrongs done to him:

> Great injuries are not so soon forgot
>
> (I.ii.209)
>
> I am not of the tribe of Levi, I,
> That can so soon forget an injury.
>
> (II.iii.18–19)

---

81. *The Historie of Guicciardin*, trans. G. Fenton (London, 1579), pp. 307–308.

82. *Discorsi*, III, 6 (Bertelli ed., p. 410). There is no reference to poison in *The Prince*.

83. Guicciardini's accusation of incest against Alexander VI and his children was censored from the early editions of *Storia d'Italia*, but it was printed at Basel in 1561 in Italian, French, and Latin, and translated into English in 1595.

Marlowe may have had in mind Machiavelli's dictum at the end of chapter vii of *The Prince:*

E chi crede che ne' personaggi grandi e' benefizii nuovi faccino dimenticare le iniurie vecchie, s'inganna.[84]

The idea was obviously important to Machiavelli, since he repeated it in the *Discourses,* Book III, chapter iv, and elsewhere. But Gentillet had noticed this, and stated it as one of Machiavelli's maxims that "It is folly to thinke, that with princes and great lords, new pleasures will cause them to forget old offences." [85] Gentillet gave the references to *The Prince* and *Discourses* which have just been mentioned and interpreted the maxim as meaning that we ought never to become reconciled to our enemies, which seems to be the sense of Barabas' line.

Similarly, Barabas' remark later in the play:

> And he from whom my most advantage comes,
> Shall be my friend.
>
> (V.ii.113–114)

may derive ultimately from Machiavelli's remark in chapter xviii of *The Prince* that princes should not keep their faith when to do so would be to their disadvantage:

Non può per tanto uno signore prudente, né debbe, osservare la fede, quando tale osservanzia li torni contro, e che sono spente le cagioni che la feciono promettere.[86]

But this idea provoked violent indignation in numerous opponents of Machiavelli, especially French writers on politics, who rephrased it into forms that are perhaps a little closer to Marlowe. The anonymous author of *Le Reveille-Matin des Francois* refers to

. . . vne des leçons de Machiauelli, qui est de ne garder aucune foy, qu'autant qu'on la cuidera tourner à son aduantage.[87]

Gentillet said much the same thing:

84. *Il Principe,* Bertelli ed., p. 40.
85. Gentillet, *Discourse,* Book III, Maxim 6, pp. 176–178.
86. *Il Principe,* Bertelli ed., pp. 72–73.
87. *Le Reveille-Matin des Francois,* pt. I, p. 107.

. . . doth not hee [i.e., Machiavelli] say, That a prince, nor any other ought to observe his faith but for his profit? [88]

though elsewhere he translated Machiavelli's Italian with reasonable accuracy, and offered it as one of his maxims.[89]

One or two other possible parallels between Marlowe and Machiavelli can be found, though I do not put them forward with much conviction. Barabas' remark that

> . . . Crowns come either by succession,
>   Or urg'd by force . . .
>
> (I.i.129–130)

may be a faint echo of the early chapters of *The Prince,* where Machiavelli distinguishes between hereditary kingdoms and those acquired by force or fraud. When Barabas has been deprived of his property, he asks whether his persecutors now intend to kill him, and when they say that they do not wish to shed blood, he comments:

> Why, I esteem the injury far less,
> To take the lives of miserable men
> Than be the causers of their misery.
>
> (I.ii.147–149)

This could conceivably have been inspired by chapter xvii of *The Prince,* where Machiavelli argued that the worst offense a prince can commit is to confiscate his subjects' property, since (to use his own words) men sooner forget the death of their father than the loss of their patrimony.[90]

It is, of course, the prologue to *The Jew of Malta* which contains what purports to be a condensation of Machiavelli's opinions, and we must now consider it in more detail. One convention which I shall adopt for the sake of clarity will be to refer to the speaker of the prologue as Machiavel, reserving the form Machiavelli for the real, historical figure.

Clearly the prologue is not a scholarly and accurate presentation of Machiavelli's actual beliefs. Nor, for that matter, is it simply a collection of borrowings from Aristotle or any other classical author; though Marlowe translated the first book of Lucan, there are no clear verbal borrowings from Lucan in *The Jew of Malta,* and there are only one or two not very

88. Gentillet, *Discourse,* p. 135. Cf. also p. 69.
89. *Ibid.,* Book III, Maxim 21, p. 255.
90. *Il Principe,* Bertelli ed., p. 70.

striking parallels with Seneca. Yet the prologue has a certain connection with Machiavelli in that it deals with some of the fundamental issues that preoccupied him: how states and kingdoms should be founded and ordered, and by what means they should be strengthened and preserved. But these preoccupations may be found in dozens of other writers on politics, from Aristotle onwards, and it should come as no surprise, in view of what has been said in the previous section of this essay, that Marlowe, if we assume for the moment that he had read Machiavelli, did not confine himself strictly to the attitudes and illustrations to be found in his works. Furthermore, on many of these issues it was possible to take up a variety of attitudes, and my impression is that Marlowe always chose the harshest and most cynical extreme, either because he wished to shock his audience or else because he genuinely believed, like many others in the sixteenth century, that Machiavelli gave his approval to the utmost extremes of human wickedness.

The first four lines of the prologue deal with the transmigration of Machiavelli's soul from Italy to France and thence to England. To some sixteenth-century writers this movement seemed like the gradual spread of a horrifying disease, an image used, for example, by the anonymous Huguenot who translated Gentillet into Latin in 1577 for the benefit of English readers, in his dedication of the work to Francis Hastings and Edward Bacon:

But O how happy are yee, both because you have so gratious a Queene, & also for that the infectious Machiavelian doctrine, hath not breathed nor penetrated the intrails of most happy England. But that it might not so doe, I haue done my endeavour, to provide an Antidote and present remedie, to expell the force of so deadly poyson, if at any time it chance to infect you.[91]

(I quote from the English translation of Gentillet by Simon Patericke, 1602; it is usually assumed that this dedication was written by Patericke himself, but it is in fact a straightforward translation from the Latin dedication of 1577.) [92] Case provides a closer analogy to Marlowe:

Reliquiae euocatae ab inferis Machiauelli, postquam diu adoratae fuerunt in Italia, translatae sunt tandem in Galliam, & alias nobis propinquas nationes.

91. Gentillet, *Discourse,* The Epistle Dedicatorie, fol. ¶ iv.
92. See *Commentariorum de regno libri tres . . . adversus Nicolaum Machiauellum Florentinum* (n.p., 1577), fol.✠ iiiᵛ–iiij. The relationship was first noted by Adolf Hauffen, "Zu Machiavelli in England," *SJ,* XXXV (1899), 274–276.

Quot, deus bone, seditiones? Quot intestina bella? Quot strages? Quot funestas & miserabiles tragoedias monstri cineres excitarunt? Quot iam mouent? Quot intendunt? Christum precor vt nos praemoniti & praemuniti id dictum audiamus:

Tunc tua res agitur paries cum proxima ardet.[93]

I suspect that the jaunty, even flippant, tone of Machiavel ("To view this land, and frolic with his friends") was deliberately intended by Marlowe as a shocking contrast to the horror with which the orthodox moralists viewed the spread of Machiavelli's influence.

The next nine lines of the prologue (ll. 5–13) do not perhaps require a detailed commentary; they may not say much about Machiavelli himself, but they certainly show that Marlowe had a shrewd and penetrating knowledge of the muddled and often hypocritical response to Machiavelli of many of his contemporaries. Machiavel claims that:

> To some perhaps my name is odious,
> But such as love me, guard me from their tongues . . .

I take this to mean that the true followers of Machiavelli make full use of his doctrines but scrupulously refrain from mentioning his name so as not to frighten the conventionally minded. This could in fact happen; the best English example I know of is too late for Marlowe to have seen, Richard Beacon's *Solon His Folly,* 1594. Machiavelli's name is never mentioned, and at first sight the book appears to have no connection with him, but there are many allusions to Roman and Italian history and various cryptic references to "a subtile writer" and "a man of great vnderstanding." On closer examination it becomes clear that several of these references are to Machiavelli and that Beacon was well acquainted with his writings and quoted from them fairly frequently in a Latin translation.[94]

In line 14 of the prologue Machiavel says:

> I count religion but a childish toy . . .

and this line has been used to illustrate what many critics regard as Marlowe's perversion of Machiavelli's real beliefs. Irving Ribner comments:

93. Case, *Sphaera civitatis,* Prolegomena, p. 3.
94. R. Beacon, *Solon His Folly* (Oxford, 1594), pp. 19, 43, 47, 60, 109, etc.

In *Discourses,* Book I, Chapters xi and xii, religion is described, not as "a childish toy," but as one of the chief causes of the prosperity of Rome and as an essential factor in the well-being of any state.[95]

This rather misses the point. If we want an authentic and detailed Elizabethan response to precisely the chapters in the *Discourses* (Book I, chapters xi–xiv) in which Machiavelli dealt with the function of religion in the state, we cannot do better than turn to the beginning of Book V of Hooker's *Of the Laws of Ecclesiastical Polity.* This text is so easily available that it is unnecessary to examine it here at length; all that needs to be said is that Hooker gave an accurate reference to those chapters in the *Discourses* and had obviously read them carefully and that he plainly felt that Machiavelli regarded religion (which Machiavelli was prepared to accept in some very dubious forms) simply as a tool in the hands of a politician. To Hooker such an approach showed no real feeling for religion at all:

Such are the counsels of men godles, when they would shew themselues politique deuisers able to create God in man by arte.[96]

If this was the opinion of the humane and learned Hooker, it is not surprising that lesser men should have put the matter more bluntly. In addition, in one of the earliest biographies of Machiavelli (if it deserves such a dignified title), Paulus Jovius described him as "irrisor & atheos," [97] and this comment, with others by Jovius, was picked up by later writers. Bodin said that Machiavelli was a man

. . . *lequel Paul Ioue ayant mis au rang des hommes signalez, l'appelle neantmoins Atheiste, & ignorant des bonnes lettres.*[98]

Exactly the same idea can be found in Coignet, who said that Machiavelli

. . . hath not without iuste cause had his qualityes paynted out by *Paulus Iouius* as one ignorant both of GOD, and learning, and so censured by the counsell of *Trente.*[99]

95. Ribner, "Marlowe and Machiavelli," p. 352.

96. *Of The Lawes of Ecclesiasticall Politie, The fift Booke* (London, 1597), p. 7.

97. Paulus Jovius, *Elogia doctorum virorum* (Antwerp, 1557), p. 194.

98. J. Bodin, *Les Six Livres de la republique* (Paris, 1576), Preface, fol. Aiiᵛ. (This preface was not translated into English.)

99. Coignet, *Politique discourses,* p. 120.

Marlowe was in fact being relatively conventional in line 14 of the prologue; it would have required far more daring and courage in the sixteenth century to assert that Machiavelli had a genuine concern for religion than to call him an atheist.

At first sight we may perhaps wonder why Marlowe included lines 16–17 in the prologue:

> Birds of the air will tell of murders past:
> I am asham'd to hear such fooleries.

but the lines can be shown, I think, to have a relevance to their context. It is not unmistakably clear precisely which birds Marlowe had in mind; probably most modern readers are reminded of Macbeth's

> It will have blood; they say blood will have blood.
> Stones have been known to move, and trees to speak;
> Augurs and understood relations have
> By maggot-pies and choughs and rooks brought forth
> The secret'st man of blood.
>
> (III.iv.122–126)

Bennett in his commentary to *The Jew of Malta* recalls the classical legend of the cranes which revealed the death of Ibycus, and this seems to lead in the right direction. Fitzherbert told the story of the cranes of Ibycus (borrowed in his case from Plutarch's *De garrulitate*) and also the story of the swallows who revealed Bessus' murder of his father (from Plutarch's *De sera numinis vindicta*), both as examples of God's providence and justice.[100] The quotation from *Macbeth* shows how profoundly the Elizabethans believed in a world in which all created objects were related to each other and to God. Nothing can be kept hidden indefinitely; murder will out, sometimes by totally unexpected means. Machiavel, therefore, is not simply mocking an obscure pagan superstition; having already belittled religion and argued that ignorance (presumably of the Machiavellian rules for worldly success) is the only sin, he quite appropriately goes on to reject the idea that God's providence is at work in the world. Murder can be concealed, and men need have less constraint in their evildoing. At first sight all this may appear not to have the slightest connection with the real Machiavelli. Yet Raab re-

---

100. Fitzherbert, *First Part of a Treatise,* pp. 262, 441–442. The general theme of Plutarch's *De sera numinis vindicta* is obviously relevant in this connection.

peatedly argues that one aspect of Machiavelli's modernity is that he rejects the Augustinian, theocentric world view of earlier writers; could
Marlowe's lines, for all their oddity, be to some extent a recognition of
this fact?

The next two lines of the prologue:

> Many will talk of title to a crown:
> What right had Caesar to the empery?

have already received some comment (see above, p. 5) and could be
said to represent a movement towards a more directly political theme. Political writers said repeatedly that a ruler with no legal title to his power
must be regarded as a tyrant; did Julius Caesar worry unduly about such
niceties? Machiavelli himself made several references to Julius Caesar;
he does not appear to have been bitterly hostile to him, but in the *Discourses*, Book I, chapter xxix, he treated Caesar as a tyrant who seized
power by force.[101] Marlowe may perhaps have been influenced by Lucan,
who consistently portrayed Caesar as an unscrupulous and hypocritical
power-seeker.

This leads to the problem of the ultimate origin of political power:

> Might first made kings, and laws were then most sure
> When, like the Draco's, they were writ in blood.

> (ll. 20–21)

It had long been debated, from classical times onwards, whether king-
ship originated through the violent seizure of rule by the most powerful, or had been established by the community, once men came together
to live in society, through a voluntary surrender of power to the man
most fitted to rule. De la Primaudaye summarized the debate in the following way:

The first soueraign gouernment was established either by the violence of the
mightiest, as *Thucidides, Caesar, Plutarke,* and others write: and the holy
historie testifieth the same vnto vs, and putteth this opinion out of doubt,
where it is said that *Nimrod Chams* nephewe, was the first that brought men
into subiection by force and violence, establishing his principalitie in the kingdome of Assyria: Or if any will beleeue *Demosthenes, Aristotle,* and *Cicero,*
the first soueraigntie was instituted upon their will and good liking, who for

---

101. *Discorsi,* Bertelli ed., p. 199.

their owne commoditie, rest, & securitie, submitted themselues to such as excelled most in vertue in those times, which they called heroicall.[102]

The difficulties of tracking down ideas to their sources in sixteenth-century writers will be made clearer if we realize that this is in fact a plagiarism from Bodin, who expressed himself rather more forcefully:

Yea Reason, and the verie light of nature, leadeth vs to beleeue very force and violence to haue giuen course and beginning vnto Commonweals. And albeit that there were no reason therefore, it shal be hereafter declared by the vndoubted testimonies of the most credible historiographers, that is to say, of *Thucydides, Plutarch, Caesar,* & also by the laws of *Solon,* That the first men that bare rule, had no greater honour and vertue, than to kill, massacre and rob men, or bring them in slauerie. These be the words of *Plutarch.* Yet haue we more also the witnesse of the sacred history, where it is said, that *Nimroth* the nephew of *Cham,* was the first that by force and violence brought men into his subiection, establishing his kingdome in the countrey of *Assyria:* and for this cause they called him the *Mightie hunter,* which the Hebrews interpret to be a theefe and robber. . . . Wherein it appeareth *Demosthenes, Aristotle,* and *Cicero,* to haue mistaken themselues, in following the errour of *Herodotus,* who saith, That the first kings were chosen for their iustice and vertue; and haue hereof faigned vnto vs I wot not what heroicall and golden worlds: an opinion by me by most certaine arguments and testimonies else-where refelled . . .[103]

Machiavel, of course, prefers the more brutal interpretation. Machiavelli himself did not say a great deal about the ultimate origins of power in prehistorical times; in the *Discourses,* Book I, chapter ii, he leaned more towards the second theory:

. . . nel principio del mondo, sendo gli abitatori radi, vissono un tempo dispersi a similitudine delle bestie; dipoi moltiplicando la generazione si ragunarono insieme, e per potersi meglio difendere cominciarono a riguardare infra loro quello che fusse più robusto e di maggiore cuore, e fecionlo come capo e lo ubedivano.[104]

It is again characteristic that Machiavel should choose as his lawgiver the Athenian Draco, whose laws were so ferociously rigorous that his

---

102. Pierre de la Primaudaye, *The French Academie,* trans. T. Bowes (London, 1586), pp. 585–586. This parallel was noted by P. H. Kocher, *Christopher Marlowe,* 2d ed. (New York, 1962), p. 198.

103. Bodin, *Six Bookes of a Commonweale,* p. 47. Cf. also pp. 200, 362, 412.

104. *Discorsi,* Bertelli ed., p. 131.

name became a byword for cruelty. Machiavelli never mentioned Draco, but he was deeply interested in the ordering of society, especially in the *Discourses,* and referred fairly frequently to lawgivers like Romulus, Numa Pompilius, "Moises, Licurgo, Solone ed altri fondatori di regni e di republiche." [105]

The remaining lines of the prologue that require commentary should be treated as a unit:

> Hence comes it that a strong built citadel
> Commands much more than letters can import:
> Which maxim had but Phalaris observ'd,
> H'ad never bellow'd, in a brazen bull,
> Of great ones' envy: o' the poor petty wights
> Let me be envied and not pitied.

Valuable work has been done on the sources of this passage by Antonio D'Andrea; [106] my approach to the lines, however, will be somewhat different from his. It could be argued, with some justification, that Marlowe completely distorted the true opinions of Machiavelli, who expressed contempt for Phalaris in the *Discourses,* Book I, chapter x, and whose attitude towards the use of fortresses, as expressed in *The Prince,* chapter xx, and *Discourses,* Book II, chapter xxiv, is much more complicated and subtle than Marlowe suggests. But one of the main points of the previous section of this paper was that Machiavelli was frequently seen in terms of the traditional view of the tyrant and his behavior, [107] and lines 22–27 of Marlowe's prologue show to my mind that Marlowe, whether or not he had read Machiavelli, certainly knew about the stock attributes of the tyrant. The Sicilian tyrants in particular, of whom Phalaris was one, were repeatedly mentioned by political writers; it is noteworthy that De la Noue said that Alexander VI and Cesare Borgia "in all crueltie, dissolution, and infidelitie were equall with the auncient *Sicilian* tyrants," [108] and I do not think it accidental that later in *The Jew of Malta* (V.iii.10) Marlowe refers briefly to "Syracusian Dionysius," presumably Dionysius I,

105. *Ibid.,* Book I, chap. 9, p. 154.
106. A. D'Andrea, "Studies on Machiavelli and His Reputation in the Sixteenth Century: I, Marlowe's Prologue to *The Jew of Malta*," *Mediaeval and Renaissance Studies,* V (1960), 214–248.
107. See particularly Gentillet on fortresses (quoted above, p. 24).
108. De la Noue, *Politicke and Militarie Discourses,* fol. K7–7ᵛ.

another notorious Sicilian tyrant who was frequently mentioned together with Phalaris.

In effect Machiavel rebukes Phalaris for not behaving like a true tyrant. Fortresses or citadels were the traditional means by which a tyrant kept his subjects under control; Bodin, for example, refers to

. . . Cittadels, which the people called Tyrants nests; and tyrants tearmed them a scourge for villaines, in contempt and scorne of the poore subiects.[109]

Phalaris, however, wastes his time with belles-lettres and thereby weakens his position; the reference is almost certainly, as D'Andrea has shown, to the *Letters of Phalaris,* now regarded as spurious, but in Marlowe's time accepted as authentic writings of Phalaris.[110] Marlowe could have made Machiavel express a contempt for learning for a variety of reasons. One may simply be that the traditional tyrant, as described by Aristotle, hated learning and closed down schools and academies as potential centers of opposition. Another may be that various writers in Marlowe's time argued that too great a preoccupation with learning had a corrupting and debilitating effect, both on the individual and on society, and that the less learned nations were more efficient in war. One of the most striking expressions of this view comes at the conclusion of Montaigne's essay *Of Pedantisme:*

Examples teach us both in this martiall policie, and in all such like, that the studie of sciences doth more weaken and effeminate mens minds, than corroborate and adapt them to warre. The mightiest, yea the best setled estate, that is now in the world, is that of the Turkes, a nation equally instructed to the esteeme of armes, and disesteeme of letters. I find *Rome* to have beene most valiant, when it was least learned. The most warlike nations of our daies, are the rudest and most ignorant.[111]

The only relevant passage in Machiavelli's writings is quoted by D'Andrea and is from *The Art of War;* in it Fabrizio Colona rebuked the Italian princes of his day for being unprepared for war:

Our Italian Princes beleved, before thei tasted the blowes of the outlandishe warre, that it should suffice a Prince to knowe by writynges, how to make a subtell answere, to write a goodly letter, to shewe in saiynges, and in woordes,

109. Bodin, *Six Bookes of a Commonweale,* p. 597.
110. D'Andrea, "Studies on Machiavelli," pp. 217 ff.
111. Montaigne, *Essays,* Everyman's Library, no. 24 (London, 1910), I, 147.

witte and promptenesse . . . nor the sely wretches were not aware, that thei prepared theim selves to bee a praie, to whom so ever should assaulte theim.[112]

This is remarkably similar to the last sentence of the essay by Montaigne referred to above, and possibly Montaigne was writing within a current of thought set in motion by Machiavelli:

When our King *Charles* the eight, in a manner without unsheathing his sword, saw himselfe absolute Lord of the whole Kingdome of Naples, and of a great part of *Thuscanie,* the Princes and Lords of his traine ascribed this sodaine, and unhoped for victorie, and facilitie of so noble and prodigious a conquest, only to this, that most of the Princes and nobilitie of *Italie* ammused themselves rather to become ingenious and wise by learning, than vigorous and warriers by militarie exercises.[113]

A final point to be made in this connection may seem rather odd. Paulus Jovius, in the account of Machiavelli referred to earlier, stated authoritatively that Machiavelli had little or no knowledge of Latin letters, and that Machiavelli himself had admitted to Jovius that he had been supplied by his friend Marcello Virgilio with passages from Greek and Latin ("Graecae atque Latinae linguae flores") which he inserted into his writings.[114] We have already seen that Jovius' account was accepted by later writers such as Bodin and Coignet, but in their hands it takes the blunt form that Machiavelli was "ignorant des bonnes lettres." If Marlowe came across a statement of this kind, he may have believed that Machiavelli had little learning himself and was in fact somewhat contemptuous of learning. (If this was true it would surely clash with the assertion that Machiavelli borrowed his main ideas from Aristotle, but sixteenth-century opponents of Machiavelli do not seem to have been troubled by discrepancies of this kind.)

I am, unfortunately, quite unable to agree with D'Andrea in his argument that the "petty wights" of line 26 of the prologue are Marlowe's personal literary enemies.[115] This interpretation strikes me as strained and implausible, and I would prefer to argue that Marlowe intended an

112. Machiavelli, *The Arte of Warre,* trans. Peter Whitehorne (London, 1560); Tudor Translations (London, 1905), p. 230.
113. Montaigne, *Essays,* I, 148.
114. Jovius, *Elogia,* p. 193.
115. D'Andrea, "Studies on Machiavelli," pp. 227 ff.

antithesis between the "great ones," the nobility and leading men, and the "petty wights," the common people. In chapter ix of *The Prince* Machiavelli discussed whether the prince who came to power by legal means should rely for support more on the great men (the "grandi") or the people ("el populo"). His argument is subtle and complicated and cannot be easily summarized; Machiavel, on the other hand, pushes the argument violently to one extreme, asserting that if Phalaris had relied on a strong citadel he would have been safe from the conspiracies of the great ones and would have been regarded with impotent envy by the ordinary people. He would not, in other words, have needed support from anyone. I am assuming, obviously, that by the end of the passage Machiavel has more or less come to identify himself with Phalaris and that this accounts for the shift from the third person to the first. One point, incidentally, that D'Andrea does not explain (and I am unable to do so) is why Marlowe implies that Phalaris was brought down by the "great ones"; probably the most widely known account of the downfall of Phalaris, in Cicero's *De officiis,* Book II, asserts that he perished in a general uprising of the people of Agrigentum.

One of Marlowe's motives for including the passage on Phalaris may have been a desire to be paradoxical, to turn accepted opinion upside down. Erasmus, for example, condemned Phalaris but praised his love of letters, which to some extent redeemed his character.[116] Marlowe inverts this and presents the love of letters as a fatal weakness; Phalaris would have done better to act like a true tyrant. I would also suggest, rather tentatively, that there is a Machiavellian element of a kind in the passage. Machiavelli was notorious in the sixteenth century for analyzing political conduct in terms of expediency and disregarding moral considerations. Even today some scholars would argue, perhaps wrongly, that Machiavelli is the scientifically detached observer who asks, in effect, what means are necessary in a given situation to bring about a desired result, without considering whether or not they are compatible with traditional morality. Marlowe may have felt that he was making a truly Machiavellian analysis of the reasons for the downfall of Phalaris and of the means he should have used to maintain his power.

116. Erasmus, *The Education of a Christian Prince,* trans. L. K. Born (New York, 1936), p. 201.

In view of this discussion of the prologue I would argue that in writing it Marlowe was not merely butchering Machiavelli for the sake of the ignorant groundlings; indeed, it would have been difficult for a completely unlearned audience to understand allusions to Caesar, Draco, and Phalaris, and Marlowe must have assumed that his listeners had some knowledge, however superficial, of the political ideas commonly expressed at the time.

Nor can it be said that the prologue is totally without relationship to the rest of the play. I have already discussed the lines in the prologue that deal with the attitude of Machiavel towards religion, and most readers have noticed that religious hypocrisy, the use of religion as a mask for unscrupulous cunning, is one of the major themes of *The Jew of Malta*. We should also note the couplet used by the governor of Malta to end the play:

> So, march away; and let due praise be given
> Neither to Fate nor Fortune, but to Heaven.
>
> (V.v.123–124)

This is, of course, a nice touch of irony; the governor, having been quite as "Machiavellian" as Barabas, sanctimoniously sees the hand of God at work on his behalf. Yet it may have a significance which is not always fully appreciated. The theme is an old one; the early Fathers of the church had attacked the pagan concept of Fortune and argued that events were brought about by divine providence. Yet the stress laid by Machiavelli, and to some extent by Guicciardini also, on Fortune rather than providence, gave the debate a fresh importance, and Gentillet rebuked Machiavelli for exaggerating the role of Fortune in human affairs.[117] The closest parallel to Marlowe I have come across is in Fitzherbert, who quotes an assertion by St. Augustine that everything happens through divine providence, and then comments:

What then would he say if he were now liuing, and saw the writinges of some Christians of no smal estimation, aswel historiographers as others, who not with standing the aboundant matter, and occasion that the subiects which they handle doe offer vnto them, to obserue the course of Gods prouidence; doe seldome or neuer speake therof, but referre al kind of effects and ac-

117. Gentillet, *Discourse*, pp. 138–139.

cidents to *fate* or *fortune,* more prophanely then many of the Painyms were wont to doe, in whom a man shal find very pious and religious obseruations of Gods infinit wisdome, prouidence, and iustice; Truly if *S. Augustine* (I say) were liuing and should see such workes, he would not thinke them fit to be read of Christians.[118]

This of course is too late for Marlowe to have seen, but I am sure that ideas of this kind were circulating in his day.

IV

The kind of background I have tried to provide for *The Jew of Malta* does not provoke any fundamental re-evaluation of the play; it does, however, show that many of the ideas in the play are Machiavellian or relevant to Machiavelli in a way that a number of sixteenth-century writers would have considered quite legitimate, though nowadays they appear to have no connection with him at all. Barabas, for example, is utterly self-centered; and just as the tyrant, in contrast to the good king, thinks only of his own interest, so the followers of Machiavelli, according to Fitzherbert, obey the law of self-love:

And *Machiavel* whose workes are so highly esteemed of many states-men at this day; doth he teach any other gouerment, then that which proceedeth from the principles of this law, to wit from self loue and particular interest? [119]

We have seen that sixteenth-century Machiavellianism is of a composite nature, with many aspects that do not derive directly from the writings of Machiavelli; and Barabas himself is very much a composite character, with elements in him of the Machiavellian, the Jew (in the traditionally hostile portrait),[120] the usurer, and the vice of the morality play. This odd mixture would probably have seemed less surprising at first sight to an Elizabethan than to someone of the twentieth century. Jewel stressed the variety of evils associated with usury:

118. Fitzherbert, *First Part of a Treatise,* p. 109.
119. *Ibid.,* p. 82.
120. See G. K. Hunter, "The Theology of Marlowe's *The Jew of Malta,*" *JWCI,* XXVII (1964), 211–240.

Couetousnesse, desire of monie, vnsatiable greedinesse, deceitfulnesse, vnmer-
cifulnesse, iniury, oppression, extortion, contempt of God, hatred to the
brethren, and hatred of al men, are the nurces and breeders of Usurie.[121]

and Elizabethan moralists frequently discussed what might be called the
interconnections of evil, the way in which one vice inevitably led to another. Machiavellianism had its own particular characteristics, such as
treachery and hypocrisy, but it was not rigorously set apart from other
kinds of sinful behavior.

We may be inclined to ask whether there is any serious conception of
politics behind *The Jew of Malta*. There was always something of the
enfant terrible about Marlowe, and in all his plays it is hard to judge how
far the ideas in them are there for effect and display, and how much they
represent passionately held convictions. He seems to have had no conception of society as organic, as a system of mutual relationships and in-
terdependencies, and this may help to explain why *Edward II* seems
fragmentary in comparison with Shakespeare's history plays. *The Jew of
Malta* presents a world of greed, hypocrisy, and selfishness, where faith
and justice are conspicuously lacking, and an isolated example of decency,
such as Abigail, is soon destroyed. Yet in this play, we might argue, it
is quite appropriate, since the orthodox moralists like Case proclaimed
that precisely this kind of world would come into existence if Machiavelli's principles were to be extensively applied. If so, it follows that Marlowe was basically in sympathy with the orthodox position, though obviously his mind was too subtle and contradictory for him to have written
a simple moralizing tract.

I have not been able to prove that Marlowe read Machiavelli, though
I have a strong suspicion that he knew *The Prince;* I am, however, convinced that he had a good knowledge of the French and English political
writings of his time, writings that provide the context in which allusions
to Machiavelli and discussions of his ideas are most commonly found.
But it is usually impossible to say authoritatively that Marlowe derived
his ideas from any one particular source, and I have sometimes quoted
several illustrations of the same point in order to show the wide diffusion
of the kind of idea Marlowe drew upon. He may possibly have used

121. John Jewel, *An Exposition vpon the two Epistles . . . to the Thessalonians*
(London, 1583), p. 115.

Gentillet; Machiavel claims in the prologue, line 32, that Barabas' money "was not got without my means," and Gentillet lays more stress than any other opponent of Machiavelli on the unscrupulous avarice of Machiavelli's followers. There may even be one direct verbal echo of Gentillet in the play; Barabas' confession that as a usurer he took exorbitant interest:

> A hundred for a hundred I have ta'en . . .
>
>   (IV.i.57)

is similar to Gentillet's indignant protest at Italian usury:

> . . . the Italians doe often returne their money with the gaine of fiftie, yea often of an hundreth, for an hundreth.[122]

I have not come across this particular accusation elsewhere, though on further investigation it might prove to be a commonplace.

I hope that this study has at least made clear the complexity and variety of the sixteenth-century response to Machiavelli. Any attempt to examine Machiavelli's influence on writers of the sixteenth century which does not take this complexity into account in as much detail as possible and relies simply on twentieth-century approaches and attitudes, is likely, it seems to me, to be misdirected from the very beginning.

122. Gentillet, *Discourse*, Preface, fol. Avi. The French text reads: "Les Italiens font souuent reuenir leurs deniers à raison de cinquante voire de cent pour cent," *Discours sur les moyens*, Preface, p. 16.

The Theology of Marlowe's Doctor Faustus

MICHAEL HATTAWAY

Oh men most braine-sick and miserable, that endevour to be worse than they can!

Montaigne, *Essays,* II.xii
(trans. Florio)

EVER SINCE Eliot described *The Jew of Malta* as a "tragic farce," critics have been trying hard to define the particular conjunctions of contradictory impulses in Marlowe's works. It is difficult now to regard Doctor Faustus simply as a great soul struggling to free himself from the fetters of his age, an interpretation incidentally that dates only from about the time of Byron's *Manfred,* nor do most of us want to follow the severely moralistic interpretations of the play that destroy it as a tragedy. Yet the more one reads the writings of Marlowe's contemporaries, the more one is forced to the opinion that his audiences adopted a more stringent attitude towards his heroes than most modern critics have done and that the plays work in large part by irony, by invoking traditional ideas or icons and using them as formative principles of meaning. If we know some orthodox answers to the problems raised by the play, we are far more likely to understand its full significance, for there is a continual interplay taking place in the minds of the audience between icon and scene.[1] Even though our involvement with the hero and the intensity of

---

1. See Michael Hattaway, "Marlowe and Brecht," in *Christopher Marlowe,* ed. Brian Morris (London, 1968), pp. 95–112. Cf. Max Bluestone, "Libido Speculandi,"

the verse may threaten the orthodox reference of the presented image, it is hard to believe that Marlowe was skeptical of its validity as a summary of human experience.

Professor Bradbrook has suggested some icons for *Tamburlaine,* and Professor Hunter has interpreted Barabas' life as "a parody of Job's spiritual Odyssey." [2] As a point of departure for this chronicle of Faustus' pursuit of wisdom, I should like to put forward the figure of Solomon, king of Israel, who in sixteenth-century literature was frequently referred to as "the wise man." As an emblem of wisdom, however, Solomon presented a paradox, for after being preeminent among men for his God-given wisdom, he had turned from his learning, fame, and wealth to write the Book of Ecclesiastes, the book that begins "Vanity of vanities; all is vanity." (No Renaissance scholars questioned his authorship of this work.) Some commentators read Ecclesiastes as a lament for man's state, some as a plea for the wise folly of Christ that they opposed to ratiocination and vain speculation, and some as a testimony of repentance written by Solomon after he had been seduced by strange women or after he had renounced his magic.[3] We remember that he had appeared to Robert Greene in his *Vision* to admonish him for his vain life. Now Solomon's skepticism led him to humility and a stronger faith: Faustus, after far less intellectual agony, came to this same conclusion of the vanity of worldly learning in the first scene of the play, but instead of formulating a skeptical philosophy and erecting his faith upon it as did Montaigne, Ralegh, and Greville, he gave himself to his lust and was unable to repent. Ecclesiastes 1:13 describes his dilemma: "And I haue giuen mine heart to search and finde out wisedome by all thinges that are done vnder the heauen." But he would not accept the conclusion drawn from this

in *Reinterpretations of Elizabethan Drama,* ed. Norman Rabkin (New York, 1969), which contains a bibliography of *Faustus* criticism. In "The Philosophy of *Dr. Faustus,*" *Essays in Criticism,* XX (1970), 123–142, A. L. French argues that the irony of the play destroys its tragic potential.

2. M. C. Bradbrook, *English Dramatic Form* (London, 1965), pp. 41–59; G. K. Hunter, "The Theology of Marlowe's *The Jew of Malta,*" *JWCI,* XXVII (1964), 211–240. See also Eugene M. Waith, *The Herculean Hero* (London, 1962).

3. See Michael Hattaway, "Paradoxes of Solomon: Learning in the English Renaissance," *JHI,* XXIX (1968), 499–530. For Solomon the magician, see J. P. Migne, *Troisième et dernière encyclopédie théologique* (Paris, 1854–1867), XXIV, cols. 839 ff.

chapter that we find in a gloss in the 1578 Geneva Bible: "Man of nature hath a desire to know, and yet is not able to come to the perfection of knowledge, which is the punishment of sinne, to humble man, and to teach him to depend only vpon God." Faustus would overleap the obstacles placed before Man as a consequence of his sin, try a short cut to wisdom and power—witchcraft.

There is evidence that connects Faustus directly with Solomon. As has been noticed, Solomon was often listed among the great magicians, and it is not surprising to find Marlowe's source, "P.F.'s" translation of the *Faustbuch,* reporting:

Belial . . . deceiued King *Salomon* that worshipped the Gods of the heathen: and there are such Spirits innumerable that can come by men and tempt them, driue them to sinne, weaken their beliefe . . . and to this intent doe wee spread our selues throughout all the world, as the vtter enemies of God, and his Sonne Christ, yea & all those that worship them: and that thou knowest by thy selfe *Faustus,* how we haue dealt with thee.[4]

Second, when Faustus asks for books of conjuring and for "one booke more . . . wherein I might see al plants, hearbes and trees that grow vpon the earth," [5] it might be that he is asking for Solomon's "lost books" of natural philosophy.[6] Third, Mephostophilis offers to bring Faustus a courtesan "as wise as *Saba*"—the Queen of Sheba (B.456), and Faustus' offer to burn his books may be connected with the legend that Solomon buried his magic book after using it to make the devils serve him in building the temple.[7] In any case Faustus turns from skepticism to the pursuit of knowledge, power, and riches as Solomon turned from these vanities to skepticism and repentance.

However much the critic admires Faustus, he must, as I shall attempt

4. *Sources of the Faust Tradition,* ed. P. M. Palmer and R. P. More (New York, 1936), pp. 152–153.

5. 1604 Quarto (A), ll. 622–623; quotations are taken from *Marlowe's "Doctor Faustus," 1604–1616: Parallel Texts,* ed. W. W. Greg (Oxford, 1950).

6. See 1 Kings 4:33: "And he spake of trees, from the cedar tree that is in Lebanon euen vnto the hyssope that springeth out of the wall." Bacon several times laments the "loss" of this book: *New Atlantis,* p. 145; *De augmentis,* VIII.i (*Works,* ed. J. Spedding, R. L. Ellis, and D. D. Heath [London, 1857–1874]); and *Gesta Grayorum,* ed. W. W. Greg (Oxford, 1914), p. 34.

7. See M. D. Conway, *Solomon and Solomonic Literature* (London, 1899), p. 236.

to do, place the wisdom Faustus craves against the knowledge he attains, weigh omniscience against man's possible knowledge, consider whether Faustus confounds two kinds of knowledge, the contemplation of divine mysteries with the active investigation of the world. I shall also seek to show how closely the end of the play, Faustus' denial of Christ (those scenes that receive most attention from the moralists), is related to the scenes that show the scholar at the height of his fame (those that the romantics like), for it is Faustus' obdurate denial of the highest wisdom, symbolized in the figure of Christ, that damns Faustus as a scholar and as a man.

I

The play opens on Faustus seated in his study reviewing the divisions of learning. His speech is a short treatise on a familiar Renaissance theme, the vanity of human knowledge, and lies in the tradition that runs from Solomon's Ecclesiastes to Agrippa's *De vanitate* and beyond. The setting recalls countless pictures of St. Jerome in his study which, because of the legend that the saint turned from pagan learning, were often regarded as vanity pictures. Although there may be a specific echo of Lyly's *Euphues,* Faustus' debate with himself follows the pattern of the *De vanitate*—but Faustus, who would be "as cunning as *Agrippa* was" (B.139), does not come to Agrippa's conclusion. The famous German magician Henry Cornelius Agrippa was certainly known to Marlowe. He had written his *De vanitate* partly as a retraction of his unpublished but notorious book on magic, the *De occulta philosophia,* but as the *De vanitate* was a rhetorical set piece, a *declamatio invectiva,* he included in it a review of all the sciences. (How sincere he was about magic is in doubt, for he later published the *De occulta philosophia* with the retractions perfunctorily appended.[8]) His purpose, he claimed, was not to condemn all learning but to reform the abuses that had "crept in, through the peruerse doings of men." He inveighs against the deification

8. See D. P. Walker, *Spiritual and Demonic Magic from Ficino to Campanella* (London, 1958), p. 190; compare with Faustus' speech the invective in Nashe's *Summer's Last Will and Testament,* ll. 1394 ff. (*Works,* ed. R. B. McKerrow [Oxford, 1958], vol. III).

of the schoolmen and says that knowledge must begin with pious humility, must be lodged in good men, and must be used for the good of the common weal. Knowledge will bring no happiness of itself, but as we have been possessed since the Fall of the knowledge of good and evil, we shall be made happy only by knowing that we are leading a good life in accordance with God's Word. "For not the good vnderstanding, but the good wyll, ioyneth men vnto God." [9]

Such sentiments were the basis of practically all humanist writings on knowledge, and the reflections of Euphues and Faustus on the vanity of worldly learning would be familiar to an Elizabethan audience. But whereas Agrippa "retracted" his magic and Euphues after ten years' unprofitable study turned from "al learninge which is not spronge from the bowels of the holy Bible," [10] Faustus dismisses divinity and embraces necromancy. To have recourse to the devil and the forbidden arts instead of to God and His Word, to devote his energies to his own good instead of the good of the common weal, would be a shocking course of action, directed against the pious tradition of Christian humanism. The scholarly saint has turned sorcerer before our eyes. But it is necessary to look at the speech in more detail.

The first subject Faustus surveys is logic. He would "leuell at the end of euery Art," would "liue and die in *Aristotles* workes." This line might be an ironic jibe at the scholastic logicians, but when Faustus defines the end of logic he derives his formulation not from Aristotle but from Ramus: "Bene disserere est finis logices." [11] It had been Ramus' ambition to sweep away the study of analytics for its own sake and to apply it instead to all forms of discourse, the material of history, antiquity, oratory, and poetry, and in Faustus' one line Marlowe shows a succinct appreciation of Ramus' intention. As is well known, moreover, he portrayed the

9. Agrippa, *Of the Vanitie and vncertaintie of Artes and Sciences,* trans. James Sanford (London, 1575), Sig. ¶ iii[r], fols. 2[r]–3[r].

10. Lyly, *Works,* ed. R. W. Bond (Oxford, 1902), I, 289; this was first quoted by Paul H. Kocher, *Christopher Marlowe* (Chapel Hill, N. C., 1946).

11. This was first pointed out in A. W. Ward's edition of the play (Oxford, 1901), p. 130; in William Temple's edition of Ramus' *Dialecticae libri duo* (Cambridge, Eng., 1584), we find the text "Bene disserere est finis dialecticae," p. 4. The end of "analytics" was thus defined by Aristotle: "Versatur autem in demonstratione, ac de demonstrandi scientia est instituta," *Logica* (Paris, 1567), p. 100.

slaughter of Ramus by the Guise in *The Massacre at Paris*. There before he dies Ramus asks his murderer, "Wherein hath *Ramus* been so offencious?" to which the Guise replies:

> Marry sir, in hauing a smack in all,
> And yet didst neuer sound anything to the depth.
> Was it not thou that scoftes the Organon,
> And said it was a heape of vanities?
> He that will be a flat dicotamest,
> And seen in nothing but Epitomies:
> Is in your iudgment thought a learned man.[12]

Now these were common charges against Ramus and Ramists: that seeking to be scholars "in shew" they used their knowledge only for display and mastered no discipline thoroughly. Most university men who had spent years mastering Aristotelian logic would have no truck with the short cuts indicated by Ramus. In an attack on Ramism in *The Anatomie of Absurditie* (1589) Nashe had censured those who, "out of looue with the obscuritie wherein they liue," sought to shine by parading new-fangled and slapdash opinions quickly learned, "becomming the Maisters of the ignorant before they be the Schollers of the learned." And five years later Hooker sarcastically defined Ramism as "an Art which teacheth the way of speedy discourse, and restraineth the mind of man that it may not wax over-wise." [13] It is probable, therefore, that a university man would detect an element of criticism of Faustus in this line: instead of being as learned as he could claim, Marlowe is suggesting that Faustus, having given his allegiance to Ramus, was swollen with a "selfe conceit," that he still had much to learn in logic alone.

Faustus' sweeping dismissals of medicine and law contain ironies that are as important as the *hubris* they reveal. His lament that he cannot raise

12. Marlowe, *Works,* ed. C. F. Tucker Brooke (Oxford, 1910), ll. 389–396. In the play Ramus counters by saying that he had reduced the confusion of the *Organon* and that he had been reviled because "the blockish Sorbonests" regarded Aristotle's works as sacrosanct. One cannot claim that Marlowe opposed any reform of logic, but as I shall suggest he, like Fraunce, who supported Ramus, disliked the universal dissemination of half-digested learning. See the preface to *The Lawiers Logike* (London, 1588).

13. Nashe, *Works,* I, 43–44. See also Thomas Lodge: "In his hood and habit [the devil] will prooue RAMUS to be a deeper Philosopher then ARISTOTLE," *Wits Miserie* (London, 1596), p. 5; Hooker, *Laws,* I.vi.4.

the dead to life is bitterly echoed in the last speech, when he says he would rather be buried under mountains and hills than live in hell for ever. Similarly his signing of the deed of gift, a "paltry legacy," brings him into confrontation with the eternal law at the end of the play. But when he turns to divinity, the highest learning, he propounds questions so well known to the audience that his unorthodox conclusion must have cast a shadow of condemnation over his actions from the first. He picks up Jerome's Bible and with seeming skill proves syllogistically from scriptural texts (Rom. 6:23 and I John 1:8) that all men are condemned to everlasting death. The audience would have been thoroughly familiar with this argument, for it is found in the Homilies that by law were read each Sunday in every church in the land. In "The First Part of the Sermon Of the miserie of man" the same texts are clearly expounded to conclude: "Wherfore the wyse man in the booke called Ecclesiastes, maketh this true & generall confession. There is not one iust man vppon the earth that doth good & sinneth not." [14] The first reaction of the audience would have been that Faustus' deduction from Solomon's "confession" was false, for, having come to the above conclusion, the homily continues:

It hath bene manifestly declared vnto you, that no man can fulfill the law of God, and therfore by the lawe all men are condemned, whereupon it folowed necessarilye, that some other thinge should be required for our saluatiō, then the lawe: and that is, a true and liuely fayth in Chryst, bringinge foorth good workes, and a lyfe accordinge to Gods commaundementes . . . For the right and true Christian fayth is, not onely to beleue that holy scripture, & al the foresaid articles of our faith are true, but also to haue a sure trust and cōfidence in gods mercifull promises, to be saued from euerlasting damnation by Christ: wherof doth folow a louing hart, to obey his commaundementes. [15]

At the end of the play Mephostophilis boasts that he led Faustus' eye to the scriptural passages that caused him to despair, and we find that the logical proof of universal damnation was a favorite figure of Luther's— he regarded it as the "devil's syllogism." [16] So although Marlowe could

14. *Homilies* (London, 1587), Sig. B2^r-v.

15. *Ibid.,* Sigs. C3^r, C4^v. Cf. *The Merchant of Venice:* "in the course of justice, none of us / Should see salvation" (IV.i.194–195), and *Measure for Measure:* "all the souls that were were forfeit once" (II.ii.73).

16. It was also used by Spenser's Despaire against Redcrosse (*Faerie Queen,* I.ix.28 ff.); see Susan Snyder, "The Left Hand of God: Despair in Medieval and

hardly have been expected to demonstrate his hero's learning conclusively in one short scene, it does seem that Faustus is parading the imperfection rather than the perfection of his learning,[17] since his logic and divinity would ring hollow to anyone who had been to university or even to church. He has not undergone that purification by dialectic and moral philosophy that Pico said gave observation of things divine by the light of theology.[18]

Yet one should not be too severe. Faustus has other accomplishments—he is "grounded in Astrologie, Inricht with tongues, well seene in Minerals" (B.160–161)—although he means to turn them to an evil end. He has heard the music of Homer and Amphion, his far-ranging mind contemns fiddling detail, and there is a hint that he would put his learning to practical use. So too he is loyal to his profession—in Tudor England scholars enjoyed none of the prestige and influence of their counterparts in Italy. Faustus would clothe his fellow students in silk; he knew how

> . . . to this day is euerie scholler poore,
> Grosse gold from them runs headlong to the boore.[19]

These lines from *Hero and Leander* occur when Marlowe is narrating the struggle between the Destinies and Mercury, one of the patrons of learning, and are quoted by Burton, who lists poverty, too much study, and social ostracism among the causes of melancholy and madness.[20] Faustus

---

Renaissance Tradition," *Studies in the Renaissance,* XII (1965), pp. 18–59; and cf. Calvin, *Institutes,* II.vii.9: "Man being condemned of sin by the law, the effect thereof in the good is the crauing of helpe from God, in the bad their despairing of themselues without aspiring to any helper" (trans. T. Norton [London, 1599]).

17. Two morality plays, Redford's *Wit and Science* (before 1547) and its derivative, the anonymous *The Marriage of Wit and Science* (ca. 1570), are devoted to this argument—that true wisdom comes only after long and assiduous study. The orthodox steps to wisdom are also set out in *An Interlude of the Four Elements,* ed. J. O. Halliwell (London, 1848), pp. 5–6. Another parallel can be found in Donne's Third Satyre, where the poet (possibly as early as 1593) urges his contemporaries to resist the temptations of the world, the flesh, and the devil, the temptations to which Faustus succumbs, and urges them to be, unlike Faustus, busy to seek truth, to "doubt wisely."

18. *Oration,* 16.

19. *Hero and Leander,* I. 471–472.

20. *The Anatomy of Melancholy,* I.ii.3.xv.

is determined to break from the tedium and unprofitability of scholarship; he longs for an act of self-affirmation—and spends the rest of the play coming to grips with his intellectual freedom.

After he has committed himself to magic, Faustus embarks eagerly on conjectures as to what his power will bring. There are two problems here: what is Marlowe's attitude to Faustus' "speculations," and what sort of magician is Faustus? The play was written at a boom time for Elizabethan capitalists, and a time when conspicuous expenditure and consumption were not only symptoms of indulgence but the means of attracting the sovereign's favor, the prerequisites of power. Lawrence Stone has drawn up revealing accounts for the enormous amounts spent on display and prodigal living, the extravagance that naturally provoked the satirists of the time.[21] Although there is little direct satire in *Doctor Faustus*, it is continually implied that learning is being subsumed in the pursuit of wealth and power. This theme of Prodigality is not new to drama: Thomas Lupton's morality *All for Money* (printed 1578) has characters that anticipate the themes of Marlowe's tragedy. As well as Sin, Damnation, and Pleasure, there is a Satan whose delight it is to exclude man from salvation and a set called Learning with Money, Learning without Money, Money without Learning, and Neither Money nor Learning. The conclusion is that he who is content with what he has has the greatest riches.[22]

Another play that deals in large part with the prostitution of learning and the pursuit of magnificence is Nashe's *Summer's Last Will and Testament*. It was written in 1592, probably the same year as *Faustus*,[23] an exceptionally bad year for the plague. The values of society are crumbling, there is great store set by material things, and Summer, racked with disease, calls his servants to account and finds them all guilty of extortion,

21. *The Crisis of the Aristocracy, 1558–1641* (Oxford, 1965), pp. 184–186, 547–586.

22. The play is reprinted in *SJ*, XL (1904), 129–186. Cf. W. Wager's *Enough is as Good as a Feast* (printed ca. 1565), where Contentation argues with the Worldly Man, and Dekker's *Old Fortunatus*, the hero of which chooses riches before wisdom.

23. I accept the opinions of W. W. Greg, *Marlowe's "Doctor Faustus,"* pp. vii, 5–11, that the case for the later dating in 1592 is stronger; Kocher, *Christopher Marlowe*, puts the case for 1588–1589.

arrogance, and self-interest. Knowledge has bred pride, pride discontent, "Conscience but few respect, all hunt for gaine":

> Familiaritie and conference,
> That were the sinewes of societies,
> Are now for vnderminings onely vsde,
> And nouell wits, that loue none but themselues,
> Thinke wisedomes height as falshood slily couch't,
> Seeking each other to o'rethrow his mate.
>
> (ll.1157, 1193–1198)

This is the world of the despised comic scenes of *Faustus,* where the scholars sit down to a great feast, where Pride will "not speake an other worde, except the ground were perfumde and couered with cloth of arras" (A.788–780), and where Faustus expends his energies on cozening a horsecourser. *"Wisdome* without honesty," said Jonson quoting from Vives, "is meere craft, and coosinage. And therefore the reputation of Honesty must first be gotten; which cannot be, but by living well. A good life is a maine Argument." [24]

Faustus' adventures moreover are not to be read as just the diversions of a man glutted with pleasure, for they serve to modify our admiration of his Promethean vision. His Epicure Mammonish trances confound his desire for knowledge with his desire for wealth:

> Shall I make spirits fetch me what I please,
> Resolue me of all ambiguities?
> Performe what desperate enterprise I will?
> I'le haue them flie to *India* for gold,
> Ransacke the Ocean for Orient Pearle,
> And search all corners of the new-found-world
> For pleasant fruites and Princely delicates.
> I'le haue them read me strange Philosophy . . .
>
> (B.106–113)

The world will be desperately ransacked for its riches, and knowledge has become another commodity, dissociated from wonder which, as Bacon said, is the "seed of knowledge." Faustus' mind, "steeped and infused in

---

24. Jonson, *Timber,* in *Works,* ed. C. H. Herford and P. and E. Simpson (Oxford, 1925–1952), VIII, 566.

the humours of the affections," [25] can never rise to the contemplation of the highest mysteries.

The evidence Marlowe supplies in the play for an evaluation of Faustus' magic is inconclusive, and our judgment must depend on our widest conception of the play's meaning. It was usual in the Renaissance to define carefully different kinds of magic, since some, like Ficino's and Pico's, were serious philosophic systems, extensions of theology and natural philosophy, while others were the hocus-pocus of sorcerers and conjurors. Many treatises could be cited; the *De vanitate* is convenient. Agrippa begins by dividing magic into natural and ceremonial magic:

Naturall Magicke then is that, whiche hauing intentiuely behelde the forces of all naturall things, and celestiall, and with curious search sought out theyr order, doth in suche sort publish abroade the hidden and secret powers of nature: coupling the inferiour things wyth the qualityes of the superiour as if it were certaine enticements by a naturall ioyning of them togither, that thereof oftentymes doe arise maruellous miracles: not so much by Art as nature whereunto this Arte doeth proffer hir selfe a seruaunt, when shee worketh these things.[26]

Natural magic includes mathematical magic, which is the bringing forth of "things lyke to the woorkes of nature" (as one example he mentions the brazen head that spoke forged by Albert the Great—like the one in *Friar Bacon and Friar Bungay*), and "witching magic," which has to do with potions and transformations and the control of natural phenomena. One of the examples he gives is Orpheus, who with his "Hymne" could, like Prospero, "assuage the stormie tempest." Control of the elements is one of the things Faustus dreams of. Agrippa's attitude to all this is ex-

---

25. *Advancement*, I.i.3. See also James Smith, "Marlowe's *Dr. Faustus*," *Scrutiny*, VIII (1939), 36–55, for some illuminating comparisons with Augustine's strictures against the unbounded appetite for experience and learning. Marlowe often knowingly confuses the motives of his characters in this way to point a moral. The obvious example is the speech in *I Tamburlaine*, "Nature that fram'd vs of foure Elements . . . Doth teach vs all to haue aspyring minds" (ll. 869–880). This is the highest common factor in all romantic interpretations of Marlowe, but it invokes in the reader a measure of detachment when Tamburlaine reveals that the "perfect blisse and sole felicitie" is "The sweet fruition of an earthly crowne." The speech has become a blasphemous prescription for a mystic ecstasy. Cf. Greene's *Selimus* (1594), in *Works*, ed. Grosart (n.p., 1881–1886), XIV, ll. 281–285.

26. *Of the Vanitie*, fol. 55^r.

tremely ambivalent. Like Scot,[27] he gives as much information as confutation and says that "this naturall *Magicke* sometymes enclineth to Geocie and [sometimes to] *Theurgie.*" He notes that Solomon condemned natural magic, claims that the products of natural magic cannot partake of "the veritie, & diuinitie," and expresses incredulity that "the secretes of hidden verity" can be discovered by magic.

What distinguishes natural magic from ceremonial magic is that, whereas the former is concerned with phenomena and the harnessing of the powers or "virtues" of natural objects like the stars, the latter is concerned with the investigation of other worlds and the employment of supernatural agents. Whether the agents are angels or demons determines whether ceremonial magic is white or black, theurgy or goecy. Agrippa says that theurgy is ideally "gouerned by good Angelles, and by the diuine power" but that in effect it is "bounde with wicked deceytes of the Diuels." Goecy is "grounded vpon the entereours of wicked sprites made with the rites of detestable curiositie, with vnleful coniurations, and with defensiue prayers, bannished & accursed by the decrees of al lawes." [28]

Now Faustus wanted to prophesy, to control the elements and bring forth wonders: "make a bridge through the mouing Aire, To passe the Ocean with a band of men" (B.330–331). He is versed in astrology and mineralogy and would make "the subiects of euery element" [29] serve him. He asks Mephostophilis for a book containing the "characters" of the planets (such figures are given in Agrippa and Scot[30]) that he might draw down their virtues, and also one containing "al plants, hearbes and trees that grow vpon the earth" (A.623–624). This last is interesting, for it suggests that Faustus would wield power over things by knowing their names, an idea that was commonly held.[31] Plato suggested that "a power more than human gave things their first names, and that the names which

27. Reginald Scot, *The Discouerie of Witchcraft* (London, 1584).

28. *Of the Vanitie,* fols. 55ᵛ–59ᵛ.

29. A.155; B reads "spirits of euery element."

30. Agrippa, *De occulta philosophia, passim;* and Scot, *Discouerie of Witchcraft,* pp. 397 ff.

31. E. R. Curtius, *European Literature and the Latin Middle Ages* (New York, 1953), pp. 495 ff., has pointed out how ancient and medieval writers (especially Isidore of Seville in his *Etymologiarum libri*) felt that the essence of a thing could be found in its designation.

are thus given are necessarily their true names" [32]—the similarity between *nomen* and *numen* also suggested a mystical relationship. In the Bible it is reported that Adam before the Fall gave names to the whole of Creation (Genesis 2:19–20). These sources stimulated many Renaissance thinkers. Agrippa devoted a chapter of the *De occulta philosophia* (I.lxx) to the subject:

For as the great operator doth produce divers species, and particular things by the influencies of the Heavens, and by the Elements, together with the vertues of Planets; so according to the properties of the influencies proper names result to things, and are put upon them by him who numbers the multitude of the Stars, calling them all by their names.[33]

Bacon wrote:

And therefore it is not the pleasure of curiosity, nor the quiet of resolution, nor the raising of the spirit, nor victory of wit, nor faculty of speech, nor lucre of profession, nor ambition of honour or fame, nor inablement for business, that are the true ends of knowledge; some of these being more worthy than other, though all inferior and degenerate: but it is a restitution and reinvesting (in great part) of man to the sovereignty and power (for whensoever he shall be able to call the creatures by their true names he shall again command them) which he had in his first state of creation.[34]

Before his rebellion Caliban had been taught words that made his purposes known,[35] and Greville wrote that Adam's sin dimmed "that piercing light, Which from their inward natures, gave the name, To euery creature, and describ'd the same." [36] So Faustus is trying to regain prelapsarian knowledge (in vain, of course, for Mephostophilis fobs him off with commonplaces), and although we are aware that immoderate knowledge can lead to the deadly sin of pride, Faustus' desires could pass for theurgic natural magic and be interpreted as quasi-serious and nonblameworthy activities.

But other passages in the play make it impossible for us to condone

---

32. *Cratylus,* 438 (trans. Jowett).
33. *Three Books of Occult Philosophy,* trans. J. F. (London, 1651), p. 153.
34. *Valerius terminus,* in *Works,* III, 222.
35. *The Tempest,* I.ii.357.
36. "A Treatie of Humane Learning," st. 50, *Poems and Dramas,* ed. G. Bullough (Edinburgh, 1939); cf. *Piers the Plowman,* ed. W. W. Skeat (Oxford, 1886), C.xvii. 206–211.

Faustus' magic. The conjuring scene in which Alleyn wore a surplice and cross [37] and used Psalters and New Testaments, Faustus' journeys through the air, his employment of diabolic agents, and the pact with the devil that makes him specifically a witch [38] involve practices that all serious magicians would condemn. Critics who have read a Baconian optimism into the play have overlooked the impression that the elements of witchcraft made upon contemporaries, the horrific seriousness that underlies the comic antics.

Yet this is not the end of the matter, for it can be argued that Faustus does not attain even the stature of a sorcerer or diviner but is merely an illusionist or juggler, duped by the devil. Although it would not be possible to perform on stage the miracles Faustus planned, those that he does perform, the tricks with the horsecorser and soldiers, and the illusions wrought at court, are the lowest form of magical art. Illusions, said Agrippa, are the stock in trade of stage players and

are onely done according to the outwarde apparance: wyth these the Magitiens do shewe vaine visions, and with Iugling casts do play many myracles, and cause dreams, which thing is not so muche done by *Geoticall* inchauntments, and prayers, and deceytes of the Diuell, as also with certaine vapours of perfumes, lightes, medicines, colleries, bindings, and hangings, moreouer with rings, Images, glasses & other like receyts and instruments of Magicke, and with a natural and celestial vertue.[39]

We are reminded of how Marlowe, as the Baines note reports, sneered at Moses, who was held to have wrought his miracles by means of the cabala he had received from God: "He affirmeth that Moyses was but a Jugler & that one Heriots being Sir W. Raleighs man Can do more than he." It would seem, therefore, that Faustus can be seen not as a mighty magician but only as an illusionist and would-be sorcerer. For even his conjuring is ineffective because Mephostophilis tells him that he came to Faustus of his own accord and then only because he heard the blasphemies in the spells—Pico quotes Plotinus' opinion that only he who has the spirits in his power and not vice versa can be graced with the

37. See Samuel Rowlands, *The Knave of Clubbs* (London, 1615?), Sig. D2ᵛ.

38. As opposed to a sorcerer who merely conjured the devil. King James and others made this distinction.

39. *Of the Vanitie,* fol. 62ᵛ. Cf. Lodge, *The Divil Coniured,* in *Works* (New York, 1963), p. 25.

name of "magus." [40] The devil's book may have the power to summon Mephostophilis from Constantinople, but he and his companions carry off the magician at the end of the play. So, like Scot, Marlowe was showing that a witch was powerless except to unleash the forces of evil. He could count on the terror these would arouse in the audience as the reports of the visible appearance of the devil on the stage testify, and he knew that his hero's black magic would be regarded as both crime and sin.

Although the state of the text makes any firm decision impossible, I believe with Greg that most of the comic scenes were planned, if not written, by Marlowe. [41] Instead of gaining the wisdom and power he had hoped for from magic, Faustus is fobbed off by diabolic fraud with a series of tricks and illusions, fun to watch on the stage, but terrifyingly ominous in the foretaste they provide with their false legs and heads of the devils tearing Faustus apart at the end of the play. Even the Pope's feast, so obvious an occasion for knockabout farce, has moral overtones as a banquet of sense. In production its staging could well allude visually to the first scene where Faustus devours the "courses" of learning before they are snatched away. [42] Certainly the Wagner scenes cannot be dismissed lightly. Lines like "the Villaines . . . so hungry, that I know he would giue his soule to the deuill, for a shoulder of Mutton, tho it were bloud raw" [43] place Faustus' blind appetite grotesquely in the tradition that Curtius has called "kitchen humor." [44] And it is significant that Marlowe does not follow *The Damnable Life* which makes Wagner one

40. *Oration*, 33. Cf. Agrippa, *Of the Vanitie*, fol. 58ʳ: "For the diuels also beeing constreyned do always lie in wayte to the ende that they may deceyue vs going astray."

41. Cf. Paul H. Kocher, "Nashe's Authorship of the Prose Scenes in *Faustus*," *MLQ*, III (1942), 17–40.

42. See M. C. Bradbrook, "Marlowe's *Doctor Faustus* and the Eldritch Tradition," in *Essays in Honour of Hardin Craig* (London, 1963), pp. 83–90; J. F. Kermode, "The Banquet of Sense," *Bulletin of the John Rylands Library*, XLIV (1961), pp. 68–99.

43. B.346–348; images connected with appetite are frequent in the play: "How am I glutted with conceipt of this?" (B.105); "The God thou seru'st is thine owne appetite" (B.398); "O this feedes my soule" (A.797); also B.25–26, B.1864, B.1932.

44. See E. R. Curtius, "Jest and Earnest in Medieval Literature," in *European Literature and the Latin Middle Ages* (New York, 1953), pp. 417–435.

"which had studied also at the *Vniversitie of Wittenberg*" (chap. 56). He is instead a servant, from which we may infer that Marlowe had in mind a burlesque of elements in the main plot, played by characters of inferior class. The other juggling scenes, besides dramatizing the failure of Faustus' aspirations, have a thematic relationship to the central scenes. For whereas the great scenes display the connection between wisdom and faith, the comic scenes display the connection between wisdom and works. Marlowe's attitude to them is ambiguous for they not only suggest a falling off from humanist ideals but also, with their antipapist satire, evoke the audience's indulgence. Unable to believe, Faustus "embraces magic rituals, they are something he can *do*."[45] But horrific rituals and comic antics contribute in no way to Faustus' damnation. This comes because Faustus ignores true wisdom, what Calvin called "certaine knowledge," that feeling of godhead that even a reprobate experiences.[46] Faustus must be justified by his faith alone.

Faustus signs the deed with the devil, ignores the warnings of both Mephostophilis and the Good Angel, and proceeds to his diabolic catechism, a scene that echoes Nature's speech to Humanyte in *An Interlude of the Four Elements* and foreshadows Lear's questioning of Edgar.[47] If Faustus hopes to plumb the secrets of the cosmos, he is deceived. To his questions about hell, Mephostophilis points out that it is not only a place, but a condition, a familiar Protestant doctrine. As a place it is circumscribed by local limits, but its existence is coextensive with its essence. Faustus' reason rejects this seeming sophistry: "I thinke Hel's a fable" (B.519), he says, just as he had disproved by reason the possibility of salvation in the first scene. Mephostophilis will provide material for his rational deductions, but his rejoinder to Faustus' conclusion ("I, thinke so still, till experience change thy minde") suggests that Marlowe is affirming the Protestant and skeptical conviction that saving wisdom comes not from reason but from faith. The passage recalls Montaigne, who wrote against rational atheists:

45. Quoted from C. L. Barber, "The Form of Faustus' Fortunes Good or Bad," *TDR*, VIII (1964), 92–119. Barber also notes that "*Doctor Faustus* reflects the tension involved in the Protestant's world's denying itself miracle in a central area of experience."

46. *Institutes*, III.ii.11, 14.

47. See Muir's important note to III.iv.159 in the Arden edition of *King Lear*.

They establish . . . by the reason of their judgement, that whatsoever is re-ported of hell, or of after-comming paines, is but a fiction; but the occasions to make triall of it, offering it selfe, at what time age or sickenes doth sommon them to death: the [terrour] of the same, through the horrour of their future condition, doth then replenish with another kinde of beleefe.[48]

Faustus is replenished with "another kinde of beleefe" at the end of the play, but it is not the faith which he has repeatedly abjured and which alone could have enlightened and saved him.

Mephostophilis' refusal to propound Copernican theories has bothered many critics. But we can reasonably conjecture that Marlowe, who dis-played a far more expert knowledge of astronomy than the author of the *Faustbuch,* was aware of Copernican thought and that he either dismissed the theory as false or, which is more probable, chose to reject it for dra-matic reasons. For although Johnston pointed out that no textbook widely used in Marlowe's youth contained a detailed description of the Coperni-can system,[49] it would be surprising if he had not heard of the writings of Thomas Digges in the 1570's, Bruno's advocacy of Copernicus during his visit to England, or the Copernican ideas discussed by Richard Har-vey,[50] Dr Dee, and Thomas Harriot. Three years after Marlowe's death Nashe, his fellow student at Cambridge and coauthor of *Dido,* wrote of Gabriel Harvey's "hatching such another Paradoxe as that of *Nicholaus Copernicus* was, who held that the Sun remains immoueable in the cen-ter of the World, & that the Earth is moou'd about the Sunne." [51]

Yet if Marlowe did in fact know of Copernicus there is not a trace of the new cosmology in Faustus' dialogue with Mephostophilis (or in the rest of his work):

> Come *Mephostophilis* let vs dispute againe,
> And reason of diuine Astrology.
> Speake, are there many Spheares aboue the Moone?

48. Montaigne, *Apologie,* Everyman's Library (New York, 1923–1928), II, 134. Cf. Calvin, *Institutes,* I.iv.4. For the *ubiquism* of the Lutheran heretic John Brenz, see D. C. Allen, "Paradise Lost I, 254–255," *MLN,* LXXI (1956), 324–326.

49. F. R. Johnston, "Marlowe's Astronomy and Renaissance Skepticism," *ELH,* XIII (1946), 241–254. Cf. Kocher: "either Marlowe did not know Copernican thought, or, if he did, he had already irrevocably given his allegiance to the system of Aristotle and Ptolemy," *Marlowe,* p. 214.

50. *Lamb of God* (London, 1590), p. 176.

51. *Works,* III, 94.

> Are all Celestiall bodies but one Globe,
> As is the substance of this centricke earth?
>   MEPHOSTOPHILIS
> As are the elements, such are the heauens,
> Euen from the Moone vnto the Emperiall Orbe,
> Mutually folded in each others Spheares,
> And iontly moue vpon one Axle-tree,
> Whose terminem, is tearmed the worlds wide Pole.
>
>   (B.602–611)

Obviously Mephostophilis is repeating Ptolemaic commonplaces [52] and dismisses Faustus' probings as offhandedly as does the simple carter in one of the later scenes:

>   FAUSTUS
> Nay, hearke you, can you tell me where you are?
>   CARTER
> I marry can I, we are vnder heauen.
>
>   (B.1708–1709)

The debate proceeds with Faustus trying to make Mephostophilis reveal whether God made the world, but the only pronouncement he can draw from him is a denial of the existence of the crystalline sphere (which had been introduced to account for the phenomenon of trepidation) and of the elementary sphere of fire. The crystalline sphere had been discarded by Augustinus Ricius in his *De motu octauae sphaerae,* which Johnston suggests might have been known to Marlowe [53]—it was also to be discarded by Ralegh.[54] Johnston makes the point that Mephostophilis is therefore propounding an unorthodox modification of Ptolemaic cosmology that was notable for its stress on empirical observation, since the two spheres it rejected were unfurnished with visible bodies. But to have let Mephostophilis impart more revolutionary theories to Faustus would have been to destroy the argument of the play. Diabolic knowledge is not wisdom.

It is notable, moreover, that throughout the play Faustus does not believe *anything* that he does not experience with his senses. (In fact, Coper-

52. The strongly placed word *centricke* suggests Faustus is expecting something more revolutionary.

53. But Ricius' theory had been mentioned by Thomas Digges in 1576 (see Kocher, *Marlowe,* p. 218 n), and by Agrippa, *Vanitie,* fol. 42ᵛ.

54. *Works* (Oxford, 1829), II, 23.

nican cosmology, which was at that time based not on empirical observation but on mathematical convenience, would have been beyond his comprehension). Mephostophilis leads Faustus' eyes to the relevant scriptures and afterwards is careful to keep his senses gratified and his mind diverted. Faustus disregards all counsel and the promptings of his own conscience. He could not see as Anselm did that belief might come before comprehension—*credo ut intelligam*. This point is developed by Thomas Lodge in *The Divel Coniured* (1596), an admirable discourse on magic and witchcraft:

> worldlie mens delight is tied to their knowledge, and what they sée, they commend, & what they heare, they suspect: They onlie that know the world trulie, trust it not in well knowing it, by faith they apprehend things vnséene, and by the profit are assured of their vncertainties: Christ by becomming man, prooueth that nothing is vnpossible to God: by partaking infirmity, nourisheth our faiths: & we that know his sufferance excéedeth our senses, must cōclude, that onelie faith must apprehend his Deitie. To them that beléeue, he maketh all things possible; the holie Ghost helpeth them, who breedeth charitie; their charitie inflameth them, which norisheth faith; their faith assureth them being grounded in charitie. To them that beléeue not that which they sée not, he giueth ouer to trust in that which they should not: in blindness they liue, in obstinacie they continue, & desperat they die.
>
> (p. 18)

Faustus' death stands for the death of the intellect enclosed by the senses; his "friuolous demaunds," his proud and obtuse refusal to concede the existence of the truth that is apprehended by faith, strike in us as in Mephostophilis himself the terrible impulse to retreat from a man with whom we might otherwise be in sympathy. As Heilman points out in a penetrating article, Faustus neither brings self-knowledge to the play, nor, which is more terrifying, does he attain it at the end.[55]

From academic disputation Faustus is easily diverted, first by his desire for a wife, then by the show of the seven deadly sins. He has already succumbed to the medieval temptations of the world and the devil; his temptation of the flesh culminates with a second banquet of sense and in his vision of Helen. His sexual appetite must be titillated with the exotic; he must sleep where Paris lay. Of course his vision of Helen *does* redeem

55. R. B. Heilman, " 'Twere Best not Know Myself': Othello, Lear, Macbeth," in *Shakespeare 400*, ed. J. G. McManaway (New York, 1964), pp. 89–98.

the bathos of the preceding scenes, and the quality and intensity of the verse celebrate something that is remarkably absent from the cold-hearted bargaining that passes on both sides for the processes of religion. One must concede a positive here, but it is a positive that transmutes various highly ironic statements. For we must remember that Helen has been an ambiguous figure from the times of Stesichorus and Euripides,[56] and that in many sixteenth-century poems she was often, if not a whore, at least a symbol of fickleness and mutability as well as being the destroyer of the home of the mythical ancestor of Elizabeth.[57] And, as W. W. Greg pointed out, "in making [Helen] his paramour, Faustus commits the sin of demoniality, that is, bodily intercourse with demons."[58] By seeing Helen as a succuba, the lines

> Sweet *Hellen* make me immortall with a kisse:
> Her lips sucke forth my soule, see where it flies
>
> (B.1876–1877)

have an ominous ring, since it was commonly believed that "a witch could not die until his familiar was passed on by a breath or kiss to someone living"; and there was a more rarely expressed belief "that the gift must be from a man to a woman and from a woman to a man."[59] Although Faustus was already "a spirit in forme and substance," the presence on the stage of real actors probably suggested a demonic tryst to the audience. But the Helen scene has a deeper symbolic value, for it is here that Faustus definitively renounces the honorable lives of action and contemplation for the dishonorable one of voluptuousness. "He that preferred Helena, quitted the gifts of Juno and Pallas."[60]

56. See A. W. Ward's edition of *Faustus*, pp. 122–124. For the false Helen in Spenser, see T. Roche, *The Kindly Flame* (Princeton, N. J., 1964), pp. 152–162.

57. See Proctor's "The Reward of whoredome by the fall of Helen," in *A Gorgeous Gallery of Gallant Inventions* [1578], ed. H. E. Rollins (Cambridge, Mass., 1926), p. 81. Rollins lists other poems, p. 187 n.

58. "The Damnation of Faustus," *MLR*, XLI (1946), 97–107; Greg's article must be read in conjunction with T. W. Craik's "Faustus' Damnation Reconsidered," *Ren D*, N.S. II (1969), 189–196, which doubts Greg's literal interpretation of the text and rightly doubts whether it is here that "the nice balance between possible salvation and imminent damnation is upset."

59. K. M. Briggs, *Pale Hecate's Team* (London, 1962), p. 37.

60. Bacon, *Essays*, "Of Love," *Works*, p. 398. W. S. Hecksher, "Was this the face . . .?", *JWCI*, I (1937), 295–297, suggests that there is an echo of Lucian's

II

Doctor Faustus opens on to social and intellectual reality, but its theological and philosophical meaning is, I believe, best examined with reference to the medieval plays from which it is directly descended. Its hero, unlike Edward II and Tamburlaine, who are monarchs, is Everyman whose fame depends on his wisdom. He is confronted by powers of good and evil, clownage alternates with graver scenes, and the play works by tableau and set debate in a way that looks back to the moralities. But beside the structural debt, certain doctrines that appear in earlier plays help the understanding of the themes of Marlowe's play. It is not possible to point to direct borrowing—the ideas were too commonplace—but these didactic plays project an orthodoxy that may elude a modern audience.

The "Macro" morality play *Wisdom Who Is Christ,* subtitled "How Lucifer tempts the Mind, Will, and Understanding of Man to sin" (ca. 1460), is a debate on the very issues of *Doctor Faustus.* The play opens with the entry of Wisdom clad in purple cloth of gold, wearing an imperial crown set with precious stones, and carrying an orb and scepter. He proclaims himself as "Euerlastynge Wysdom" and as Christ explains why this name is especially given to the Son:

> All-thow eche persone of þe trinyte be wysdam eternall,
>   And all thre, on euerlastynge wysdome to-gedyr present,
> Neuer-þe-les, for-as-moche as wysdom ys propyrly
>   Applyede to þe sune by resune,
> And als yt fallyt to hym specyally,
>   By-cause of hys hye generacion,
> Therfor þe belowyde sone hathe þis sygnyficacion
>   Custummaly 'Wysdom', nowe Gode, now man,
> Spows of þe chyrche, & wery patrone,
> Wyffe of eche chose sowle: thus Wysdom be-gane.[61]

18th Dialogue of the Dead on the theme *mors omnia aequat,* in which the cynic Menippus discourses with Hermes over Helen's skull.

61. *The Macro Plays,* ed. F. J. Furnivall and A. W. Pollard (London, 1904), ll. 7–16. The idea of *sophia,* the active wisdom that Paul contrasted with the intellectual wisdom of the Greeks, derives from 1 Cor. 1:24. For a history of the *topos* of Christ as Wisdom and its iconography, see M. T. d'Alverny, "La Sainte Sagesse et le Christ," *The Bodleian Library Record,* V (1956), 232–244. Cf. Sidney's

Anima enters accompanied by Mind, Will, and Understanding, and asks Wisdom what she may give Him; He desires her to give Him her heart. When she asks Him to "Teche me þe scholys of yowur dyvynyte," he replies:

> Dysyer not to sauour in cunnynge to excellent,
>   But drede and conforme yowur wyll to me,
>   For yt ys þe heelfull dyscyplyne þat in Wysdom may be,
>   The drede of God, þat ys begynnynge;
>   The wedis of synne, þat makyt to flee,
>   And swete wertuus herbys in þe sowll sprynge.

(ll. 87–92)

And when Anima asks Wisdom how she may know God, He replies:

> By knowynge of yowur sylff, ye may haue felynge
>   Wat God ys is yowur sowle sensyble;
>   The more knowynge of yowur selff passyble,
>   þe more veryly ye xall God knowe.

(ll. 95–98)

Wisdom goes out, and in His absence Lucifer enters "in a dewyllys [a]ray, with-owt & with-in, as a prowde galonte" and boasts of his knowledge of "all compleccions of a man" (l. 343). He dupes the three "mights," urging Mind to leave his studies, to dress well, do many deeds, get riches, see the world, seek a mistress, and breed children. Like Faustus, Mind is turned from the Wisdom of God to knowledge of the flesh. Understanding and Will cheerfully join Mind, and Lucifer plans to steer them to three of the deadly sins, Pride, Lechery, and Covetousness, the perversions of the virtues with which they are respectively associated. They glory in their misdeeds, but when Wisdom returns like the Old Man in *Faustus* and bids Mind think on his end, Anima after some hesitation repents and calls on Christ for mercy. She comes to "Salomonys conclusyon": "Timor domini inicium sapiencie" (ll. 1157–1158).

---

translation of de Mornay's *A Woorke concerning the trewnesse of the Christian Religion* [1587]: "In the Trinitie we call the Sonne, the Word, or the Speech; namely, the lively and perfect image and wisedome of the Father," (Sidney, *Works*, ed. Feuillerat [Cambridge, Eng., 1912–1926], III, 325). For further examples in medieval drama, see M. F. Smith, *Wisdom and Personification of Wisdom* (Washington, D. C., 1935), pp. 145–163.

The parallels to the events in the Faustus story are apparent, and the parallels in doctrine, although perhaps only present by implication in the later play, are suggestive. Faustus' denial of Christ, "the power of God and the wisdom of God" (I Cor. 1:24), is a final denial of wisdom. In the last scene we see Faustus obtusely refusing the highest wisdom and power he had dreamed of. He has cut himself off from the Christian tradition of learning, the tradition established by Luther and Colet, for whom wisdom was above all Christ, and can find no other to replace it. He has sought infinite knowledge but does not realize that this is built upon the saving wisdom of repentance and contrition, the Knowledge personified in Everyman. His "selfe conceit" has supplanted his fear of the Lord.[62] Unable because of this pride to comprehend "þe scholys of dyvynyte," he tries a short cut to wisdom—sorcery. His lack of self-knowledge, dramatized by his failure to measure his achievements against his aspirations, prevents him from winning higher knowledge. Ignorance of himself produces pride, ignorance of God, despair. And by letting his sensuality triumph over his reason, by giving himself to Helen rather than heeding the Old Man's counsel, he deprives himself of heavenly grace and is unable to repent. True, his proud daring and the breadth of his vision surpass the simple delights of the morality play and turn their jingles into felt desires, but the agony of the final scene is so much the greater.

Wisdom Who Is Christ contains more doctrine relevant to *Doctor Faustus* than the other Macro plays, but these do provide some useful insights. *The Castle of Perseverance* contains elements that parallel the high scenes in *Faustus*. It is a play about the art of dying. Mankind appears between a good and an evil angel; the Good Angel urges him to think on his end so that he will not sin, but Mankind accepts the counsel of the Bad Angel —there will be time enough for repentance when he is old and his fleshly fires have burned low. As Pleasure says later:

> With þis werld he schal haue lond & house;
> þis werldys wysdom geueth not a louse
> of God, nyn of hye heuene.

$$(ll.489-492)$$

62. Like the characters in *The White Devil,* Faustus' world finishes beneath the moon: he refuses to contemplate the highest wisdom which is spiritual and not terrestrial, to confound knowledge with knowledge, as Flamineo says.

The play continues with a long series of debates, in which the following, spoken by Humilitas to Pride, the primal sin, is important. Pride was the insuperable bar to salvation until Christ's death—since His death it has become the way to hell:

> for, whann Lucyfer to helle fyl,
>   Pride, þer-of þou were chesun;
> & þou, deuyl, with wyckyd wyl,
>   In paradys trappyd us with tresun,
> So þou us bond in balys Ille;
>   þis may I preue be ryth resun.
> tyl þis Duke þat dyed on hylle,
>   in heuene man myth neuere han sesun;
>   þe gospel þus declaryt.
> for who-so lowe hym, schal ben hy;
> þerfore þou schalt not comen us ny;
> & þou þou be neuere so sly,
>   I schal felle al þi fare.
>   qui se exaltat, humiliabitur, & cetera.

(ll. 2096–2109)

For although the devil's power is great, man can be saved by Christ's sacrifice—if he repents:

> Lord, þou þat man hathe don more mysse þanne good,
>   if he dey in very contricioun,
> Lord, þe lest drope of þi blod,
>   For hys synne makyth satisfaccioun.

(ll. 3367–3370)

Despite his apostasy Faustus could have called on Christ until the last moment. But he succumbs to Lucifer's threats and temptations, and by calling on Lucifer to spare him, instead of on Christ to save him, he is damned:

> See see where Christs blood streames in the firmament,
> One drop would saue my soule, halfe a drop, ah my Christ.
> Ah rend not my heart for naming of my Christ,
> Yet wil I call on him, oh spare me *Lucifer!*
> Where is it now? tis gone:
> And see where God stretcheth out his arme,
> And bends his irefull browes.

(A.1463–1469)

Faustus' "Knowledge of Good bought dear by knowing ill"[63] comes too late to save him.

The third of the Macro moralities, *Mankind* (ca. 1470), helps us to understand the comic scenes of *Faustus* and the hero's relationship with Mephostophilis. More worldly than the other two plays, *Mankind* demonstrates how, after the Fall, Man can be saved only by Christ's mercy. Mercy appears to Mankind at the beginning of the play and is greeted as the incarnation of saving knowledge:

> All heyll, semely father! ye be welcome to þis house!
> Of þe very wysdam ye haue partycypacyon.
>
> (ll. 202–203)

Mankind takes counsel from Mercy and resolves to live by the sweat of his brow and delve with his spade. In this way he is sure he can resist the blandishments of Titivillus the devil. But his resolution[64] does not save him from the wily Titivillus and his fellows New Guise, Nought, and Nowadays, and he accepts the fleshly delights they offer him. Mercy, however, expostulates with Mankind, who at first refuses to listen, and then falls into despair. He goes to hang himself, and Mischief like Mephostophilis is promptly at hand with a rope just when he would despair and die.

> The egall justyse of God wyll not permytte such a synfull wrech
> To be rewyvyd & restoryd a-geyn; yt were Impossibyll

he laments. But Mercy, like the Old Man shows how God does not work merely according to His law:

> The justice of God wyll as I wyll, as hym selfe doth precyse:
> Nolo mortem peccatoris, inquit, & yff he wyll be reducyble.[65]
>
> (ll. 824–827)

Here Mercy triumphs over despair, and the play ends with a sermon *De contemptu mundi*. But although the play ends happily and although the

---

63. *Paradise Lost*, IV, 222.

64. Nicholas Brooke has argued that *Doctor Faustus* is a perversion of the morality pattern in that Faustus resolves to be damned and succeeds despite the warnings of Mephostophilis: "The Moral Tragedy of Dr. Faustus," *The Cambridge Journal*, V (1952), 662–687.

65. Cf. *Faerie Queene*, I, ix.39.

devils appear as a crew of merry fellows, good companions as Mephostophilis is to Faustus, there is an awful difference between the cheerful
vice and the implacable enemy of mankind, between their familiar appearance and their evil nature. The audience's laughter at Mankind's pitiful attempts to resist them floats on a deep sense of unease, and like the comic
scenes of *Faustus* the play is a parable of the pettiness of man without
God.

III

But what *was* Faustus' sin, and did he bring his punishment upon himself, or was it inflicted by a vengeful God, a symbol of all the beliefs he
had outraged? It is possible to show that it was not the conjuring (or
rather juggling), nor even the diabolic pact that cost Faustus his salvation. For the mere presence of the Old Man and Good Angel would be
ridiculous if Faustus had been damned from the beginning of the play,
or if there were no possibility of his repentance.[66] His fellow scholars regretfully leave him in the penultimate scene for embracing goecy, but
even after he has excluded "the grace of heauen" from his soul by taking
Helen as his paramour, there is no reason to believe that this loss of grace
has made salvation impossible, since he is granted the vision of Christ's
blood in his last agony. For Faustus is damned not for his works—Marlowe could indulge Faustus in the comic scenes without causing us to
worry about his salvation—but for his loss of faith. In terms of the in-
forming allegory of the play, Faustus has blindly ignored Christ, the incomprehensible mysteries of the highest wisdom. By this act he has at
once damned himself as a scholar and been made to realize that, as at the

66. Scot, *Discouerie* (1584), notes (pp. 40 ff.) that bargains between witches and
devils are not binding. Nor would orthodox theologians allow that the devil by his
strength alone would overcome a penitent Christian: see St. John Chrysostom, "De
Diabolo Tentatore": "Unum igitur hoc primum didicimus, eum per vim aut
necessitatem non vincere," *Homiliae LXXVII* (Paris, 1609), p. 319D; also his
Sermon that no man is hurted but of hym selfe, trans. T. Lupset (London, 1542).
Chrysostom's sermons contain several specific points that Marlowe included in his
play (see J. D. Jump's edition [London, 1962], p. 21 n). For Faustus' despair, see
Chrysostom's *Treatise touching the restoring againe of him that is fallen,* trans.
R. Wolcomb (London, 1609), esp. pp. 6, 139.

beginning of the play, he is "still but *Faustus,* and a man." We fear his punishment, but we pity his fate and realize that human comprehension will rise no higher than his. Specifically, however, in sixteenth-century terms, Faustus is a man who has fallen away from God, who has committed the sin of sins, the sin against the Holy Ghost, by his repeated abjurations of Christ, and who finally falls into despair. As Luther knew, despair could lead to salvation, but he also knew the other despair, the sin against hope, the denial of Christ, the repudiation of saving wisdom.

Until the last moments of the play we are in suspense over whether Faustus will recover his faith. At the beginning of the play he had planned to

> . . . make a bridge through the moouing ayre,
> To passe the *Ocean* with a band of men,
> Ile ioyne the hills that binde the *Affricke* shore,
> And make that land continent to Spaine.
>
> (A.350–353)

These are parodies of miracles that could be wrought only by those who possessed the strongest faith [67]—Faustus' aspirations are in fact similar to the powers of Fidelia in *The Faerie Queene.* She alone could teach Redcrosse the mysteries of heavenly learning, and she alone had the cosmic power Faustus craved:

> And when she list poure out her larger spright,
> She would commaund the hastie Sunne to stay,
> Or backward turne his course from heauens hight;
> Sometimes great hostes of men she could dismay,
> Dry-shod to passe, she parts the flouds in tway;
> And eke huge mountains from their natiue seat
> She could commaund, themselues to beare away,
> And throw in raging sea with roaring threat.
> Almightie God he gaue such powre, and puissance great.
>
> (I.x.20)

These are also like the miracles that the magician Antichrist in the Chester play boasts of but can never perform and for which he is damned

---

67. See Matt. 7:20: "if ye haue fayth . . . ye shall saye vnto this mountaine, Remoue hence to yonder place, and it shall remoue: and nothing shalbe vnpossible vnto you."

and borne away by devils.[68] But Faustus succumbs, and his last call for
the mountains and hills to fall on him, an image taken from Luke 23:30
and Revelation 6:15–16, has a special irony. Without faith he could not
perform miracles; without faith he could not be saved.

The movement of *The Tragicall Historie of Doctor Faustus* is therefore inevitably towards orthodoxy rather than iconoclasm. The great
scenes re-enact and reassert the emblems of Christian learning, the saint in
his study, Solomon's conviction of vanity, the moralizations of the Helen
story, the saving wisdom of Christ, and the apocalypse that will destroy
all monuments to man's knowledge. But when pointing the moral of
this play we must not let the weight of censure fall too heavily on the
hero, for he is the representative of a tradition of learning which was
essentially self-destructive. Until men could find conviction in their study
of the world for its own sake, which implies a retreat from divine wisdom
as well as a retreat from the humanist ideals of wisdom as a moral virtue
and of the priority of self-knowledge, Faustus' attempt to resolve the
predicament of Solomon had to end in tragedy. Yet the intensity of
Faustus' vision that culminates in his conjuring of Helen and his whole
grand temerity affects us far more deeply than Bacon's rationalizations
or a critic's moralizings. *Doctor Faustus,* like all great tragedies, defies
philosophy.

68. See *The Play of Antichrist from the Chester Cycle,* ed. W. W. Greg (Oxford, 1935). Faustus' death scene is similar to that of Philologus in Woodes's *The
Conflict of Conscience.* See also Lily B. Campbell, *"Doctor Faustus:* A Case of Conscience," *PMLA,* LXVII (1952), 219–239.

"The Sobbing Deer":
As You Like It, *II.i.21–66*
and the Historical Context

CLAUS UHLIG

T HE ACHIEVEMENTS of historical scholarship in Shakespearean research
are indisputable. Hardly less obvious, however, are its dangers. Nowadays, it is true, they do not seem to consist so much in ". . . the scholar's
attempt to confine the writer within the pale of the age's commonplace
. . . ," as Wilbur Sanders put it not long ago,[1] as in an undue broadening
of the historical perspective to a point where the term "historical" loses
all significance. This blurring of necessary distinctions seems to underlie
the same writer's concluding remarks on "the proper uses of historical
material in the study of literature" in his otherwise suggestive and penetrating, although somewhat disorganized, book, especially when he makes
the use of historical material depend on an "act of critical definition,"
inferring:

This is an expanded version of an article which originally appeared in Germany
(*SJ* [*West*] [1968], pp. 141–168). It is reprinted with the permission of the pub-
lisher, Quelle & Meyer. I wish to thank Miss Deborah Engländer (University College, London) for her kind help with the English translation.
1. Cf. his *The Dramatist and the Received Idea: Studies in the Plays of Marlowe
and Shakespeare* (Cambridge, Eng., 1968), p. 321.

. . . material drawn from the dramatist's own culture has no more intrinsic claim to be regarded as relevant than material from our own, or some earlier culture. Hooker has no more authority than Jean-Paul Sartre in the interpretation of Shakespeare, because what has to be established in each case is a mutually illuminating congruence of thought.[2]

Such a conviction endorses unlimited freedom of association on the part of scholars and critics, and may, in the end, lead to unchecked subjectivity in the interpretation of Shakespeare's plays. Instead, it seems wiser and more objective to start from a particular Shakespearean passage and to establish its immediate historical context by trying to find out how it is related to corresponding passages which belong to the Renaissance literary heritage and consciousness and can therefore be shown to be relevant to the interpretation of the Shakespearean text under discussion. When we have acquired some degree of insight into a coherent pattern of related texts, we may then ask what use Shakespeare made of the historical material at his disposal. The historical approach thus conceived might pave the way to a correct interpretation of the dramatist and bring us closer to the real meaning of any given text in his work. It goes without saying that highly reflective passages, of the kind found in the tragedies and history plays as well as in the comedies, are particularly suited to this purpose. Shakespeare's comedy *As You Like It* is a case in point.

As You Like It can only be compared with *Love's Labour's Lost* as far as poverty of action is concerned.[3] The central elements in the play consist of what is said and reported, not of what happens. One could therefore justifiably say: "It is a play of comment rather than of action."[4] Even if the predominantly static character of the comedy is disadvantageous to its immediate scenic effectiveness, it is, from the historical point of view and as seen against the background of Shakespeare's entire work, certainly to be understood as the expression of a definite stylistic intention. Maynard Mack differentiated between two aspects of Shakespeare's artistic method, the psychological and the emblematic, making the point that the former serves engagement, the latter detachment, by—as for example in the garden scene in *Richard II* (III.iv)—creating distance from the dramatic

2. *Ibid.,* p. 318.

3. Cf. Harold Jenkins, *"As You Like It,"* ShS, VIII (1955), 40–51, esp. 42.

4. Cf. *Narrative and Dramatic Sources of Shakespeare,* ed. Geoffrey Bullough, (London and New York, 1958), II, 157.

events and enhancing their significance.[5] A recognition of these differences in method not only enables us to understand the characteristic style of *As You Like It* but at the same time obliges us to examine Shakespeare's emblematic style with reference to a play where comment, creating distance, and not infrequently ironic speech dominate so clearly. This can be achieved by concentrating on a selected textual example.

The first scene of the second act leads us into the Forest of Arden, where we meet for the first time the banished Duke and his lords, disguised as foresters. After the Duke has praised his new situation eloquently, making a virtue out of necessity and voicing the opinion that, though exposed to the inclemency of the weather, he is now safe from the dangers of court life (1–18), he suddenly changes the subject:

DUKE SENIOR
Come, shall we go and kill us venison?
And yet it irks me the poor dappled fools,
Being native burghers of this desert city,
Should, in their own confines, with forked heads
Have their round haunches gor'd.

FIRST LORD
                        Indeed, my lord,
The melancholy Jaques grieves at that;
And, in that kind, swears you do more usurp
Than doth your brother that hath banish'd you.
To-day my Lord of Amiens and myself
Did steal behind him as he lay along
Under an oak whose antique root peeps out
Upon the brook that brawls along this wood!
To the which place a poor sequest'red stag,
That from the hunter's aim had ta'en a hurt,
Did come to languish; and, indeed, my lord,
The wretched animal heav'd forth such groans
That their discharge did stretch his leathern coat
Almost to bursting; and the big round tears
Cours'd one another down his innocent nose
In piteous chase; and thus the hairy fool,

5. "Engagement and Detachment in Shakespeare's Plays," *Essays on Shakespeare and Elizabethan Drama in Honour of Hardin Craig,* ed. R. Hosley (London, 1963), pp. 275–296.

Much marked of the melancholy Jaques,
Stood on th' extremest verge of the swift brook,
Augmenting it with tears.

DUKE S[ENIOR]
                    But what said Jaques?
Did he not moralize this spectacle?

FIRST LORD
O, yes, into a thousand similes.
First, for his weeping into the needless stream:
"Poor deer," quoth he "thou mak'st a testament
As worldlings do, giving thy sum of more
To that which had too much." Then, being there alone,
Left and abandoned of his velvet friends:
" 'Tis right;" quoth he "thus misery doth part
The flux of company." Anon, a careless herd,
Full of the pasture, jumps along by him
And never stays to greet him. "Ay," quoth Jaques
"Sweep on, you fat and greasy citizens;
'Tis just the fashion. Wherefore do you look
Upon that poor and broken bankrupt there?"
Thus most invectively he pierceth through
The body of the country, city, court,
Yea, and of this our life; swearing that we
Are mere usurpers, tyrants, and what's worse,
To fright the animals, and to kill them up
In their assign'd and native dwelling-place.

DUKE S[ENIOR]
And did you leave him in this contemplation?

SECOND LORD
We did, my lord, weeping and commenting
Upon the sobbing deer.[6]

                                                    (II.i.21–66)
If one now calls to mind that the outward form of an emblem consists
of three parts, that is, firstly, the *pictura,* the woodcut or engraving,

---

6. Citations from Shakespeare are to *The Complete Works,* ed. Peter Alexander,
The Tudor Edition (London and Glasgow, 1951; repr. 1966).

secondly, the Greek, Latin, or vernacular motto of the *inscriptio* on top of the picture, and, thirdly, the *subscriptio* below, in most cases an epigrammatic explanation and interpretation of the contents of the picture,[7] then it is not difficult to see that the section of the text we have quoted also follows such a tripartite division. The short expository dialogue between the Duke and the first lord, which revolves around the theme of "uneasiness about hunting" and "hunting as an usurpation" (ll.22–28) may be considered as the motto for the following scene, which places the melancholy Jaques in the same surroundings as the wounded and sobbing deer by the brook (ll.29–43). The Duke's question: "But what said Jaques? / Did he not moralize this spectacle?" (ll.43–44) then leads to Jaques' comment (cf. l.65: "commenting") on what he saw (ll.45–63), which, also in a tripartite structure (ll. 46–49, 49–52, 52–57), culminates in the passionate condemnation of the tyrannical cruelty of hunting (ll. 58–63). The fact that Shakespeare uses the verb "to moralize" in the Duke's question supports our thesis that the structure of the quoted text is emblematic, for this verb is positively a *terminus technicus* in the emblem literature of the period. In order to confirm this, we have only to look at the title of Geoffrey Whitney's collection of emblems, which he published in Leyden in 1586, while he was in the Netherlands in the Earl of Leicester's suite: *A Choice of Emblemes, and other Devises, For the moste parte gathered out of sundrie writers, Englished and Moralized and divers newly devised, by Geffrey Whitney.*[8] "To moralize" means, for the authors of emblem books as well as for Shakespeare in this particular passage, to illuminate the inherent sense of a scene, in our case that of the wounded and sobbing deer by the brook, by referring what was presented to generally acknowledged conditions and events of human life—"applying this to that and so to so," as Shakespeare has it in *Venus and Adonis* (l. 713) (cf. also the *OED*, s.v.*moralize*, 1).

7. Cf. Albrecht Schöne, *Emblematik und Drama im Zeitalter des Barock* (Munich, 1964), pp. 18–19; and also *Emblemata: Handbuch zur Sinnbildkunst des XVI. und XVII. Jahrhunderts,* ed. Arthur Henkel and Albrecht Schöne (Stuttgart, 1967), pp. xii–xiii; hereafter cited as *Emblemata.*

8. Citations from Whitney are from the following edition: Geoffrey Whitney, *A Choice of Emblemes,* ed. Henry Green [London, 1866], with an introduction by Frank Fieler (New York, 1967).

I

Indeed, no scholar has as yet been able to provide a valid historical interpretation of the lines quoted.[9] Henry Green, for example, tried as early as 1870 to establish a connection between the pathetic scene which the first lord's report evokes and a common love emblem. This was unjustified, as we hope to show. Green referred to an emblem illustrating incurable love from Gabriele Symeoni's *Imprese heroiche et morali* (Lyon, 1559), which shows a deer wounded by an arrow chewing the Cretan healing herb *dictamnum* (white dittany) under the Spanish motto: "Esto tiene su remedio, y non yo." The *subscriptio* elucidates further:

> Troua il ceruio ferito al suo gran male
> Nel dittamo Creteo fido ricorso,
> Ma lasso (io 'l sò) rimedio ne soccorso
> All' amoroso colpo alcun non vale.[10]

Claude Paradin, whose *Devises heroïques* (Lyon, 1551) appeared together with Symeoni's collection in Antwerp in 1561, explains this emblem by reference to a line of Ovid's: "Hei mihi, quod nullis amor est medicabilis herbis" [*sic*] (cf. *Metamorphoses,* I.523). The same line also provides the motto for a similar emblem in Otho Vaenius' *Amorum emblemata* ([Antwerp, 1608], pp. 154–155), where a wounded Cupid points to a doe which heals itself by chewing white dittany.[11] The ancient conviction that

9. This applies especially to Horace Howard Furness' New Variorum Edition of *As You Like It* (Philadelphia, Pa., 1890), which provides factual explanations and elucidations of various words in our quotation but no help with its interpretation. The same is valid for the edition of the comedy in the series The New Shakespeare, ed. Sir Arthur Quiller-Couch and J. Dover Wilson (Cambridge, Eng., 1926).

10. Cf. Green's *Shakespeare and the Emblem Writers: An Exposition of their Similarities of Thought and Expression, preceded by a view of Emblem-Literature down to A.D. 1616* (London, 1870), pp. 397–398. Green's rather free English translation of this subscription runs (p. 398):

> The smitten stag hath found sad pains to feel,
> No trusted Cretan dittany is near,
> Wearied, for succour there is only fear,—
> The wounds of love no remedy can heal.

11. *Ibid.,* p. 399. See also Mario Praz, *Studies in Seventeenth-Century Imagery,* 2d ed., Sussidi eruditi, XVI (Rome, 1964), 110. See esp. Praz's bibliography of emblem books (pp. 235–576). Subsequent references to Praz are to this considerably

the Cretan herb *dictamnum* possessed miraculous powers of healing is also spoken of by both Virgil (*Aeneid,* XII.411–424) and Pliny (*Natural History,* VIII.27; XXV.8).[12] The motif on which the love emblem is based can, as one might expect, be found as well in the work of Shakespeare's contemporaries, for example in John Lyly [13] or Thomas Lodge,[14] but not—and even a rapid glance shows this—in our quotation from *As You Like It.* For this reason it is incomprehensible why Rosemary Freeman repeated Green's misleading parallel.[15]

There are other deer emblems which could possibly have contributed to the situation we have described, but not to the main theme of the melancholy Jaques' lament. We will examine briefly the symbolic images possible here, in order to contrast our Shakespearean text to them. When Petrarch, for instance, in his sonnet "I dolci colli . . .", following Virgil (*Aeneid,*IV.68–73), proffers the comparison:

> Et qual cervo ferito di saetta,
> col ferro avelenato dentr' al fianco,
> fugge, et piú duolsi quanto piú s'affretta,
>
> tal io, con quello stral dal lato manco,
> che mi consuma, et parte mi diletta,
> di duol mi struggo, e di fuggir mi stanco,[16]

expanded edition. The emblem from Vaenius is reproduced in *Emblemata,* col. 473. Joachim Camerarius' *Symbolorum et emblematum ex animalibus quadrupedibus desumtorum centuria altera collecta* (Nuremberg, 1595), p. 71, no. 69, tells us that the wild goat pierced by an arrow knew how to cure itself with the help of the Cretan herb *dictamnum* (cf. *Emblemata,* col. 476).

12. For further references cf. *Emblemata,* col. 476, s.v. "Wildziege."

13. Cf. *Euphues: The Anatomy of Wit* (1578), in *The Complete Works,* ed. R. Warwick Bond, 3 vols. (Oxford, 1902), I, 208, ll. 24–26: ". . . the Harte beeing pearced with the darte, runneth out of hande to the hearbe *Dictanum* [*sic*], and is healed."

14. Cf. *The Famous, true and historicall life of Robert second Duke of Normandy* (1591), in *The Complete Works,* ed. E. Gosse, The Hunterian Club, 4 vols. (Glasgow, 1883; repr. New York, 1963), II, Sig. 25ʳ ("The first Sonnet," ll. 3–4): "Now like the Hart my bosome hath been pearsed, / Yet no Dictamnum seru'd when I was pained."

15. *English Emblem Books* (London, 1948; repr. New York, 1966), p. 100.

16. Francesco Petrarca, *Canzoniere,* introd. Gianfranco Contini, notes Daniele Ponchiroli (Turin, 1964), p. 270, no. ccix, ll.9–14. R. G. Macgregor's translation of these lines reads:

we may ascertain that it provided, after having been used by Ariosto in his *Orlando furioso* (XVI.iii.5–6: "Vorria il miser fuggire; e come cervo / Ferito, ovunque va, porta la freccia"),[17] both picture and motto for an emblem in Hadrianus Junius' *Emblemata* ([Antwerp, 1565], no. 47) [18] symbolizing love's inescapable agony. Its diffusion and popularity are vouched for by its further use in the same moral meaning in Gabriel Rollenhagen's *Selectorum emblematum centuria secunda* ([Arnheim, 1613], no. 56) and in Daniel Heinsius' *Het Ambacht van Cupido* ([Leyden, 1615], no. 39), where as well as the *pictura* there is a motto from the previously quoted Petrarchan sonnet (*ET PIU DOLSI*),[19] but as far as Shakespeare's comedy *As You Like It* (ca. 1599) is concerned, it is, for mere reasons of chronology, just as irrelevant as Green's and Freeman's reference to Vaenius—not to mention that Jaques does not introduce the subject of love in his contemplation of the wounded and sobbing deer.

However, Shakespeare's deer sheds his flood of tears into a brook (II.i.32, 42). Thus one could be tempted to call on a further emblem for

> And as a stag, sore struck by hunter's dart,
> Whose poison'd iron rankles in his breast,
> Flies and more grieves the more the chase is press'd,
> So I, with Love's keen arrow in my heart,
> Endure at once my death and my delight,
> Rack'd with long grief, and weary with vain flight.

Cf. *The Sonnets, Triumphs, and other Poems of Petrarch, now first completely translated into English Verse by Various Hands*, Bohn's Illustrated Library (London, 1859), p. 190, no. clxxiv.

17. Ludovico Ariosto, *Orlando Furioso*, ed. Pietro Papini, new presentation by Giovanni Nencioni (Florence, 1964), p. 189. For an English version, see *Orlando Furioso in English Heroical Verse, by John Harington* (London, 1591), p. 121: "Like wounded deare in vaine he seekes to flie, / And in his thigh the shaft about doth beare." Cf. Abd-El-Kader Salza, "Imprese e divise d'arme e d'amore nell' 'Orlando Furioso' con notizia di alcuni trattati del 500 sui colori," *Giornale storico della letteratura italiana*, XXXVIII (1901), 310–363, esp. 333–334. We note in passing that Salza's references to Symeoni's above-mentioned stag emblem and the deer hurrying towards the spring of Psalm 42 do not provide a satisfactory explanation of the quotation from Ariosto, which, without mingling thematically separate emblems, goes back quite clearly to Virgil via Petrarch.

18. Cf. Praz, p. 95, as well as the reproduction from Junius in *Emblemata*, col. 471.

19. On both authors cf. *Emblemata*, col. 472; on Heinsius cf. also Praz, pp. 88–89, 95.

comment on this scene, namely, that of the stag hurrying with longing to a spring, which we find, for example, in Joannes Sambucus' *Emblemata* (*Altera editio* [Antwerp, 1566], p. 72) or in Joachim Camerarius' *Symbolorum et emblematum ex animalibus quadrupedibus desumtorum centuria altera collecta* ([Nuremberg, 1595], no. 42).[20] But quite apart from the fact that Camerarius shows a stag at a spring entwined by snakes, it is first and foremost the *significatio* of this emblem which makes it impossible for us to identify *As You Like It*, II.i.29–43, with it. The second verse of Psalm 42 illuminates the meaning: "Quemadmodum desiderat cervus ad fontes aquarum, / Ita desiderat anima mea ad te, Deus."[21] This line of the psalm, which also reappears in the *Physiologus* (no. 30),[22] became fused in Spanish and Portuguese poetry of the *siglo de oro*, since Juan Boscán, with the passage from the *Aeneid* (IV.68–73) used by Petrarch and Ariosto, where Dido, inflamed by incurable love, is compared to a hind pierced by an arrow, a fusion which can, according to María Rosa Lida, express such different themes as ". . . la sed [scil. de Dios], el ansia mística, el impulso animal y todas las sutilezas del amor petrarquesco."[23] A feeble echo of the religious intensity with which a St. Juan de la Cruz uses the image of the wounded deer at the spring as a mystic circumscription of the endless longing for God within a lonely Christian soul can be found in England as late as in Francis Quarles's *Emblemes* (1635).[24] It hardly need be emphasized that this motif and its reflection in contemporary emblem literature are not thematically reconcilable with the Shakespearean text in question.

In the above remarks we have attempted to reach our goal by a circui-

20. Cf. *Emblemata*, col. 1471, resp. 470–471. Whitney took over the emblem we mentioned from Sambucus into his collection: cf. *A Choice of Emblemes*, p. 43 (not p. 41, as is wrongly stated in *Emblemata*, col. 1471).

21. Quoted from the *Biblia sacra iuxta vulgatam Clementinam*, ed. Alberto Colunga and Laurentio Turrado, 3d ed. (Madrid, 1959).

22. Cf. *Der Physiologus*, trans. and with commentary by Otto Seel (Zürich and Stuttgart, 1960), p. 26.

23. "Transmisión y recreación de temas grecolatinos en la poesía lírica española: 2. El ciervo herido y la fuente," *Revista de Filología Hispánica*, I (1939), 31–52, esp. 33. It is clear from Heinsius' *Het Ambacht van Cupido*, no. 40, that this particular picture (no. 16 of the undated Amsterdam edition) can just as well serve to illustrate profane love. Cf. Praz, pp. 95–96; also *Emblemata*, col. 471.

24. Cf. *Emblemes* (London, 1635), Book V, no. xi, pp. 284–287.

tous path rendered necessary by the lack of method displayed by previous scholars. Without depreciating Green's pioneer achievement, one may, with Mario Praz,[25] criticize his unwary habit of tracing back Shakespearean images and motifs directly to particular emblem books. This criticism is all the more appropriate since there are now more recent emblematic studies available which do not differ in essentials, if at all, from Green's precedent.[26] They were, moreover, specifically requested in order to elucidate Shakespearean stage imagery.[27] But in considering this, one must not, however, forget that the large majority of emblems—and the examples we have discussed make this sufficiently clear—are nothing but visualized *topoi,* or, to be more precise, symbolized *topoi.*[28] Consequently, emblem books form only one link in a chain of tradition which reaches from antiquity through the Middle Ages and the Renaissance to the Baroque age. Hence the study of the processes of literary borrowing must take this circumstance into account and avoid overhasty deductions. In any case, however tempting any given analogy may be, we must bear in mind the context of the passage we are attempting to interpret in its entirety. For *As You Like It* this means that the wounded and sobbing deer by the brook does not, in Jaques' eyes, symbolize love's incurable agony, but the tyrannical cruelty of the hunt. And this theme belongs to quite a different historical context, which we now intend to examine.

25. Praz, pp. 207–208, 220. Cf. also F. Fieler's critical remark in his introduction to Green's edition of Whitney, p. xvii.

26. Cf. for instance John M. Steadman, "Falstaff as Actaeon: A Dramatic Emblem," *SQ,* XIV (1963), 231–244; John Doebler, "A Submerged Emblem in Sonnet 116," *SQ,* XV (1964), 109–110; and esp. G. Pellegrini, "Symbols and Significances: 'All such emblems,'" *ShS,* XVII (1964), 180–187, who cannot be excused his lack of methodological circumspection (cf. esp. pp. 185–187). A notable exception, however, is Dieter Mehl's article "Emblematik im englischen Drama der Shakespearezeit," *Anglia,* LXXXVII (1969), 126–146, where the functional aspect of emblem studies in works of dramatic art is duly stressed (cf. esp. p. 132). This article is also available in English: "Emblems in English Renaissance Drama," *Ren D,* N.S. II (1969), 39–57.

27. Cf. Martha Hester Golden, "Stage Imagery in Shakespearean Studies," *Shakespearean Research Opportunities,* I (1965), 10–20.

28. Golden, by the way, is as conscious of this fact (*ibid.,* p. 13) as are (of course) Praz, pp. 206–207; and Mehl, "Emblems in English Renaissance Drama," p. 42.

II

In contrast to the Greeks, the Romans did not conceive of hunting as an *officium virile,* i.e., an occupation worthy of a free man; they left the pursuit of game to professional hunters of the slave and freedman classes.[29] Cicero accordingly places *venatores* on a level with athletes and gladiators (*Tusculanae disputationes,* II.18.40–41), and Sallust judges the hunt to be a purely material occupation comparable to agriculture: ". . . agrum colundo aut venando, servilibus officiis . . ." (*Catilina,* IV.1). Seneca's opinion is scarcely more positive when, in *De constantia sapientis* (II.2–3), he praises Cato as a man of perfect wisdom, not least because he never killed animals, for he thinks hunting them the task of a professional hunter or a simple countryman. In *De vita beata* (XIV.4) he compares the hunter to a sensualist who neglects his duty for the sake of passion. The hunt is also seen negatively in the *Praetexta Octavia,* which we cannot with certainty ascribe to Seneca; it is regarded as proof of the increasing depravity of humanity which this play laments:

> Alia sed suboles, minus
> experta mitis, tertium sollers genus
> novas ad artes extitit, sanctum tamen;
> mox inquietum, quod sequi cursu feras
> auderet acres, fluctibus tectos gravi
> extrahere pisces rete vel calamo levi,
> decipere volucres turbidos forti canes
> tenere laqueo. . . .[30]

(ll. 406–413)

Although Seneca concedes that hunting requires physical prowess and moral qualities (*De vita beata,* XIV.2; *De ira,* I.11–12), he cannot bring

29. Cf. F. Orth's article "Jagd" in Pauly-Wissowa-Kroll, *Realencyclopädie der classischen Altertumswissenschaft,* IX, pt. 1 (Stuttgart, 1914), cols. 558–604, esp. col. 562.

30. *Seneca's Tragedies,* with an English translation by Frank Justus Miller, The Loeb Classical Library, 2 vols. (London and New York, 1917), II, 438–441. The English translation faces the Latin text:

But another race arose which proved less gentle; another yet, cunning in unknown arts, but holy still; then came a restless race, which dared pursue the wild beasts in the chase, draw fish from their coverts 'neath the sea with weighted net or slender rod, catch birds, on a strong leash hold unruly dogs. . . .

himself to like it and still feels that it is unnaturally cruel and sympto-
matic of an irreligious society (cf. *Praetexta Octavia*, l. 393: "genus
impium").[31]

One of the spiritual authorities of the high Middle Ages shares Seneca's
opinion of hunting—namely, John of Salisbury in his *Policraticus* (1159).
Chapter four of the first book of this influential mirror for princes can
certainly be regarded as the *locus classicus* of humanistic criticism of
hunting and as a source of similar attitudes expressed in times that followed. John does not disallow hunting entirely, but countenances it,
using Virgil's Aeneas as an example, when it is essential for subsistence:
". . . res quippe decora est, si honesta causa praecesserit." [32] As pure
sport, however, he definitely includes it among the "curialium nugas"
(p. 31) which he exposes in the first three books of the *Policraticus*. When
the sole object of the hunt consists of elaborate preparations for it, and
the whole becomes an end in itself and is merely thought of as a frolic
(and John's own time gives him due cause for the complaint: "Haec sunt
temporibus nostris liberalia nobilium studia" [33]), one must ask the question: "Quomodo ergo dignus est uita, qui nichil aliud in uita nouit, nisi
uanitatis studio saeuire in bestias?" [34] According to John, to wreak havoc

31. For the references quoted from Latin literature cf. Aurèle Cattin, *Les Thèmes
lyriques dans les tragédies de Sénèque* (Diss., Univ. of Fribourg, Neuchâtel, 1963),
pp. 98, 115, n. 33. The reference to Varro's *Rerum rusticarum libri tres* (II.ix.5),
also found there, is, however, thematically misleading.

32. *Ioannis Saresberiensis Episcopi Carnotensis Policratici sive de nugis curialium
et vestigiis philosophorum libri VIII*, rec. Clemens C. I. Webb, 2 vols. (Oxford,
1909), I, 22. For an English translation, see Joseph B. Pike, *Frivolities of Courtiers
and Footprints of Philosophers: Being a translation of the First, Second and Third
Books and Selections from the Seventh and Eighth Books of the "Policraticus" of
John of Salisbury* (Minneapolis, Minn., 1938), p. 15: "An act is seemly if the cause
that preceded it is honorable." The same sentiment occurs again somewhat later in
John's chapter on hunting (p. 31): "Potest igitur uenatica esse utilis et honesta; sed
ex loco, tempore, modo, persona, et causa." Cf. the Pike translation, p. 23: "Therefore it is quite possible, depending upon the circumstances, time, manner, individual, and purpose, for hunting to be a useful and honorable occupation." See also p.
32 (Pike trans., p. 24).

33. *Ibid.*, p. 23 (Pike trans., p. 16): "In our day this knowledge constitutes the
liberal studies of the higher class."

34. *Ibid.*, p. 24 (Pike trans., p. 16): "Is one then worthy of life, whose sole interest in it is the trivial one of waging cruel warfare against beasts?"

among animals, as did Achilles, taught by the centaur Chiron and consequently lacking in respect for nature, reduces man to a state of bestiality:

Nempe qui his studiis aut desidiis insistunt, semiferi sunt, et abiecta potiore
humanitatis parte, ratione morum prodigiis conformantur.[35]

These words do not only contain criticism; we can also feel the implicit
concern of the humanist for the preservation of humanity. This concern
takes on a political overtone when John puts forward the example of
Nimrod, who appears in the Bible as "robustus venator coram Domino"
(Gen. 10:9: "a stout hunter before the Lord"), to demonstrate that the
source of tyranny springs from hunting and hunting alone:

Tyrannidis ergo fastigium in contumeliam creatoris a uenatore incipiens,
alium non inuenit auctorem, quam eum qui in caede ferarum et uolutabro
sanguinis Domini contemptum didicisset.[36]

His reproach that hunters are godless stems from the historical fact that,
apart from the previously mentioned Thebans (p. 21), who were in any
case thought of as infamous, only heathen peoples went hunting, and
never saints or wise men (pp. 29–30).

Moreover, John of Salisbury's satirical innuendo, "In our day this
knowledge constitutes the liberal studies of the higher class," would not
have gone unnoticed by his contemporaries, however much he disguised
it by Biblical and mythological allusions, and to us, indeed, he seems to
have presented his case effectively enough. In fact, almost one third of
England became forest land under the Angevin kings, so that they could
indulge in the royal sport of hunting, and severe punishment was inflicted on any poacher who violated the king's game rights.[37] Henry II's
passion for the chase is sufficiently well known and, since John had the
conditions at Henry's court particularly in mind when writing his
Policraticus, we may feel justified in assuming that his deprecating re-

35. *Ibid.,* p. 26 (Pike trans., p. 18): "In truth those who have such inclinations
and desires are half-beast. They have shed the desirable element, their humanity,
and in the sphere of conduct have made themselves like unto monsters."
36. *Ibid.,* p. 27 (Pike trans., p. 19): "Therefore tyranny, initiated by a huntsman
to insult the Creator, finds its sole source in one who, amid the slaughter of beasts,
wallowing in blood, learned to feel contempt for the Lord."
37. Cf. Austin Lane Poole, *From Domesday Book to Magna Carta 1087–1216,*
The Oxford History of England, 2d ed. (Oxford, 1955), pp. 28–35.

marks on hunting were prompted by intense dislike of the king's ways in general. As further confirmation, we should remember that especially at the time of writing the *Policraticus* John, the loyal secretary and friend of Thomas Becket, did not enjoy untroubled relations with his king. John's view of the royal pastime is not, of course, shared by courtiers and members of Henry II's household. Thus, for instance, the royal treasurer and author of the *Dialogus de Scaccario* (begun in 1176), Richard Fitz Neal (also known as Richard of Ely), is in sympathy with the king's desire to forget the cares of government in enjoyment of the delights of the forest;[38] and another member of the royal court, the imaginative Walter Map, who, in his *De nugis curialium* (1181–1193), may follow John of Salisbury to the letter—indeed, the title of his fragmentary collection of anecdotes echoes the subtitle of the latter's work—but certainly does not do so in spirit, even wishes us to believe that the king, himself a victim of courtly intrigues, was on occasion sent off to hunt by his own courtiers, so that they could pursue their sinister cabals:

Ad ludendum in auibus et canibus eum foras fraudulenter eiciunt, ne videat quod ab eis interim intro fit. Dum ipsum ludere faciunt, ipsi seriis intendunt, rostris insidunt, et ad unum finem iudicant equitates et iniusticias. Cum autem rex a uenatu vel aucupio redit, predas suas eis ostendit, et partitur; ipsi suas ei non reuelant.[39]

Poor king, or could there be a higher degree of courtly flattery on the part of one close to him? It becomes obvious, then, that the condemnation of the hunt implies a certain aloofness from courtly, i.e., worldly, activities,

---

38. *Dialogus de Scaccario,* I.11; quoted from A. L. Poole, *From Domesday Book to Magna Carta,* p. 29, n. 1.

39. *Walteri Map de nugis curialium,* ed. Montague Rhodes James, Anecdota Oxoniensia, Mediaeval and Modern Series, pt. XIV (Oxford, 1914), Book V, chap. vii, p. 254. For an English translation, see *Master Walter Map's Book De nugis curialium (Courtiers' Trifles),* trans. Frederick Tupper and Marbury Bladen Ogle (London, 1924), p. 320:

The courtiers slily send him forth to sport among birds and hounds to prevent his seeing what they do within during his absence. While they make him take his sport, they themselves are busy with serious matters; they sit upon their tribunals and bring both righteousness and unrighteousness to the same judgement. When, however, the king returneth from his hunting or his hawking, he showeth his spoils to them and giveth them a share; they do not disclose theirs to him.

and surely it is indicative not only of a truly humanistic attitude but also of a genuinely scholarly and contemplative mind.

The fact that the main representatives of humanism proper share John of Salisbury's outlook on hunting illustrates the continuity of humanistic attitudes of mind from the twelfth century, which has often been seen as a prelude to the Renaissance,[40] to the sixteenth century. Erasmus, like John (pp. 22–23), mocks the hunters for their rites and code of honor in his *Praise of Folly* (written in 1509 and published in 1511) and includes ardent hunters in his army of fools on earth, at the same time noting, as John did, their degeneration into bestiality:

Itaque cum isti [scil. qui prae venatu ferarum omnia contemnunt] assidua ferarum insectatione atque esu nihil aliud assequantur, nisi ut ipsi propemodum in feras degenerent, tamen interea regiam vitam agere se putant.[41]

At the same time this sentence contains a covert and sly dig at the princes of the time, for Erasmus claims later in his delightful exposition of human folly that they felt they were fulfilling their role sufficiently if they "constantly hunted" and indulged in other carefree pastimes.[42] The fact

40. On this question one may consult Charles Homer Haskins, *The Renaissance of the Twelfth Century* (Cambridge, Mass., 1927), whose position, however, was politely but firmly challenged by Johan Huizinga in his lecture on Abelard (1935), incorporated in *Men and Ideas: History, the Middle Ages, the Renaissance*, Essays by Johan Huizinga, trans. James S. Holmes and Hans van Marle (London, 1960), pp. 178–195, esp. pp. 181–183.

41. Μωρίας ἐγκώμιον: *Stultitiae laus, Des. Erasmi Rot. declamatio*, rec. I. B. Kan (The Hague, 1898), chap. XXXIX, pp. 73–74. For an English version, see Sir Thomas Chaloner, *The Praise of Folie* [1549], ed. Clarence H. Miller, EETS, no. 257 (Oxford, 1965), p. 54, ll. 25–30: "So therfore, wheras these hunters through continuall chasyng and eatyng of theyr venerie, gaine nothyng, but in a maner dooe them selfes also degenerate into wilde and saluage propretees, ye maie see yet, how through this errour of mine, thei repute theyr lyues ledde in more than princely pleasure."

42. *Ibid.*, chap. LV, p. 142. Later on (1515) Erasmus ventured to be more outspoken in his strictures on the behavior of the princes and rulers of his time, witness his bitter comments on the adage "Scarabeus aquilam quaerit" ("The beetle searches for the eagle") (*Adagia*, III.vii.1). Cf. *Desiderii Erasmi Roterodami opera omnia*, rec. Joannes Clericus, 10 vols. (Leyden, 1703–1706), II, col. 871A: "Atque his divis, inclytis, triumphatoribus, si quid est ocii ab alea, à poculis, à venatu, à scortis, id omne jam vere regiis cogitationibus dicant." For an English rendering

that his English translator, Sir Thomas Chaloner, did not translate this rebuke out of regard for the political situation under Edward VI proves that it was justified.[43] As Erasmus also criticizes the inanity of dicing together with the passion for hunting (pp. 75–76), he seems in this respect to be under the influence of the *Policraticus,* which was available in print during his lifetime,[44] for we find the same connection there (on dicing see *Policraticus,* I.5, pp. 35–38).[45] We can thus see that we are dealing with a specific *topos* of humanist writing. It reappears in Sir Thomas More's *Utopia* (1516), this time directly inspired by Erasmus, who did not only dedicate the *Praise of Folly* to his friend More but actually wrote it in the latter's London home in Bucklersbury. Accordingly, hunting and dicing are likewise despised by the Utopians. They see hunting—and this is in line with the Roman view already mentioned—as mere slaughter, unworthy of a free man and better left to slaves. More says of the Utopians:

. . . animalia necessitatis dumtaxat gratia perimant, quum uenator ab miseri animalculi caede ac laniatu, nihil nisi uoluptatem petat, quam spectandae necis libidinem in ipsis etiam bestijs, aut ab animi crudelis affectu censent exoriri, aut in crudelitatem denique, assiduo tam efferae uoluptatis usu defluere.[46]

see Margaret Mann Phillips, *The "Adages" of Erasmus: A Study with Translations* (Cambridge, Eng., 1964), p. 234: "And if these gods, these heroes, these triumphal leaders have any leisure left over from dicing, drinking, hunting and whoring, they do give every bit of it to truly regal considerations."

43. For this information see C. H. Miller's edition of Chaloner's *Praise of Folie,* p. 182, note to p. 93, l. 34.

44. Here we should like to mention that the Brussels edition (ca. 1476) which appeared without place or year of publication and was soon followed by another in Paris and Lyon (1513) should be particularly considered. Cf. Webb's "Prolegomena" to his edition of the *Policraticus,* p. xvii ff.; and Ernst Robert Curtius, *European Literature and the Latin Middle Ages,* trans. Willard R. Trask (London, 1953), p. 140.

45. Such a similarity in thought seems to be more than mere coincidence. Therefore, one wonders why I. B. Kan in his notes to the passages from Erasmus discussed above does not draw attention to John of Salisbury.

46. *Utopia,* ed. Edward Surtz, S. J. and J. H. Hexter, The Yale Edition of the *Complete Works of St. Thomas More,* IV (New Haven, Conn. and London, 1965), p. 170. The English translation faces the Latin text (p. 171): ". . . they . . . kill animals only from necessity, whereas the hunter seeks nothing but pleasure from the killing and mangling of a poor animal. Even in the case of brute beasts, this

The thoughts expressed here admit of the possibility that Thomas More, via Erasmus, is echoing John of Salisbury;[47] in any case his statement that the desire to watch blood being shed springs from, or leads to, cruelty shows greater moral seriousness than Erasmus' witty mockery about the closeness of the hunter's nature to that of the beast he pursues. And More's sympathy with the hunter's victims also reveals deeper concern (pp. 170–171). The fact that all free Utopians are forbidden to kill animals themselves, ". . . cuius usu, clementiam humanissimum naturae nostrae affectum paulatim deperire putant,"[48] fits into the same pattern, as does the lament of the rabbit caught in the hunter's net on the cruelty of his torturers in More's *Epigrams* (1518): "O durum genus, atque fera truculentius omni, / Nex cui crudelem praebet acerba iocum."[49] The three humanists considered thus far aim at a similar target when criticizing hunting: princes and courtiers. The marginal note to the passage quoted from the *Utopia* removes all possibility of doubt: "At haec hodie ars est deorum aulicorum."[50] Yet another contemporary voice joins the unanimous humanist chorus in rejection of hunting, namely, Agrippa of Nettesheim, who loosely summarizes the by now familiar objections of his predecessors in chapter 77 of his treatise *De incertitudine et vanitate scientiarum* (1530). He too is of the opinion that hunting undermines humane attitudes, and characterizes its practice as follows:

---

desire of looking on bloodshed, in their estimation, either arises from a cruel disposition or degenerates finally into cruelty through the constant practice of such brutal pleasure."

47. The influence of medieval mirrors for princes, especially of the *Policraticus*, on the *Utopia* still awaits further investigation. Cf. E. Surtz's introduction to the edition quoted, p. clxvii. For the influence of Erasmus' writings on the *Utopia*, cf. pp. cliv–clvi and clxxix–clxxxi.

48. *Ibid.*, p. 138 (Eng. trans., p. 139): ". . . by the practice of which they think that mercy, the finest feeling of our human nature, is gradually killed off."

49. Cf. *The Latin Epigrams of Thomas More*, ed. Leicester Bradner and Charles Arthur Lynch (Chicago, 1953), p. 27, no. 19. The English translation is to be found on p. 149: "Insensate breed, more savage than any beast, to find cruel amusement in bitter slaughter!" Cf. also Epigram 65. On the above-mentioned passages from the *Utopia*, one should consult the excellent commentary in the Yale Edition, pp. 418 f.; 457 f.

50. *Utopia*, p. 170 (Eng. trans., p. 171): "Yet This Is Today the Art of the Superior Beings at Court."

Ars profectò detestabilis, studium vanum, certamen infoelix. . . . Ars crudelis, et tota tragica, cuius voluptas est in morte & in sanguine, quam ipsa
deberet refugere humanitas.[51]

Here again, by the use of Biblical *exempla* (of course including Nimrod),
as with John of Salisbury, Agrippa demonstrates that only those peoples
who denied God's existence indulged in hunting and that hunting was
the very beginning of tyranny. Erasmus must have been reminded, with
a smile of amusement and satisfaction, of his own remarks in the *Praise
of Folly* when he heard the well-known magician and occultist's eloquent
mockery of the ceremonial rites of hunters and their relapse into bestiality (Agrippa's treatise was read to him at meals [52] owing to pressure of
work):

Insignis profectò venatorum stultitia, insigne bellum, cui dum nimium insistunt, ipsi abiecta humanitate ferae efficiuntur, morumque prodigiosa per-
uersitate, tanquam Acteon mutantur in naturas belluarum.[53]

Agrippa further laments that hunting practices, ". . . in se reuera seruilia
& mechanica," [54] had found too much favor with the nobility, more precisely with both secular and ecclesiastical princes, and had practically
ousted the study of the liberal arts; thus, he too imbues his own horror of
hunting with criticism of his time. Agrippa concludes his discussion with

51. *Henr. Cornelii Agrippa ab Nettesheym De incertitvdine et vanitate omnium
scientiarum & artium liber* . . . (Cologne, 1598), Sig. [R 11ʳ]. James Sanford's
English translation reads: "A detestable Arte, no doubte, a vaine studie, an vnhap-
pie strife. . . . A cruell Arte, and altogeather tragicall, whose pleasure is in deathe,
and bloude, whiche oure humanitie ought to eschewe" (*Henrie Cornelius Agrippa,
of the Vanitie and Uncertaintie of Artes and Sciences, Englished by Ja. San. Gent.*
[London, 1569], p. 121ʳ).

52. Cf. Agrippa of Nettesheim, *Die Eitelkeit und Unsicherheit der Wissenschaften
und die Verteidigungsschrift,* ed. Fritz Mauthner, 2 vols. (Munich, 1913), I, II. On
the whole, however, it should be noted that Agrippa's 77th chapter "Of Huntinge
and Fowlinge" reads very much like a condensed reproduction of John of Salisbury's treatment of the theme in the *Policraticus.*

53. *De incertitvdine* . . . , Sig. [R11ʳ]; Sanford trans., p. 121ᵛ: ". . . a notable
foly of Hunters doubtlesse, and a worthy battaile, about which, whilest they are too
busie, they, settinge all humanitie apart, become saluage beastes, and through
monstruous naughtinesse of nature, are changed like *Acteon* into the nature of
Beasts."

54. *Ibid.,* Sig. [R 12ᵛ]; Sanford trans., p. 122ʳ: ". . . of themselves seruile and
base."

the remark that original sin destroyed the paradisaic harmony between man and animal; the conflict between them has been raging ever since: ". . . venationum orta est pugna, hominum scilicet cum caeteris animalibus." [55] We do not need to look for further similarities between *De incertitudine et vanitate scientiarum* and the preceding literature, for it must have already become perfectly clear from our choice of representative literary humanist texts that the condemnation of hunting as a cruel, inhuman occupation, leading to barbarism and not befitting a free man, is a stereotyped *topos,* which, as we saw, has its roots in a basically bourgeois attitude which disapproves of court life. One is therefore all the more surprised—and this certainly testifies to the literary effectiveness and ubiquity of the *topos*—to find it also present in the volume *The Noble Arte of Venerie or Hunting,* which appeared anonymously in London in 1575 and was not only intended for court circles, but in all probability was written by one of their spokesmen, George Gascoigne.[56] In Gascoigne's dedicatory poem to the *Noble Arte of Venerie* we find a significant reference to the public he had in mind: "For my part (being one) I must needes say my minde, / *That Hunting was ordeyned first, for Men of Noble Kinde.*" [57] The work itself is a translation from the French, i.e., of Jacques du Fouilloux' *La Vénerie* (Paris, 1573). This edition contains among other things a "Complainte du Cerf . . ." (Fol. 70ʳ), which was considerably extended in the English version and became the moralizing "Looking Glasse for lessons lewde, wherein all Hunters may looke." In it the deer curses the cruel hunter and hopes that war and plague will lay him low, so that he will hunt no more. Gascoigne was inspired by this "Lament of the Deer" to write five further poems, in

55. *Ibid.,* Sig. S2ʳ; Sanford trans., p. 123ʳ: ". . . the battaile of huntinge tooke his beginning, to weete, of men with other liuinge creatures."

56. The contents and tone of this volume, when seen in relation to his other works, imply that Gascoigne is the author and not George Turbervile. Cf. Felix E. Schelling, *The Life and Writings of George Gascoigne,* Publications of the University of Pennsylvania, Series in Philology, Literature and Archaeology, II, no. 4 (Boston, 1893), p. 81; as well as Charles and Ruth Prouty, "George Gascoigne, *The Noble Arte of Venerie,* and Queen Elizabeth at Kenilworth," *Joseph Quincy Adams Memorial Studies,* ed. James G. McManaway et al. (Washington, D. C., 1948), pp. 639–664, esp. pp. 650 ff.

57. Cf. *The Complete Works of George Gascoigne,* ed. John W. Cunliffe, 2 vols. (Cambridge, Eng., 1907–1910), II, 560.

which the hare, the fox, and the otter pillory man's pitilessness.[58] The
same spirit is present in these poems as in More's Epigram 19. Surprised
as we may be, then, to find the humanistic *topos* of condemnation of
hunting used by a courtier and soldier like Gascoigne, we can predict its
occurrence in the work of a scholar like Robert Burton. And in fact the
uncontrollable passion for the hunt is given, with reference to authorities
by now familiar to us (John of Salisbury and Agrippa of Nettesheim), as
one of the reasons for "grief of mind" and even "madness itself" in the
Anatomy of Melancholy (1621), although Burton, out of regard for
English social conditions, excludes the ruling classes of society from his
criticism when he specifies "those mad sports of Hawking and Hunting"
as "honest recreations, and fit for some great men, but not for every base
inferior person." [59] Of course Burton's book was published too late to be
a possible "source" for Shakespeare.

III

It is now our task to ascertain whether Shakespeare, when working on
As You Like It, had direct access to the humanistic tradition in which the
topos we have examined belongs. We can see that Jaques' lengthy observations about the sobbing deer are already foreshadowed in the hunting scene (IV.i,ii) of *Love's Labour's Lost* (ca. 1594), which—and this is
one of the sociological assumptions necessary when considering Shakespearean comedy [60]—was modeled on the aristocratic festivities customary
at the time. It is usual to refer back to Lyly's *Honorable Entertainment
giuen to the Queenes Maiestie in Progresse, at Cowdrey in Sussex, by the
right Honorable the Lord Montacute* (1591) [61] when discussing *Love's*

58. This information is based on the essay by Charles and Ruth Prouty, "George
Gascoigne," esp. pp. 643–649, 653.
59. Cf. Robert Burton, *The Anatomy of Melancholy,* ed. A. R. Shilleto, The York
Library, 3 vols. (London, 1904), I.iii.3.13 (I, 332–338, esp. 333 f.).
60. Cf. C. L. Barber, *Shakespeare's Festive Comedy: A Study of Dramatic Form
and its Relation to Social Custom* (Princeton, N. J., 1959), pp. 30–35, 110.
61. *The Complete Works of John Lyly,* ed. R. W. Bond (Oxford, 1902), I,
421–430.

Labour's Lost.[62] However, it is not without irony that Shakespeare, in contrast to Lyly, lets the French princess, in whose honor the hunt for red deer has been arranged, express horror and pity: "Then, forester, my friend, where is the bush / That we must stand and play the murderer in?" (IV.i.7–8; cf. ll. 24–35, esp. l. 24: "Now mercy goes to kill"), while the learned pedant Holofernes, from whom we would, on account of the tradition we have discussed, expect such expressions, praises the princess' good fortune in the hunt in lines rendered unbearable by alliteration (IV.ii.53–59, esp. l. 53: "The preyful Princess pierc'd and prick'd a pretty pleasing pricket") which expose the speaker, and together with him a mode of speech which was fast disappearing to ridicule,[63] but do not unmask the cruelty of the hunt. This conscious irony, a particularly subtle comic effect, reveals Shakespeare's knowledge of the tradition we have discussed, but in the case of *Love's Labour's Lost* it is still not clear exactly which source the poet used, for *The Queen's Entertainment at Cowdrey,* which we are not even sure that Shakespeare used, contains, as indicated, no criticism of the hunt.

At this juncture we receive unexpected help from Sir John Harington, godson of Queen Elizabeth, in whose *Metamorphosis of Ajax* (1596), which breathes the spirit of Rabelais, we read the following curious passage:

. . . look into your sportes of hauking and hunting, of which noble recreations, the noble Sir Phylip Sidney was wont to say, that next hunting, he liked hauking worst, but the faulconers and hunters would bee euen with him, and say, that these bookish fellowes, such as he, could iudge of no sports, but within the verg of the fair fields of Helicon, Pindus and Parnassus.[64]

The fact that Harington associates the rejection of hunting with "bookish fellowes" confirms our right to regard the *topos* under consideration as part of an intellectual world which does not share the values of aristocratic courtly society. It is all the more remarkable, therefore, that Sir Philip Sidney, one of its leading representatives, is an exception in this

62. Cf. *Love's Labour's Lost,* ed. Richard David, The [New] Arden Shakespeare (London, 1956; repr. 1960), pp. xxix, 62–63 (note on IV.i.8).

63. Cf. E. M. W. Tillyard, *Shakespeare's Early Comedies* (London, 1965), p. 156.

64. *The Metamorphosis of Aiax. A New Discourse of a Stale Subiect by Sir John Harington . . . ,* ed. Peter Warlock and Jack Lindsay (London, 1927), p. 44.

respect. He is able to see beyond the limits of his class, for whose physical and intellectual training hunting is recommended in educational writings like Sir Thomas Elyot's *Governor* (1531),[65] Roger Ascham's *Toxophilus* (1545),[66] or collections of essays like Robert Johnson's *Essaies or rather Imperfect Offers* (1601),[67] because he shares in the humanist heritage. Although deer and falcon hunting are described as honorable occupations in the *Arcadia* (1590),[68] there is no lack of pity for the animal on the part of the poet, who comments on the killing of the stag finally cornered by the hunters as follows: ". . . but with a Crossebowe [scil. *Kalander*] sent a death to the poore beast, who with teares shewed the unkindnesse he tooke of mans crueltie" (*Works,* I, 61). This moralizing commentary corresponds to the intellectual content of the humanistic *topos* of criticism of hunting, which we meet yet again in the song of the melancholy shepherd Philisides, abandoned in Arcadia, behind whom is concealed no less a figure than Sir Philip Sidney himself.[69] The song, which Philisides— and this again is a reference to the humanist origin of our *topos*—learnt from "old Languet" (l. 22), a Protestant statesman and Sidney's mentor during his Continental tour, relates in the form of an animal fable how monarchy evolved and gradually changed into despotism. In doing so, man's hunting innocent animals for pleasure is branded as a particularly repulsive expression of tyranny (ll. 146–152):

65. Ed. S. E. Lehmberg, Everyman's Library, no. 227 (London, 1962), I.xviii, pp. 65–69.

66. Cf. *The English Works,* ed. William Aldis Wright (Cambridge, Eng., 1904), p. 30.

67. Cf. the essay "Of Exercise" in the edition of 1607, ed. Robert Hood Bowers, Scholars' Facsimiles and Reprints (Gainesville, Fla., 1955), Sig. C2ᵛ–C3ᵛ. For further references on the importance assigned to hunting in the educational literature of the Renaissance, cf. Yale Edition of More's *Utopia,* p. 457, note to p. 170, ll. 7–8, where, however, a sociological differentiation of the material collected is lacking.

68. *The Prose Works of Sir Philip Sidney,* ed. Albert Feuillerat, 4 vols. (Cambridge, Eng., 1912; repr. 1962), I, 59–61 and 167–168. Cf. also the catalogue of pastimes worthy of a nobleman on p. 266: "Musicke, Daunsing, Hunting, Feasting, Riding, & such like."

69. In the first version of the *Arcadia,* written between 1577 and 1580, Philisides' song appears at the end of the third book (*Works,* IV, 237–242), where it is thematically in harmony with the other eclogues; however, in the extended second edition, published in 1590, it is wrongly placed among "The First Eclogues," and the singer remains anonymous (*Works,* I, 132–137).

At length for glutton taste he did them kill:
At last for sport their sillie lives did spill.
But yet ô man, rage not beyonde thy neede:
Deeme it no gloire to swell in tyrannie.
Thou art of blood; joy not to make things bleede:
Thou fearest death; thinke they are loth to die.
A plaint of guiltlesse hurt doth pierce the skie.[70]

This expressive lamentation of the tyrannical cruelty of the hunt, which, according to Harington, was in accordance with Sidney's personal conviction,[71] was by no means without effect on Shakespeare. Thus, Edwin Greenlaw could prove by a structural analysis of pastoral novels like Longus' *Daphnis and Chloe* (2d century A.D.), Boccaccio's *Ameto* (which was written about 1341 but did not appear until 1478), Sannazaro's *Arcadia* (1504), and Montemayor's *Diana* (ca. 1559) that Philisides exemplifies the standard type of the lonely shepherd, suffering from love's incurable sickness, who is not involved in the love intrigue in any of the novels listed. As such, Greenlaw holds, Philisides' successors in England are Spenser's Colin Clout (cf. *The Faerie Queene*, VI [1596]. ix.41; x.16) and Shakespeare's Jaques, as he is nowhere to be found in Lodges's *Rosalynde* (1590), the direct source of *As You Like It*.[72] Hence the dramatist here goes back beyond Lodge and even further to Sidney himself. Greenlaw's proofs are convincing not only on the grounds that Shakespeare was influenced by Sidney in other works[73] but above all because of the obvious similarity of theme in Philisides' and Jaques'

70. Quoted from *The Poems of Sir Philip Sidney*, ed. William A. Ringler, Jr. (Oxford, 1962), pp. 98–103, esp. p. 103; see also Ringler's commentary on this song, pp. 412–415.

71. When Virgil B. Heltzel shows his astonishment in "The Arcadian Hero," *PQ* XLI (1962), 173–180, at the contrast between the hunting scenes in the *Arcadia* and Sidney's personal convictions, he does so merely to make the virtues of the heroes of the novel concur with Sidney's own. But we are only entitled to do this in the case of Philisides.

72. "Shakespeare's Pastorals," *SP*, XIII (1916), 122–154, esp. pp. 123–124, 129–136 (on Jaques).

73. On this point see Greenlaw, *ibid.*, pp. 134–135; M. Poirier, "Sidney's Influence upon *A Midsummer-Night's Dream*," *SP*, XLIV (1947), 483–489; Fitzroy Pyle, "*Twelfth Night, King Lear* and *Arcadia*," *MLR*, XLIII (1948), 449–455; and Kenneth Muir, *Shakespeare's Sources, I: Comedies and Tragedies* (London, 1957; repr. 1961), p. 13.

laments. If, in addition, Sidney's melancholy "yong shepheard" lies "at the foot of a cypresse tree" (*Works,* I,132), and if, furthermore, his teacher Languet is said to have voiced his lament "in oke's true shade" (l. 41), then these indications of locality might explain the pose of "melancholy Jaques" (*As You Like It,* II.i.26) who, as Orlando in love (III.ii.220–226) or the villain Oliver (IV.iii.103–106) do later, lies down "under an oak" (II.i.31). We should not overlook the fact that this *locus amoenus,* obviously so well suited to indulging in suffering, is an essential element in the scenery of pastoral novels, which Virginia Woolf could still use in a witty and humorous fashion.[74] If, in addition to a tree, there is a spring into which tears can be shed, then we have a place which, by its very nature, is ideally suited to "melancholie and contemplation." Jorge de Montemayor describes one such:

. . . la pastora se fué derecha a la fuente de los alisos donde el día antes, con los dos pastores, avía passado la siesta. Y como vió lugar tan aparejado para tristes imaginaciones, se quiso aprovechar del tiempo, sentándose cabe la fuente, cuya agua con la de sus ojos acrecentava.[75]

The heroine Diana in the novel named after her suffers in like fashion (pp. 240–243 and 265–266). Thus it might not be erroneous to see, with John Dover Wilson,[76] a direct reference back to Montemayor in Rosa-

74. Cf. *Orlando: A Biography* [1928], 8th ed. (London, 1958), pp. 19–20.

75. *Los siete libros de la Diana.* Prólogo, edición y notas de Francisco López Estrada, Clásicos Castellanos (Madrid, 1946), p. 63. This passage reads in Bartholomew Yonge's English translation as follows: ". . . [the faire Shepherdesse] . . . went directly to the fountaine of the Sicamours, where the day before, in companie of the two Shepherds, she had passed away the noone-tide heate: and seeing the place so agreeable to melancholie, and contemplation of her sorrowes, she thought it not amisse to take the opportunitie of the time, and place, and to sit downe by the fountaine, whose waters seemed with her swelling teares to increase" (*A Critical Edition of Yong's Translation of George of Montemayor's Diana and Gil Polo's Enamoured Diana,* ed. Judith M. Kennedy [Oxford, 1968], pp. 51–52).

76. Cf. John Dover Wilson, *Shakespeare's Happy Comedies* (London, 1962), pp. 41–42, 150. Shakespeare may have used Bartholomew Yonge's English translation, which appeared in 1598 but was available in manuscript sixteen years earlier. Moreover, the *Diana* had been known to him since his work on the *Two Gentlemen of Verona* (1594–1595). As far as Shakespeare's further use of Montemayor is concerned, see T. P. Harrison, Jr., "Shakespeare and Montemayor's *Diana,*" *University of Texas Bulletin, Studies in English,* VI (1926), 72–120.

lind's playful threat to Orlando, when he is wooing her: "I will weep for nothing, like Diana in the fountain, and I will do that when you are dispos'd to be merry" (IV.i.137–138). In any case, one is on firmer ground in thinking of the scene reported by the first lord in *As You Like It* (II.i.29–43), as modeled on the pastoral *locus amoenus* of suffering from the *Diana* than on the deer emblems we have discussed above. Shakespeare's wounded deer augments the brook, by which he sought refuge, with his tears (II.i.38–43), and Jaques, lamenting the lot of the persecuted animal, lets his own tears flow as freely (l. 65). This pathetic scene is the literary effect of the fusion of Sidney and Montemayor in Shakespeare's mind.

Yet Jaques does not weep out of unfulfilled love; his tears rather spring from a kind of universal *Weltschmerz* which is revealed in his "all-embracing sympathy with living creatures." [77] Whether one thinks this sentimental or not,[78] the fact remains that Jaques' extraordinarily complex personality, which reflects the different variants of the Elizabethan "malcontent," [79] is enriched by yet another characteristic. Jaques too, if one takes the historical origin of his lament on the tyrannical cruelty of hunting into account, is a humanist. Shakespeare, in concentrated imitation, reduced his direct source, Philisides' song from the *Arcadia,* to its fundamental core: "hunting as a form of unjust usurpation." This retains the political aspect inherent in criticisms of hunting since John of Salisbury but also underlines Jaques' *humanitas* which brings out his capacity for pity. In *As You Like It* as a whole this characteristically Shakespearean assimilation of the humanistic *topos* investigated serves, especially since hunting belongs to the trifling pastimes of courtiers, to accentuate strongly the criticism of courtly life which pervades the play and is explicitly formulated by the banished duke (II.i.1–18). That is its proper function

77. Cf. Friedrich Gundolf, *Shakespeare: sein Wesen und Werk,* 2 vols. (Berlin, 1928), I, 439 ("panisches Mitgefühl mit der Kreatur").

78. Opinions as to this differ: cf., for instance, Wilson, *Shakespeare's Happy Comedies,* pp. 154–155; and for a contrasting view see Alfred Harbage, *As They Liked It: An Essay on Shakespeare and Morality* (New York, 1947), p. 178.

79. Cf. Lawrence Babb's excellently documented study, which sums up previous research, in *The Elizabethan Malady: A Study of Melancholia in English Literature from 1580 to 1642* (East Lansing, Mich., 1951), pp. 73–101, esp. pp. 92–93.

in a play thematically revolving round the contrast between court and country life.[80] If, contrary to the main body of tradition, Shakespeare does not stress the moral degeneration which the passion for hunting brings about among men, then this will most probably be accounted for by the fact that, on the one hand, he would scarcely have gone beyond Sidney when he wrote *As You Like It* and, on the other, he wanted to avail himself of the opportunity to develop the theme of Jaques' lament directly out of the play's initial situation, namely, Frederick's usurpation of his brother's rightful dukedom (cf. II.i.27–28). Admittedly, it does not enter into Jaques' mind at all that the banished courtiers are forced to hunt in order to sustain themselves, which is permitted in both the *Policraticus* and the *Utopia*. However, where Jaques, the moralist, seems weak to us, Shakespeare shows his strength as a writer of comedy, for he does not allow any statement in the play to pass without contradiction. There is, to start with, deep irony in the fact that man, as a hunter, i.e., a murderer, forces his way into a world which, according to Seneca or Agrippa of Nettesheim, should know nothing of the battle between man and animal that is unknown in paradise.[81] Apart from that, Jaques' condemnation of hunting is itself rendered questionable by Touchstone's parodistic reference to it (III.ii.69–75). Even the melancholic's pessimistic commentary on the tragic scene before his eyes is partly belied by the comedy's action. Jaques interprets the augmenting of the brook, which already has enough water, with the tears of the wounded deer as a parable of the heedless way in which "worldlings" make their testament: ". . . giving thy sum of more / To that which had too much" (II.i.48–49). In the play, on the contrary, those who suffer hardship and poverty give to those who are still poorer and more miserable (cf. II.iv.66 ff.; II.vii.88 ff.). When the forsaken deer further prompts Jaques to remark: "'thus misery doth part / The flux of company'" (ll. 51–52), the best argument to the contrary is the misery shared by all the banished in the comedy (cf. I.iii.86 ff.; II.iii.38 ff.; II.vi). The only question which is not off the mark when seen against the play's action as a whole is the sarcastic:

80. On this contrast and its significance for *As You Like It,* see the present writer's *Traditionelle Denkformen in Shakespeares tragischer Kunst,* Britannica et Americana, XV (Hamburg, 1967), pp. 48–51, 67–69.

81. On the ambiguous nature of Shakespeare's "golden world" (I.i.109), cf. Harold Jenkins' article, *"As You Like It,"* pp. 43, n. 3, and 44.

"Wherefore do you look / Upon that poor and broken bankrupt there?" (ll. 56–57), when the pitiful victim of the hunt is left in the lurch by the remainder of the fleeing herd; for it may refer to Jaques himself, who plays the role of the outsider and continues to do so until the end by refusing to return to the court (V.iv.174–190). Thus the moral interpretation which melancholy Jaques gives of the wounded deer by the brook is not proved entirely wrong.

Creative assimilation is based on the fact that the source material thematically fits into, and definitely fulfills a function within, its new context. We have attempted to clarify the extent to which this is true for *As You Like It*, II.i.21–66. If we may now summarize, Shakespeare amplifies the humanistic *topos* of criticism of hunting borrowed from Sidney's *Arcadia* into a reported "emblematic" scene, probably inspired by Montemayor's *Diana*. This scene proves with perfect clarity how meaningful it is to speak of an "emblematic style" in Shakespeare, for as the object of visual perception as well as intellectual reflection it indeed does create distance and heightens the meaning of the events on stage. The ironic refraction of melancholy Jaques' humanistic criticism, which, as we said, cannot be considered as being completely to the point, prevents the lament for the sobbing deer from lapsing into the tragic. It also reduces its moral seriousness to the enjoyable play with literary convention which (without refusing to draw on certain stale comic effects—we have the strained witticism about "the deer's horns" in IV.ii particularly in mind) is so characteristic of the subtle comedy of plays poor in action like *Love's Labour's Lost* and *As You Like It*.

IV

If we may finally be allowed to extend our notion of "historical context" slightly, we can then see from a rapid glance at English literature after Shakespeare that Jaques is not merely acting as the mouthpiece of an inherited tradition in his criticism of hunting; to a certain degree he gave it new impulse and influenced it in his turn. This widening of perspective seems to contradict the methodical principles put forward in our introductory remarks. But in reality many subsequent texts undoubtedly belong to the same literary tradition as Jaques' speech, to a period, in other words, where *topoi* are still very much in evidence and form, so to speak, intellectual nuclei around which the creative writer arranges the expression of his sometimes very personal feelings and convictions. Thus, Michael Drayton, in his geographical epic *Poly-Olbion* (of which the first eighteen cantos appeared in 1612), when depicting the county of Warwickshire and the Forest of Arden, Shakespeare's home country, which was in the dramatist's mind when he wrote *As You Like It* (in spite of the "lioness" in IV.iii.112–131), actually describes a stag hunt (XIII.93–161) in which both the idea of cruelty (l. 151: "The cruell ravenous hounds and bloody Hunters neer") and the tears of the pursued animal occur (ll. 160–161).[82] It is possible that he was writing under the influence of Shakespeare here, but there is no direct proof.[83] The description of a royal stag hunt is to be found in Sir John Denham's *Cooper's Hill* ([1642], ll. 241–322). Denham was the founder of the semi-epic genre of landscape poetry, which intersperses the depiction of scenery with political and moral observations. However, he does not condemn hunting as such, although he finds affecting words to portray the misery of the victim of the hunt, excluded from the remainder of the herd (ll. 269–276, 289), and for obvious reasons, for he wishes to gloss over its cruelty by contrasting hunting to the threat to, and oppression of, human freedom. Thus he describes the royal sport with an allusion to the political events which led to Magna Carta as follows:

> This a more innocent, and happy chase,
> Than when of old, but in the selfsame place,
> Fair Liberty pursued, and meant a prey
> To lawless power, here turn'd, and stood at bay.[84]

(ll. 323–326)

It remained for the representatives of the English Enlightenment in the eighteenth century to renew the *topos* investigated in the spirit of their

82. The Tercentenary Edition of the *Works of Michael Drayton,* ed. J. William Hebel, Kathleen Tillotson, and Bernard H. Newdigate, 2d ed., 5 vols. (Oxford, 1961), IV, 277–279.

83. The editors' note to *Poly-Olbion,* XIII.87–161, does not discuss this problem and refers to the poet's personal experience to explain the description of the hunt (*ibid.,* V, 237)—not very convincing in the case of a *poeta doctus* like Drayton.

84. Citations are to *The Poetical Works of Edmund Waller and Sir John Denham,* with Memoir and Critical Dissertation by the Rev. George Gilfillan (Edinburgh, 1857), p. 225.

humanitarian ideals.[85] Alexander Pope, whose *Windsor-Forest* (1713), however much it may be patterned on Denham's *Cooper's Hill,* couples the theme of the hunt with that of tyranny, following the precedent of the humanists we have mentioned above. He too associates the Norman conquerors of England with Nimrod, the first hunter and prototype of a tyrant, because they laid waste inhabited and cultivated land in order to lay out the New Forest in Hampshire as a royal hunting precinct (ll. 43–92, esp. ll. 61 ff.).[86] The merry hunts in Windsor Forest are sharply contrasted with those which the poet conjures up against the somber background of the New Forest, but nevertheless they mean—and the somewhat euphemistic phrase "Sylvan War" (l. 148) cannot disguise this completely—death for the animals (ll. 113–114, 131–133), and man, armed with "slaught'ring Guns" (l. 125), even trains them in the art of killing their fellows: "Beasts, urg'd by us, their Fellow Beasts pursue, / And learn of Man each other to undo" (ll. 123–124).[87] The pre-romantic James Thomson, in his seasonal poem *Autumn* (1730), lashes out even more violently than the classicist Pope at the cruelty of the hunt (ll. 360–457, esp. ll. 383–395):

> 'Tis not joy to her [scil. the peaceful muse],
> This falsely cheerful *barbarous game of death,*
> This *rage of pleasure* which the restless youth
> Awakes, impatient, with the gleaming morn;
> When beasts of prey retire that all night long,
> Urged by *necessity,* had ranged the dark,
> As if their conscious ravage shunned the light
> Ashamed. Not so the *steady tyrant, man,*
> Who, with the *thoughtless insolence of power*
> Inflamed beyond the most infuriate wrath

85. On the humanitarian ideals of the English Enlightenment see Ludwig Borinski, "Menschheit und Menschlichkeit in der englischen Literatur des achtzehnten Jahrhunderts," *Studium Generale,* XV (1962), 157–170, esp. 168.

86. This despotic procedure of the Norman rulers, already strongly resented by John of Salisbury (see *Policraticus,* I.4; pp. 30–31), is also criticized by Robert Burton in his *Anatomy of Melancholy,* I.iii.3.13 (I, 334), with reference to the medieval humanist.

87. *Pastoral Poetry and an Essay on Criticism,* ed. E. Audra and Aubrey Williams, The Twickenham Edition of the *Poems of Alexander Pope* (London and New Haven, Conn., 1961), I, 162. Cf. also the introduction to *Windsor-Forest,* esp. pp. 138–140.

Of the worst monster that e'er roamed the waste,
For *sport alone* pursues the *cruel chase*
Amid the beamings of the gentle days.[88]

The words singled out for attention show us without any great difficulty
how much this passage from the *Seasons* owes to the intellectual structure
of the humanistic *topos* of criticism of hunting. "Tyrant man" (cf. also
Autumn, ll. 1189–1191, and *Spring*, l. 703) only embarks on the chase out
of "delight in blood" (l. 399), and urges on the bloodthirsty pack of
hounds (l. 439: "inhuman rout," see also l. 432) to pursue the fleeing stag,
who, abandoned by the herd, again sheds tears in the hour of his death.
This is how the description of a stag hunt reads in *Autumn*, obviously,
except for the tears, written in imitation of *Cooper's Hill*, yet in its
humanitarian pathos much closer to *As You Like It*.[89] Finally, William
Cowper's sympathetic understanding of the animals' fate is shown to be
the deepest, when he selects the symbiosis of man and animal as a subject
for a moral discussion in broad terms in his topographical and didactic
poem *The Task* ([1785], VI.321–631). As Agrippa of Nettesheim did
before him, Cowper attributes the breakdown of this symbiosis, which he
laments in his poem, to original sin (ll. 368 ff.) whereby the "seed of
cruelty" was sown (l. 381; see also ll. 343 and 594): "Hence date the
persecution and the pain / That man inflicts on all inferior kinds, / Regardless of their plaints" (ll. 384–386). Of course the thought of tyranny
reappears in this context (ll. 406, 455), as does the key word for the whole
attitude of mind dealt with here: "humanity" (l. 566). In accordance with
this, hunting is condemned as an encroachment on an area allotted by
nature to the animals alone (ll. 577–580):

. . . and he that hunts
Or harms them there is guilty of a wrong,
Disturbs th' economy of nature's realm,
Who, when she form'd, design'd them an abode.[90]

88. *The Complete Poetical Works of James Thomson,* ed. J. Logie Robertson, Oxford Standard Authors (London, 1908; repr. 1961), p. 147. Italics added.

89. A hint at these connections is lacking in Alan Dugald McKillop's *The Background of Thomson's "Seasons"* (Minneapolis, Minn., 1942).

90. Cf. Cowper, *Poetical Works,* ed. H. S. Milford, Oxford Standard Authors,
4th ed. (London, 1934; repr. 1967), p. 232. Cowper, by the way, does not here describe a stag hunt, but he uses, as Praz points out in *Studies in Seventeenth-Century*

The evidence we have assembled proves the vitality of the humanistic *topos* of criticism of hunting, which can be traced in almost unbroken continuity from antiquity to the very threshold of the Romantic period. It would not, however, be legitimate to use the above texts as a basis for interpretation of Jaques' speech. They may corroborate what has already been said, but we cannot on any account allow the moral sensibility of a later age to intrude on our assessment of the character and function of Jaques.This would, above all, destroy the powerful effects of subtle irony which Shakespeare, as has been pointed out, intends us not to miss. Still, by seeing his lament in its appropriate historical context, Jaques gains in complexity, and through a correct understanding of his moralizing speech even the nature of his melancholy may become clearer to us. His lament at the sight of the wounded and sobbing deer by the brook is only one voice, if an important one, in the chorus of condemnation of hunting not silenced through the centuries. It reveals convictions which ennoble their spokesman, no matter how one may otherwise be disposed towards him.

Imagery, pp. 229–230, the emblem of the wounded deer, which we discussed above, elsewhere in his poem (III.ll.108–120).

"The Simetry, Which Gives a Poem Grace": Masque, Imagery, and the Fancy of The Maid's Tragedy

MICHAEL NEILL

LYSIPPUS
Strato, thou hast some skill in poetry;
What think's thou of the masque? will it be well?

The Maid's Tragedy, I.i.5–6

MASQUES ARE A COMMONPLACE FEATURE of the drama written for the private playhouses of the Jacobean and Caroline periods. Their spectacular appeal to an audience, which (whatever the statistical details of its composition) was nearly dominated in matters of taste by a genteel coterie, is obvious. Thanks to the work of Enid Welsford and M. C. Bradbrook, it is now generally recognized that in the hands of the more intelligent dramatists "these pretty devices" may also have important structural functions. Miss Welsford has shown that the ritualistic qualities of masque, as well as helping to universalize the significance of the action, may provide an essential method of controlling the audience's response to apparently melodramatic episodes.[1] Professor Bradbrook has discussed the use of masques as a variety of the play-within-the-play device, designed to create "ironic interplay" of various kinds.[2]

Oddly enough, however, very little attempt has been made until recently to examine the structural purpose of one of the most elaborate masques-within-the-play, the wedding masque in *The Maid's Tragedy.* Professor Bradbrook remarks that "the masque . . . with its description

1. Enid Welsford, *The Court Masque* (Cambridge, Eng., 1927), pp. 292 ff.
2. M. C. Bradbrook, *Themes and Conventions of Elizabethan Tragedy,* paperback edition (Cambridge, Eng., 1960), pp. 45–46.

of the sudden storm rising on the wedding night, is not entirely irrelevant";[3] and W. W. Appleton[4] finds a "prophetic irony" in Cynthia's
promise to provide such entertainment for the company

> As may for ever after force them hate
> Our brother's glorious beams, and wish the night.[5]
>
> (I.ii.153–154)

Otherwise the critical silence would suggest that Beaumont and Fletcher's
masque has been regarded as a spectacular irrelevance. In an essay printed
in *A Book of Masques*,[6] Inga-Stina Ewbank attacks this generally implicit
view: she notes the way in which the highly conventional themes and
imagery of this masque are echoed in the following scene, so that the
idealized masque ritual becomes a foil for the corrupt action of the wedding night. And she detects further heavy irony in the conventional tribute to the sovereign with which the masque concludes. In general she
claims for it "a . . . strongly ironical bearing on the action of the play,"[7]
though the scope of her paper does not allow her to argue the case in detail.

The failure of other critics to give sympathetic attention to the function
of the masque is particularly surprising since constructive skill is perhaps
the only talent that Beaumont and Fletcher are widely granted today: and
yet here, in a play that is usually cited as their most successful tragedy, we
are faced with a structural excrescence of unique proportions[8]—and in

---

3. *Ibid.*, p. 46. But see p. 47, where Professor Bradbrook speaks of a "felt fusion"
between masque and play.

4. W. W. Appleton, *Beaumont and Fletcher: A Critical Study* (London, 1956),
p. 35.

5. Citations from *The Maid's Tragedy* are to *Five Stuart Tragedies*, ed. A. K. Mc-
Ilwraith (Oxford, 1953).

6. Inga-Stina Ewbank, " 'These pretty devices': A Study of Masques in Plays," *A
Book of Masques* (Cambridge, Eng., 1967), pp. 405–448.

7. *Ibid.*, p. 416.

8. The masque takes up over one third of Act I, and this proportion would probably increase in actual performance (taking into account the various spectacular and
musical effects called for) to over one half. On the printed page it is roughly comparable in length to an early Jonson masque, like *Blacknesse* (though one would
not expect its staging to have been as elaborate as Inigo's). Its relative structural
prominence is indicated by the fact that even in print it is considerably longer than
either "The Murder of Gonzago" or any of the playlets in *The Roman Actor*.

the exposition, where dramatic economy is most important. Far from attempting to minimize the weight given the masque by its elaborate proportions, the dramatists actually go out of their way to emphasize it in the action and dialogue of Act I. Indeed, with the exception of some brief narrative which reveals Amintor's desertion of Aspatia and sketches in his friendship with Melantius, it would be fair to say that the masque is the real dramatic subject of the first act. In view of the care taken to focus the audience's attention upon the masque, it is at least reasonable to assume that its physical prominence is deliberate, that it corresponds to an intended structural significance.

The purpose of this essay is to show that the "felt fusion" between masque and play action in *The Maid's Tragedy,* of which Professor Bradbrook speaks, is a real thing; that the masque is part of a carefully worked out dramatic scheme; and that this scheme involves (among other things) the ironic manipulation of running imagery, which links the masque not only to the wedding night but to the action of the play as a whole. Elsewhere in her *Themes and Conventions,* Professor Bradbrook remarks that the final test of the decadence of the Beaumont and Fletcher plays is their lack of any kind of "verbal framework." [9] I shall argue that a complete reading of *The Maid's Tragedy* does involve the recognition of significant "linguistic patterns," though they are not perhaps of quite the kind that Professor Bradbrook meant.

I

In the first set of encomiastic verses which he contributed to the 1647 folio, William Cartwright singled out Fletcher's constructional skill for particular praise:

> None can prevent the Fancy, and see through
> At the first opening; all stand wondring how
> The thing will be untill it is; which thence
> With fresh delight still cheats, still takes the sence;
> The whole designe, the shadowes, the lights such
> That none can say he shewes or hides too much.[10]

9. Bradbrook, *Themes and Conventions,* p. 248.
10. *The Works of Francis Beaumont and John Fletcher,* ed. A. Glover and A. R. Waller (Cambridge, Eng., 1905), I, xxxvii.

By "Fancy" Cartwright apparently means something like "design" or "plot," though of a rather specialized kind.[11] The context suggests that the senses of "witty conceit" and "something delusive" are also relevant. Fletcher's "Fancy" is not only a "designe," but a thing which "with *fresh delight* still *cheats* . . . the sence." The term thus neatly embraces three of the most distinctive features of Fletcher's plots: the paradoxical perversions of familiar social situations from which the plays begin; the working out of these paradoxes in a logically articulated sequence of further structural conceits; and the elaborate tissues of deception, dissimulation, and error, rising naturally out of the situational paradoxes, which serve to keep up the audience's interest in the unfolding design.

The social conceits, on which the fancies of plays like *A King and No King* or *A Wife for a Month* are built, are immediately and more or less adequately suggested by their titles. The fancy of *The Maid's Tragedy* is rather more complicated and could be covered only partially by the subtitles which suggest themselves: "A Wife and No Wife," "A Maid and No Maid," or "A Marriage and No Marriage." But it is, I believe, only in terms of the conceited kind of design which Cartwright calls a "fancy" that we can properly discuss the dramatic method and meaning of the play, and so avoid making critical demands that are inappropriate to the dramatists' artistic intention. More specifically, I believe that it is only in its relation to such a controlling fancy that we can fully realize the function of the obtrusive wedding masque.

Of course the masque does have simple, literal functions: it is designed to set the play in a certain milieu and to establish the appropriate social tone. As part of a sequence of wedding festivities, ending with the banquet in Act IV, scene ii, it provides an ironic foil to the revenge action. But these are limited and static uses; more important is what we might call its kinetic function, as part of a dynamic pattern of verbal and dramatic ironies. It embodies, in striking visual terms, a group of images, whose equivocal significance the play exploits through a series of paradoxes and reversals, both structural and rhetorical. The ironic nature of this development compels repeated recollection and re-examination of the masque: it becomes the central and dominating image of the whole work, an epitome of its structural fancy.

11. The meaning is not recorded in *O.E.D.* but could be readily derived from a common sense of the verb.

The reason for the general critical neglect of the ironic patterns of action and imagery in *The Maid's Tragedy* seems to me to be fairly indicated by Eliot's complaint that "the blossoms of Beaumont and Fletcher's imagination draw no sustenance from the soil, but are cut and slightly withered flowers stuck into the sand." [12] The language of the Fletcher plays obviously lacks the poetic intensity of the best Elizabethan and Jacobean work, and it does not appear to be organized in patterns which can be called (except in the broadest sense) morally significant. But this is not to say that the plays lack any organizational principle except that of melodramatic opportunism. The marriage masque in *The Maid's Tragedy* is as conventional as the imagery which links it to the play as a whole: but this conventionality is appropriate to the fanciful design of the play, which consists in the juggling of equally conventional social situations. The familiarity of the rhetoric vouches for the fundamental ordinariness of the basic situations. But what the play does, of course, is to turn these situations inside out, and the language of the play is made to go through a corresponding series of inversions and perversions. The patterns are patterns of wit.

By the very nature of its conventional ritual, a wedding masque ought to define the images it presents. In its sophisticated way it remains a kind of magical rite, performed to ensure the success and fertility of the union it celebrates. The unconventional thing about this most conventional of masques is that it fails to establish the proper definitions. This means, as far as the language of the play is concerned, that it initiates a pattern of equivocation and semantic inversion which is the rhetorical analogue of the repeated peripeties of the plot structure. At the same time it ironically predicates the disasters and confusions of the subsequent action. Implicitly its action is related to the fate of the play action: it is not magic which has failed, but magic which has gone astray. I must emphasize that this connection is only implicit: if we stopped to consider it, it would seem absurd. But the implication is necessary if the ironical symmetry is to be effective. The sleight of hand is possible only because the dramatists are juggling with two levels of illusion: in life mundane reality conventionally transcends stage reality at the conclusion of a masque (the presence of the king visibly affects the actions of the masquers), but when the

12. T. S. Eliot, *Selected Essays,* 3d ed. (London, 1951), p. 155.

mundane reality is itself a play there is no felt reason why the relationship should not be reversed and the masque "determine" the fate of its audience. Queen Night, and Cynthia, after all, who control the revels and see the stage audience as their "servants" (I.ii.151), are as "real" to the theater audience as Amintor and Evadne themselves.

II

A stock theme of revels, both in England and on the Continent, as Miss Welsford points out, is the arrival of night and the gradual approach of dawn.[13] Allusion to the presence of night, whether simply in the setting (like the "obscure and cloudy nightpiece" of *Blacknesse*) or through the presence of a goddess (Queen Night herself or one of the Moon deities), is an obvious device for the blurring of artifice and reality which is essential to the effectiveness of masque. The particular appropriateness of such allusions in wedding entertainments is equally obvious. In choosing Queen Night as the presenter of their wedding masque, Beaumont and Fletcher may perhaps have been influenced by the published accounts of the entertainments at two Italian weddings in 1608. One of these, the Florentine *Notte D'Amore* was to be extensively adapted by Jonson for his *Vision of Delight* (1617) and again by Davenant in *Luminalia* (1638).[14] But the idea might just as well have been borrowed from the conventions of the epithalamium, of which this masque is in effect a dramatized version. A regular feature of epithalamia is the poet's entreaty that the departure of day be hastened and the reign of night begin;[15] and the appeal is normally followed by the announcement that the wished-for night has in fact arrived. Queen Night's "Our reign is come . . . I am the Night" (I.ii.122–124) at once signalizes the beginning of the masque and anticipates the end of the revels in the entry to the nuptial

13. Welsford, *Court Masque*, p. 111.

14. See *Court Masque*, pp. 111–114, 200–202, 235 ff. An English precedent is provided by Daniel's *The Vision of the Twelve Goddesses* (1604).

15. See Spenser, "Epithalamion" ll. 278 ff.; Herrick, "The Entertainment: or, Porche-Verse . . . , l. 10; "Conubii Flores," ll. 5–17; Donne, "An Epithalamion . . . on the Lady Elizabeth and Count Palatine being married," ll. 56–70; and cf. Jonson, *Hymenaei*, ll. 377–380.

night itself. The visual context of the announcement and the terms in which it is made suggest an ambiguity which is also native to the epithalamium tradition—an ambiguity which the dramatists go on to exploit.

The eighteenth stanza of Spenser's "Epithalamion," for instance, while welcoming Night as the friend and protectress of lovers, implies that night conceals not only love but evil: it may stand not only for the joys of marriage but for death. And stanza 19 consists of a series of charms invoked against the sinister possibilities of the dark. So, when Beaumont and Fletcher's Night "rises in *mists,*" we may take them as standing for Spenser's "deluding dreames" and phantasms (as in the Mantuan *intermezzo* of 1608) [16] or, more generally, for "misconceived dout" and "hidden feares." In fact the imagery of Night's opening lines tends to support her identification with evil and confusion:

> Our reign is come; for in the *quenching* sea
> The sun is *drown'd,* and with him *fell* the Day.
>
>   (I.ii.122–123; italics added)

There is a quite deliberate irony in the juxtaposition of this ominous visual and verbal imagery with Evadne's greeting to Melantius ("Your presence is more joyful than this *day*" l. 120; italics added), an irony which is complicated by the fact that her apparent hyperbole turns out to be a heavily sarcastic litotes.

The doubts thus created are deepened rather than dispelled when Queen Night is joined by her co presenter, the Moon Goddess, Cynthia. As the patron of virginal chastity, Cynthia/Diana may seem to preside somewhat incongruously over a ritual of consummation. In fact, of course, she has a second aspect as the patron of generation and childbirth and is so invoked in Spenser's poem and in the Epithalamium from *Hymenaei.* But in both of these her connection with fertility is given considerable emphasis, whereas here it is not so much as alluded to. [17] Indeed, Cynthia's rather tart rebuke to Night's insinuations about her relationship with Endymion (ll. 168–170) can only tend to identify her with the virgin Diana. If we make this identification, Neptune's offering of the revels as "a solemn honour to the moon" (l. 211) becomes heavily ironical; and the

---

16. See Welsford, *Court Masque,* p. 111.

17. Unless we take Night's metaphor at ll. 160–161 to involve an allusive quibble. But even if this is intended, the allusion is remarkably inconspicuous.

irony is perfectly, if perversely, fulfilled in a wedding night which remains completely chaste, though the chastity results from the vows of whoredom, not virginity. As an ironic celebration of chastity, the masque is relevant to both Amintor's love relationships: each is a match but no match which this wedding-and-no-wedding ensures will never be consummated, except in death.

The initial uncertainties concerning the nature of Queen Night herself are partially resolved by the conversation between the two goddesses, in which Night is presented as the friend, and Day as the enemy of lovers. Night's proposal that they should "hold their places and outshine the day" (l. 145) even promises to fulfil the conventional lovers' wish (expressed here in the masque songs) that the night may never end. Cynthia has to remind her that the gods' decrees may not be broken in this way but suggests instead that they "stretch their power" over fleeting time by means of an entertainment, designed

> To give our servants one contented hour,
> With such unwonted solemn grace and state,
> As may for ever after force them hate
> Our brother's glorious beams, and wish the night.
>
> (ll. 151–154)

In effect the masque is to be, like Spenser's "Epithalamion," "for short time an endlesse moniment" which will "raise to time a nobler memory / Of what these lovers are" (ll. 173–174). If we read the masque with the irony that its ambiguities invite, it can be seen to do exactly this.

Pre-eminent among the servants for whose delight the revels are offered are the lovers themselves, Evadne and Amintor; and conventionally of course it is the bride and groom who will most hate the advent of dawn and "wish the night." This defining association of Night with happiness, love, and sexual consummation is continued in the nuptial songs which separate the three dances of the revels. The masquers make repeated appeals for the extension of Night's reign:

> Joy to this great company!
>   And no day
> Come to steal this night away,
>   Till the rites of love are ended.
>
> (ll. 219–222)

Hold back thy hours, dark Night, till we have done;
    The Day will come too soon:
Young maids will curse thee, if thou steal's away,
And leav'st their losses open to the day:
    Stay, stay, and hide
    The blushes of the bride.

                                                    (ll. 233–238)

Hesperus, be long a-shining,
Whilst these lovers are a-twining.

                                                    (ll. 257–258)

By contrast with "gentle Night," Day is rude, abrupt, and inquisitive: the reward which Cynthia offers the sea-gods for their performance is flood tides which will hide their dwellings from the hateful eye of Day (ll. 265–269).

The process of definition, then, is one which inverts, according to the familiar conceit of epithalamia and love poetry in general, the conventional symbolism of night and day, light and dark. But the definition remains incomplete and equivocal. The masquers who are conjured up by Cynthia represent the winds and the sea-gods. Both wind and sea supply conventional metaphors for the passions; so that the dances in which the masquers are led by Neptune may be seen as analogous to the ordered dance in which Reason sets the rebellious humours and affections of *Hymenaei.* But this symbolism of marital harmony is upset by the escape of Boreas, who proves unamenable to the power of Neptune's "music to lay a Storm." His raising of a tempest which threatens the destruction of "many a tall ship" *before day* implicitly calls in question the real nature of Night (ll. 259–262). The storm stands for an outbreak of unbridled passion which is realized in the discord of the wedding night which follows,[18] and even more disastrously in the slaughter of the second "wedding night" in Act V. Further, the presence among the dancers of Proteus, the shape changer, may also have ironic implications, in view of the web of dissimulation and deception which complicates the subsequent action.

The conventionally circular structure of the masque[19] allows the dram-

18. See below, pp. 132–134 for a discussion of this trope.
19. It is worth noticing that this circularity is paralleled in the structure of the play itself, which (like the masque, if we include Night's promised return) both begins and ends with the descent of night.

atists to wind up its action with a recapitulation of its opening sequence, which concentrates in a single dramatic emblem the ambiguity of the whole piece. Night, now appropriately called "dead Night" (l. 273) announces her departure with a second and even more malevolent reference to her murderous quarrel with Day, and then vanishes once more "into mists" (l. 287):

> Oh, I could frown
> To see the Day, the Day that flings his light
> Upon my kingdom and condemns old Night!
> Let him go on and flame! I hope to see
> Another wildfire in his axletree,
> And all fall drench'd.
>
>   (ll. 275–280)

The immediate effect of the various uncertainties about the significance of the masque action is to give substance to the visual and verbal ambiguities surrounding the figure of Queen Night on her first appearance. Night is described by Cynthia as "queen of shadows" and in the context of a dramatic performance "shadows" may refer not only to the literal shadows of darkness but to the shadows of theatrical illusion: as the presenter of a masque, Night is queen of its actor / shadows and acted illusions. In a wider sense the "shadows" may stand (like the symbolic mists out of which she rises) for delusive appearance and concealed evil. The unfolding ironies of the plot are to reveal Night as the presiding deity of the Rhodian court, Queen of its shadows in both these senses. The whole of the ensuing play action can be seen as the process by which the ambiguities of the masque are ironically elaborated and finally resolved.

The process begins in Act II, scene i: in its opening sequence Dula's bawdy identification of night with love and consummation is contrasted with Aspatia's melancholy association of night with death (ll. 104–105). The juxtaposition extends the ambiguity of the masque-artifice to the play-reality and gives a somewhat sinister ambivalence to the removal of the wedding torches (l. 114). The ambivalence is supported by a subdued play with the two senses of "death" which, though it becomes explicit only occasionally, underlies a great deal of the action of *The Maid's Tragedy* and is an essential feature of its witty fancy. Just as the rhetoric of love poetry can convert Night, the symbol of death, so it can convert death itself to its own metaphorical ends.[20] On her wedding night a maid "dies" in two senses: there is the "death" of sexual climax and the consequent "death" of her virgin self: in the morning she is reborn as a wife.[21] These are the deaths which the bride songs of the masque lead us to expect for the supposed maid, Evadne:

> Stay, and confound her tears and her shrill cryings,
> Her weak denials, vows, and often-dyings.
>
> (I.ii.241–242)

> they may kiss while they may say a maid:
> To-morrow twill be other kissed and said.
>
> (I.ii.255–256)

Thus, the full pathos of Aspatia's rebukes to Evadne and Amintor depends on an implicit comparison between the literal death which she foresees for herself and the nuptial death of which she has been cheated (II.i.94–105, 116–118)—the allusion being clinched by the association of the funeral hearse, around which the maids will watch one night, with the marriage bed, around which maids gather to prepare the bride,[22] and of the mourning garlands of yew, ivy, and willow (ll. 77–78, 108, 124) with the bride's floral coronet.[23]

The ironic hints in the first 130 lines of the scene are partially substantiated by the ominous recurrence of tears on the wedding day, so lightly dismissed in Act I, scene i. And the omen is amply fulfilled in the

20. Herrick's "Upon a maid that dyed the day she was marryed" (like *The Maid's Tragedy* itself) seems to turn the familiar conceit back to front: the expected sexual death becomes a kind of metaphor for literal death. (Quoted below, p. 127.)

21. Cf. Donne, "Epithalamion made at Lincolnes Inne," ll. 79–80; Jonson, *The Haddington Masque,* ll. 415–425 (which may be imitated in Beaumont and Fletcher's third masque song); and Dryden, "On the marriage of Mrs. Anastasia Stafford," l. 21. All citations from Jonson are from the Herford and Simpson edition (Oxford, 1925–1952).

22. For other versions of this comparison between marriage bed and grave, see the passage cited above (n. 21) from Donne, and Herrick's "Upon a maid . . ." (quoted below, p. 127).

23. In II.ii.23–27 Aspatia, echoing Shakespeare's Cleopatra, is to pursue this comparison to the point of equating sexual and literal death. The echo of *Antony and Cleopatra* is appropriate—cf. *Antony and Cleopatra,* IV.xiv.99–101; V.ii.192–193, 293–294.

wedding night, in terms which constantly send us back to the masque. Amintor's ineffectual deprecation of "the vapours of the night" (l. 146) immediately recalls the mists surrounding Queen Night, with their symbolism of doubt, confusion, evil, and possibly also of death.[24] In one way, of course, the scene is to dispel the mists of deception and error by revealing the true nature of Amintor's "maid and wife"; but against this is set his decision that they must both dissemble (ll. 355 ff.). Again, Amintor's jocose "I mean no sleeping" (l. 154) may remind us of Cynthia's claim to be "gazed on . . . Almost of none but of *unquiet* eyes" (I.ii.159; italics added); but this night is to be unquiet for its lovers in quite another sense from the one intended. Even more important are the ways in which the scene produces a perverted realization of two of the masque's most conventional epithalamic tropes. Evadne's declaration that her refusal of conjugal rights is "not for a night / Or two . . . but ever" (ll. 210–211) amounts to an ironic fulfilment of the conventional wish for the indefinite extension of the night of bliss: these "joys of marriage," such as they are, are granted for ever. At the same time Cynthia's prediction that her servants will come to "wish the night" is morbidly realized in Amintor's desire for death at Evadne's hands (ll. 327–333). The substitution of literal for sexual death suggests an ironic equation of Amintor's situation with that of the woman he has betrayed.

If night proves as hateful as its symbolic connection with death threatens, day, nevertheless, remains as unwelcome as the masque songs predict. The two morning scenes (II.ii and III.i) contrast Aspatia's lamentation with the inner misery of Amintor. The imagery of her laments makes of the sun, Cynthia's brother and Night's antagonist, a further agent of destruction and death. Rather than credit the faith of a man, she says, one should believe the impossible, that

> the sun
> Comes but to kiss the fruit in wealthy autumn,
> When all falls blasted.
>
> (II.ii.20–22)

The image reflects, with ironic aptness, firstly on the King, whom the mandatory flattery of the masque has styled a greater sun (I.ii.283), and whose kiss has in fact blasted the fruitfulness of Evadne's marriage, and

24. Cf. *The Duchess of Malfi*, V.v.94, and *The White Devil*, V.vi.260.

next on Evadne herself, whom Amintor has previously hailed as bringing a kind of day at midnight (II.i.142–144).[25] In the second of these scenes, the hostility attributed to the searching eye of day is painfully embodied in the blundering curiosity of the courtiers and the jealous enquiries of the King. Their jokes about the troublesomeness of the night (III.i.2–4) and Diphilus' cheerful shout to his sister that "the night will come again" (ll. 16–17) are heavy with unconscious irony, an irony which is heightened by the fact that it is actually Amintor whom Diphilus has heard approaching.

In this scene (as throughout the play) the night/day antithesis is given considerable rhetorical emphasis. But the ironies are not always as clearcut as in the cases we have been considering,[26] and it would be pointless to labor them all. In general, we can say that they function chiefly as insistent reminders of the central paradoxes of the play's fancy. The final resolution of these paradoxes begins with the perverted second "weddingnight." The preparation for this begins in Act IV, scene i, Evadne's conversion scene. Here the play with the literal and metaphorical senses of death becomes brutally explicit. Evadne, who has been introduced in the hackneyed trope of love poetry as "a lady . . . that . . . strikes dead with flashes of her eye" (I.i.74–76),[27] and for whom the bridal dyings have been promised, now quite literally "has death about her." Her relationship with the King has "poisoned" her virtue and "murdered" the honor of her family; and, according to Melantius, she can redeem herself only by resolving to kill the King in fact. When she hesitates, her brother responds with a sarcasm that demands death for her "dyings":

> An 'twere to kiss him dead, thou'dst smother him:
> Be wise and kill him.
>
> (IV.i.159–160)

25. Cf. I.ii.134–137, where Night sees the eyes of the assembled beauties as shooting a light which brings a false dawn. Spenser's "Epithalamion" contains a more elaborate version of the trope at ll. 148 ff.

26. When, for instance, in III.i. Evadne is made to swear "by this light" (l. 203) and the King reminds her that "Day and Night" have heard her oaths of constancy (l. 187), we may sense an ironic undertone, without being able to define it precisely. Similarly, the context may suggest subdued ironies in Evadne's use of "days" and "evening" at IV.i.255–257 as metaphors for life and death.

27. Evadne's "strike him dead" (V.ii.24) may be meant as an ironic echo of this tribute.

The conceit is elaborately worked out in Act V, where Evadne fulfils her vow.

In Act IV, scene ii, the King presents Amintor and Evadne with a second marriage entertainment, in the shape of a banquet, which is the structural equivalent of Act II's masque. The feast ends with his urging the couple once more to the bridal chamber: "It grows somewhat late.— / Amintor, thou wouldst be a-bed again" (ll. 221–222). But the conversation which follows, between Melantius and his brother, sharply points up the difference in the two situations:

> This were a night indeed
> To do it in: the King hath sent for her.
>
> (IV.ii.276–277)

And as though Diphilus' exclamation were not sufficient to establish the night/death conceit on which their revenge is to be built, Melantius is made to echo it a few lines later (ll. 288–290).

With Act V the night, in fulfilment of Diphilus' promise to his sister in Act III, scene i, "is come again." Its opening scene[28] is evidently designed as an ironical inversion of the wedding night. The gentleman's obscene banter as he ushers the King's whore to the royal bed corresponds to the bawdy nudging of Dula during the preparation of the bride; just as the dialogue between the two gentlemen at the end of the scene, with its boasting and speculation on the King's sexual prowess, recalls the horseplay outside the bridal chamber in Act III, scene i.[29] The "good-nights" of the gentleman and Evadne ominously echo the repeated "good-nights" of Act I, scene ii and Act II, scene i; and the gentleman's farewell picks up the conventional wish for the perpetuation of the marriage night ("A good night be it, then, and a long one" V.i.11)—a wish which is about to be fulfilled for the lovers of the play with an exactitude that he scarcely anticipates. The King's insistent "to beds" (V.ii.33,38,43) ironically repeat the groom's invitations to his bride in II.i.152, 155–156, 194, 277; while his mounting horror as he becomes aware of Evadne's real purpose, his protestations that she is "too sweet and gentle for such an act"[30] and his

---

28. V.i and ii are in fact a single scene, as McIlwraith notes.

29. It is worth noting that the scene follows the second wedding entertainment of IV.ii, just as the first wedding night followed the masque.

30. Cf. especially II.i.191–194, 212, 269–271; and V.ii.60–61, 70–72, 83–84.

despairing plea for "pity"[31] all parallel Amintor's response to Evadne's unmasking. The allusions to the earlier action show the scene as a grotesque travesty of a wedding night and thus give its *doubles entendres* on love and death an intensified ironic force. As she trusses up the sleeping King, Evadne actually seems to recall Melantius' sarcastic quibble:

> I dare not trust your strength; your grace and I
> Must grapple upon even terms no more.
>
> (V.ii.25–26)

And she recklessly pursues the conceit by referring to her knife blows as "love-tricks" (l. 91). The whole perverted love act reaches its climax in the King's expiring "Oh! I die" (l. 99). In ironic fulfillment of the second masque song, Night stays to cover the kisses ("love-tricks") of the lover, to "hide all" and make the cries of the murdered King as ineffectual as those of the dying bride. In this scene the symbolism of night becomes for the first time completely unequivocal (though the context provides ironic reminders of its original association with amorous fulfilment):

> The night grows horrible; and all about me
> Like my black purpose.
>
> (V.ii.1–2)

The abortive night of love is succeeded by the consummatory night of death.[32]

In the final scene Evadne appears, "her hands bloody, with a knife," to announce to her husband

> joys,
> That in a moment can call back thy wrongs . . .
>
> (V.iv.109–110)

The joys she envisages are in fact nothing less than the "marriage-joys" so insistently referred to in the first three acts.[33] The blood and the knife she offers as tokens, not of death but of "rites" which have "washed her stains away" and, she implies (ll. 112–113, 117–123), restored her maidenhood,

---

31. The inversion by which "pity" comes to mean "death" for Amintor and "life" for the King is typical of the play's symmetrical ironies.

32. Strato's reference to "this dead time of night" (l. 131) echoes Cynthia's "dead Night" at the end of the masque (I.ii.273).

33. I.i.46; I.ii.117, 120, 219; II.i.94, 219; III.i.80, 84, 131; III.ii.80, 84.

so that their marriage may be rejoined.[34] Thus, she announces her revenge in words which echo the hymeneal shout in the first masque song:

> Joy to this great company!
>
> (I.ii.219)

> Joy to Amintor! for the King is dead.
>
> (V.iv.128)

And she goes on to make the last of the play's formal invitations to the marriage bed (ll. 152–157). When, however, Amintor rejects the symbolism of her love tokens ("Black is thy colour now"), Evadne bids her husband farewell with a speech that finally accepts death as the only consummation possible for her:

> Amintor, thou shalt love me now again:
> Go, I am calm. Farewell and peace forever!
> Evadne, whom thou hatest, will die for thee.
>
> (V.iv.169–171)

The death of Evadne, bride and no maid, is carefully contrived to parallel that of Aspatia, maid and no bride. Aspatia's equation of sexual and actual death, at II.ii.22–26, is realized through her absurd duel with Amintor in Act V, scene iv, which can be seen as an ironic literalization of the metaphorical battle of bride and groom. Quite properly, as the conventions of the trope require, Aspatia offers only a token resistance (V.iv.101 ff.). And her line as she falls recognizes a pathetic irony in her death in the house of the man who was to have become her husband:

> There is no place so fit
> For me to die as here.
>
> (ll. 106–107)

In its final act *The Maid's Tragedy* is revealed as at once dramatized epitaph and epithalamium; the disturbing ambiguities of the masque have been elaborated into a structure of verbal and dramatic ironies which, whatever the difference of scale, is fundamentally of the same order, in its witty conjunction of opposites, as Herrick's "Upon a maid that dyed the day she was marryed":

34. At this point (as perhaps in V.ii) the audience may be meant to think of the customary use of wedding knives and daggers as part of the bridal costume. See L. E. Pearson, *The Elizabethans at Home* (Stanford, Calif., 1957), p. 343.

> That Morne which saw me made a Bride,
> The Ev'ning witnest that I dy'd.
> The holy lights, wherewith they guide
> Unto the bed the bashful Bride;
> Served, but as Tapers, for to burne,
> And light my Reliques to their Urne.
> This *Epitaph,* which here you see,
> Supply'd the *Epithalamie.* [35]

Evadne's intention is that the night of death should blot out the dishonor of the actual wedding night: the blackness of the deed, by a final paradoxical twist, is to make her fair again.

> Am I not *fair?*
> Looks not Evadne beauteous in these rites now?
> Were those hours half so lovely in thine eyes
> When our hands met before the holy man:
> I was too *foul* within to look *fair* then.
>
> (V.iv.117–122; italics added)

The italicized words belong to a strain of light/dark imagery so closely related to the basic Night / Day opposition that it may be appropriate to deal with it now. The symbolic hostility of Night and Day in the masque was clearly meant to be paralleled in the staging by spectacular use of chiaroscuro.[36] The presence of the "fair Queen," "Bright Cynthia" in the company of dull, black Night, the "Queen of Shadows," calls for visual realization of the paradox which the moon goddess promises to achieve in her revels ("our music may . . . make the east break day / At midnight" I.ii.214–216). In the play action this visual opposition is continued in the alternation of nocturnal and daytime scenes; and it is a consistent theme of the poetry. The masque's paradox of brightness in blackness, fairness in foulness, is typically embodied in Evadne and in that false sun, the King. The Night Goddesses salute the assembled court beauties (among whom the bride is pre-eminent) as "a troop brighter than we," whose "eyes know how / To shoot far more and quicker rays" than Cynthia herself (ll. 136–143); and Night's figure recalls the first description of Evadne as a lady "that bears the light above her and strikes dead / With flashes of her eye"

35. *The Poems of Robert Herrick,* ed. L. C. Martin (Oxford, 1965), p. 109.
36. Such as only an indoor theater, like the Blackfriars, for which *The Maid's Tragedy* was written, was equipped to provide.

(I.i.75–76), while her comparison of their beams of beauty with the dawn (ll. 134–135) looks forward to Amintor's conventional greeting of his bride as Aurora (II.i.142–144).

The first scene, with its references to the "fair Aspatia" (l. 60) and "the fair Evadne" (l. 76) establishes the two as rivals in fairness. Evadne's triumph in this contest, signalized by Amintor's tribute to the "lustre" of her eye, proves however to be a matter of appearance only. When Amintor asks "what lady was there, that men call *fair* and virtuous . . . that would have shunned my love?" (II.i.263–265; italics added), he is in fact stumbling towards his later characterization of her as "that *foul* woman" (IV.i.206; italics added). And by Act III it is Aspatia whom he recognizes as genuinely "fair" (III.i.235). There is an irony beyond that which the King intends in his reference to Evadne's "black eye" (III.i.147) as a token of her quickness in the sports of love. For hitherto it has been the brightness, the fieriness of her eyes which has been insisted on as an epitome of her fairness. But the blackness on which the King fixes, we know by now, corresponds to an inner blackness—the foulness of illicit lust. If there is any true whiteness about Evadne it is the proverbial whiteness of leprosy (III.ii.183; IV.i.201). And once Melantius has penetrated Amintor's mask of dissimulation, her blackness becomes a persistent rhetorical theme; in Melantius' castigations:

> that desperate fool that drew thee
> From thy fair life.
>
> (IV.i.51–52)

> The burnt air, when the Dog reigns, is not fouler
> Than thy contagious name.
>
> (IV.i.60–61)

> Thy black shame . . .
>
> (IV.i.113)

and then in her own bitter self-denunciation:

> Would I could say so to my black disgrace!
> . . . .
> There is not in the compass of the light
> A more unhappy creature.
>
> (IV.i.181–186)

> A soul as white as Heaven . . .
>
> . . . .
>
> I do present myself the foulest creature . . .
>
> (IV.i.222–232)

> I am hell,
> Till you, my dear lord, shoot your light into me,
> The beams of your forgiveness.
>
> (IV.i.234–236) [37]

> All the dear joys here, and above hereafter,
> Crown thy fair soul! Thus I take leave, my lord;
> And never shall you see the foul Evadne,
> Till she have tried all honour'd means, that may
> Set her in rest and wash her stains away.
>
> (IV.i.281–285)

There is of course a special irony in the fact that the King continues to see her (IV.ii.64) as "fair Evadne" (by which he means fair to himself and foul to her husband), since her conversion has effectively restored the word from the perverted sense he gives it.

The imagery of the regicide scene carries on the fair / foul, light / dark oppositions (V.ii. 45, 50, 59, 62–65, 74–80, 87, 90), now chiefly in reference to the King whose foulness has corrupted Evadne's fairness, and whose death alone may restore it: "Am I not fair? / Looks not Evadne beauteous in these rites now?" Amintor's reply to this question is crucial: he coldly denies that one evil can cancel out another; for him Evadne remains foul beneath her fairness: "Black is thy colour now" (V.iv.135). The effect of the last scene is in fact to define beyond argument (as the masque failed to do) the key terms of the play's fancy. And in that damning "Black" (in which is concentrated the traditional symbolism of both sin and death) is implied the ultimate resolution of the central ambiguity of Night—a resolution achieved in Amintor's judgment of Evadne's murder:

> And to augment my woe,
> You now are present, stain'd with a king's blood

---

37. Cf. also V.iv.78, where the use of the conventional trope derives a peculiar irony from the fact that it is spoken by a lover who is unwittingly addressing his mistress.

> Violently shed. *This keeps night here,*
> And throws an unknown wilderness about me.
>
> (V.iv.147–150; italics added)

The lines point to the scene as the final ironic realization of the conventional epithalamic appeal which has haunted the action of the play, "Hold back thy hour, dark night . . . Stay, and hide all"; the appeal is granted as the four lovers of the play slip into the illimitable night of death.

Two further linguistic patterns, associated with the masque and important for the working out of Beaumont and Fletcher's fancy, deserve some comment. One involves images of blushing, and the other, images of storm. The second masque song, in the fashion of an epithalamium, appeals to Night to "stay, and hide / *The blushes of the bride*" (I.ii.237–238; italics added). These conventional tokens of maidenly modesty acquire an increasingly ironic significance as the play develops. In Act II, scene i, Amintor attributes Evadne's obstinacy to "the coyness of a bride" (l. 163); [38] but Evadne shortly disabuses him (ll. 213–217) and cruelly spells out the real meaning of the color on her face:

> Alas, Amintor, think'st thou I forbear
> To sleep with thee, because I have put on
> A maiden's strictness? Look upon these cheeks,
> And thou shalt find the hot and rising blood
> Unapt for such a vow.
>
> (II.i.290–294)

The revelation gives a bitterly ironic twist to Aspatia's complaint at the beginning of the scene which follows:

> Good gods, how well you look! Such a full colour
> Young bashful brides put on.
>
> (II.ii.2–3)

But the greatest ironies are reserved for Act III with Strato's unwittingly tactless banter: "O call the bride, my lord, Amintor, / That we may see her blush" (III.i.76–77) and the King's vicious probing

> I should think, by her black eye,
> And her red cheek, she would be quick and stirring . . .
>
> (III.i.147–148)

38. For this convention, see (for instance) Herrick "A Nuptiall Song, or Epithalamie, on Sir Clipseby Crew and his Lady," ll. 51–60.

As he perfectly well knows, her blushing is a token not of chastity but guilt: it is the result not of maiden bashfulness but excess of blood, in the sense of lust. Despite this, Evadne's blushes, like the fire in her eye, continue to be used for purposes of dissimulation—Amintor endeavors to fob off the curious Melantius with a complimentary reference to the "inevitable colour" of her cheeks (III.ii.76–77); while Evadne herself responds to his attacks with the tokens of bashful innocence (IV.i.3,5). The foolish old Calianax imagines the restoration of Aspatia's happiness in terms of the same image: "I shall revenge my girl, / And make her red again" (III.ii.333–334). Blushing is seen, then, as a sign of health, as well as of fairness and innocence—the health which the "leprous" Evadne, for all her superficial color, conspicuously lacks. For this reason there is an ironic appropriateness in the fact that the meaning ascribed to blushes is precisely inverted in Act IV. Melantius' reply to Evadne's "You would make me blush" (IV.i.3) implies that blushing reveals guilt rather than bashful innocence. And this cynical interpretation is maintained through Act IV, scene ii (ironically the scene of the second wedding entertainment, where the coy blushes of the bride would be appropriate):

CALIANAX
If he deny it,
I'll make him blush.

(IV.ii.7–8)

AMINTOR
Here, my love,
This wine will do thee wrong, for it will set
Blushes upon thy cheeks; and, till thou dost
A fault, 'twere pity.

(IV.ii.68–71)

KING
. . . . Calianax,
I cannot trust this: I have thrown out words,
That would have fetch'd warm blood upon the cheeks
Of guilty men, and he is never moved.

(IV.ii.95–98)

The King's is the last overt reference in the play to blushing, but I think it is clear that the red of the blood upon Evadne's hands as she enters in Act V, scene iv is meant to recall the earlier insistence upon the redness of her cheeks. The King has connected that redness with lustful excess of blood (III.i.148), and Evadne ironically describes his murder as a medicinal bleeding to purge his surfeit of passionate blood (V.ii.41–46). At the same time the bleeding is intended to "wash her stains away" (IV.ii.285), to "make her red again" in Calianax' phrase. In Act V, scene iv she offers the red upon her hands as an emblem of restored fairness and maiden innocence. The ambivalence of redness cannot, however, any more than that of blackness, survive the assassination of the King: in Amintor's eyes it stands only for lust and sanguinary corruption. Evadne has simply committed the one sin that may "outname thy other faults" and the stain of lust is deepened by the stain of "a king's blood / Violently shed" (ll. 148– 149).

In my discussion of the masque, I pointed out that its dance of wind and sea gods could be seen as symbolizing the reasonable ordering of the passions necessary to nuptial harmony, and that this symbolism was compromised by the escape of Boreas. Like the other evil auguries of the masque, his storm is realized in the play action and its realization marked by a series of images. Sea and storm imagery runs through Aspatia's extended laments in Act II, scene ii. Its first appearance, seemingly incidental, is as part of the elaborate comparative figure at Act II, scene ii, lines 17 ff. But her "ruined merchant" (merchant vessel) must recall Aeolus' prophecy of the wreck of "many a tall ship," and the recollection becomes even more apparent in the elaborate tableau of Dido and Aeneas which she sets up a few lines later (ll. 31 ff.). Aspatia identifies herself with the deserted Dido and pictures herself standing, helpless before the elements

> upon the sea-beach now,
> Mine arms thus, and mine hair blown with the wind,
> Wild as that desert . . .
>   let the rocks
> Groan with continual surges; and behind me,
> Make all a desolation.
>
> (ll. 68–77)

Amintor she casts as the faithless Aeneas, on whose departing ship she calls down a storm:

> Could the gods know of this,
> And not, of all their number, raise a storm?
>
> (ll. 49–50)

The irony is, of course, that the wind god Boreas has raised just such a tempest as she despairs of and that it has already struck Amintor in the preceding scene. The wedding night has been stormily "troublesome" in a sense that Diphilus at III.i.3 does not guess.

In Act II, scene i, Amintor feels his inner storm of passion mocked by the peacefulness of the elements. His complaint reflects ironically on Aeolus' advice to Neptune "to strike a calm" for the bridal night (I.ii.-264):

> Why is this night so calm?
> Why does not Heaven speak in thunder to us,
> And drown her voice?
>
> (II.i.253–254)

Appropriately, the height of Amintor's passion is expressed in his threat to cut the body of Evadne's lover "into motes, / And scatter it before the northern wind" (II.i.304–305)—where the reference to Boreas is felt less as a literal threat than as an ironic metaphor for his ungoverned rage. And in Act IV, scene i, when Melantius plots the revenge which Amintor's royalism has prevented, the motif occurs again as a metaphor for the revenger's unbridled fury against Evadne's seducer:

> By my just sword, h'ad safer
> Bestrid a billow when the angry North
> Ploughs up the sea . . .
>
> (ll. 76–78)

The storm so ominously raised by Boreas is not in fact to be allayed until the last scene of the play, after the destruction of "many a tall ship." For Amintor, Evadne's murder of the King has

> touch'd a life
> The very name of which had power to chain
> Up all my rage, and calm my wildest wrongs.
>
> (V.iv.136–138)

The image explicitly identifies his storm of rage on the wedding night with Boreas' breaking of his chain in the masque, and it signals the destruction of his last restraints. He finds himself in the "unknown wilderness" of Aspatia's tableau in Act II, scene ii, the psychological desert left by the violent winds of passion (V.iv.150). True calm of mind is possible

now only when all passion is finally spent in death—as Evadne, at the
last, comes to realize:

> Go; I am calm. Farewell, and peace for ever.
>
> (V.iv.170)

III

In the second of the encomiums which he contributed to the 1647 Folio,
William Cartwright returned to the praise of Fletcher's constructive
genius:

> Parts are so fitted unto parts, as doe
> Shew thou hadst wit, and Mathematicks too.

Fletcher, in Cartwright's admiring view, excelled all his contemporaries
in mastery of "the simetry, which gives a Poem grace." [39] In this essay I
have been concerned to reveal something of the formal symmetry of *The
Maid's Tragedy*. I have tried to show how it extends, as Cartwright
claims, to all the parts—to the rhetoric as much as to the characters and
the plotting. The symmetry of the whole is primarily a symmetry of inversions and oppositions—love and death, marriage and adultery, appearance and reality—produced by the dramatists' juggling of familiar social
situations. The rhetorical symmetry is designed to elaborate these structural conceits in terms of patterns of imagery whose effectiveness is para-
doxically dependent on their very conventionality. Certainly, these patterns are of a different order from those we find in, say, Webster; and
there is a good deal of force in Eliot's criticism that the language lacks a
"network of tentacular roots reaching down to the deepest terrors and desires." [40] But the criticism is only a half-truth. The imagery of *The Maid's
Tragedy* is conventional rather than imaginative, but the conventionality
is the consequence of a particular constructive function: it corresponds to
the social familiarity of the situations out of which the plot, with its
fanciful twists and witty counterturns, grows. There is a network of
roots, but not of the kind that Eliot or Professor Bradbrook were looking
for—its spread is wider and shallower.

39. Glover and Waller, *Works of Beaumont and Fletcher*, p. xxxix.
40. Eliot, *Selected Essays*, p. 155.

The wedding masque justifies its formal prominence by the way in which its fundamental oppositions and ambiguities prefigure the development of the whole elaborate edifice of structural and rhetorical conceits. It provides, in effect, the necessary exposition of the play's "fancy," an exposition which predicates the "fate" of the play. In this it combines an oracular ambivalence, ensuring that "none can prevent the fancy," with a mathematic precision that justifies Cartwright's enthusiastic puff:

> The whole designe, the shadowes, the lights such
> That none can say he shewes or hides too much.

Beaumont and Fletcher have suffered more than most from neglect of the principle that criticism should move towards, rather than from, evaluative comparisons. An attempt to set that right need not, of course, involve any radical change in our assessment of their worth as dramatic poets, but it ought to enhance our respect for their virtues as theatrical craftsmen.

Dramatic and Moral Energy
in Ben Jonson's
Bartholomew Fair

JOEL H. KAPLAN

W E DO NOT KNOW why Ben Jonson quarreled with Thomas Dekker, or even if their dispute was primarily personal or aesthetic.[1] Yet on the basis of Jonson's own work in comedy it is not hard to imagine his probable reaction to a play like *The Shoemakers' Holiday*. The magic of a Simon Eyre rests upon our readiness to accept theatrical solutions to moral dilemmas. If we are unwilling or unable to make this allowance we can see how Dekker's euphoria might be viewed as a perversion of the theater's "proper" magic, an attempt on the part of slick dramaturgy to conceal ethical ambiguities rather than throw them into high relief. This, I suggest, would have been Jonson's position; the most formidable of *his*

This article is adapted from a paper presented at the University of Western Ontario Spring Colloquium, April 10, 1969.

1. The standard works on Jonson's dispute with Marston and Dekker, Josiah Penniman's *The War of the Theaters* (Philadelphia, 1897) and Roscoe Addison Small's *The Stage-Quarrel Between Ben Jonson and the So-Called Poetasters* (Breslau, 1899), are more concerned with the manifestations of this argument in the literature of the period than with its ultimate origins.

characters partake of a "ferocious energy"[2] as outrageously vigorous as anything we can find in the period, yet unlike Dekker, Jonson seems always conscious of the limitations of extravagance and often creates situations in which it is forced to reveal its ultimate impotence—its inability to sustain a world in which it may operate successfully. Volpone's "arrogance and muscular worldliness" are ludicrous as well as enthralling, recommending the traditional values Volpone rejects by the very language that calls his new world into being.[3] From the outset we are asked to take a double view of this order, and as a result it never seems quite as permanent or inevitable as the world of Simon Eyre. Likewise, the *"indenture tripartite"* that stands at the center of *The Alchemist* is as volatile as Subtle's *magisterium* and just as likely to go up *in fumo*. Since Subtle and Face have exalted one another "out of dung" through a sequence of transformations that parodies both alchemy and creation, their partnership remains an unstable commodity held together only by the assumption of further shapes and roles until the pressure of Lovewit's return causes it to "flie out, i' the *proiection.*"

Jonson's implied skepticism towards the prospect of imposing an order upon society through exuberant will, or even towards the ability of exuberance to hold its own shape,[4] is linked to a misplaced trust that his characters often give to mimesis.[5] The protean instability of Jonson's in-

2. Jonas A. Barish, introd. to *Ben Jonson: A Collection of Critical Essays* (Englewood Cliffs, N. J., 1963), p. 12.

3. Edward B. Partridge, *The Broken Compass: A Study of the Major Comedies of Ben Jonson* (New York, 1958), p. 74. Much of what I have to say about *Volpone* is based upon Partridge's discussion of the play's double vision. See also Alvin B. Kernan's introduction to the Yale edition of *Volpone* (New Haven, Conn., 1962), p. 15.

4. This ambiguous view of energy may have developed out of Jonson's earlier use of the humours. Asper, we will recall, in the Induction to *Every Man Out of His Humour* claims:

> That what soe're hath fluxure, and humiditie,
> As *wanting power to containe it selfe,*
> Is Humour.
>
> (ll. 96–98; italics added)

and in that play's Macilente we see the same combination of intense energy and instability that animates many of Jonson's later characters.

5. Kernan, *Volpone,* esp. pp. 7–13. After the present essay was in final form, Alex Leggatt's excellent article, "The Suicide of Volpone," appeared in *UTQ,*

triguers coincides with their own restless passion for role playing, as transformations that are conscious and willed modulate into those that are imposed by external circumstances. In both *Volpone* and *The Alchemist* disguise is at first a means of initiating events, but as the action of each comedy unfolds it becomes a response to—or even a refuge from—events that have already been set in motion. Perhaps the most striking example of this shift occurs towards the close of *The Alchemist* when the frantic efforts of Subtle, Face, and Doll to keep their visitors apart drive all three through a succession of roles determined by the unpredictable order in which their customers knock on Lovewit's door.[6] As the conspirators begin to lose control over the events of the play, they also lose control over the transformations they must undergo, being for the moment ironically shaped and reshaped by a world they assumed they might manipulate for their own ends. Volpone and Mosca also view acting as a means of imposing themselves upon society at large, and they are betrayed as well. When servant and master are compelled to play their deathbed scenario in their own defense before a court of law, they too lose their initiative for action, maneuvering to extricate themselves from events rather than shape them. Thus, in spite of the victory the pair wins before the *Scrutineo,* after the verdict is pronounced the action of the play grinds to a halt, and they must inaugurate an entirely new series of deceptions if they are to regain the upper hand. Yet the part Volpone now selects only completes his abuse; as "corpse" he loses the potential for action completely, and when Mosca takes advantage of this to betray him, Volpone's only recourse is a general unmasking that sends Mosca to the galleys and forces *him* to play his former role in earnest among the inmates of a prison. Like their more fortunate counterparts in *The Alchemist,* both Volpone and Mosca fall victim to their own faith in mimesis, which is part of their greater belief in the ability of a turbulent and exuberant will to reorder society to its own liking.

In another and happier vein, Dekker could amply reward such faith,

---

XXXIX (1969), 19–32. This study deals in some detail with Volpone as a consummate actor and points out some of the problems he encounters after his role has played itself out.

6. The rising tempo of this play's action as a "progress towards collision and catastrophe" is discussed in Una Ellis-Fermor's *The Jacobean Drama* (London, 1936), pp. 43–48.

and in plays like *Old Fortunatus* and *The Shoemakers' Holiday* his magical invocation of a better world is as confidently made as it is in the civic
pageants he designed explicitly for this purpose. For Jonson such a mode
might be appropriate for masques, triumphs, or other forms of celebratory
art, but the realm of comedy was not the place to let society bask in "its
own well-being" or attain "social health" through "mimetic magic." [7] In
comedy Jonson chose rather to stress the ambiguities of exuberance and
mimesis and not simply the ways in which such energy might transform
its own environment. This is not to say that there are no subtleties in
Dekker—merely that they lie in another direction. Both dramatists are
serious moral artists disturbed by the meanness of the world about them,
but while Dekker dwells upon ways to metamorphose this world, either
ritually cursing it into oblivion or leaping to a better society through the
magic of exuberance or prayer, Jonson is more concerned with the anoma-
lies of human behavior that have created such a world and that make
Dekker's charmed solutions seem at best naïve and at worst misleading
and downright dishonest.

We can readily see this difference of approach and method if we compare the antics of Simon Eyre with the high spirits of Jonson's own version of citizen London on holiday.[8] *Bartholomew Fair,* like Dekker's
play, uses a familiar annual outing to present a state of madness sanctioned by festive license. In both comedies reason is overwhelmed by
vitality and prescriptive morality exposed for its folly; in each, under the
guise of holiday, we meet a compelling form of energy that shatters the
social and economic bonds of a workaday world, reshuffling its members
into new patterns and relationships.[9] However, while Dekker's art trans-

7. These terms are taken from Barish's definition of the Renaissance court
masque (*Ben Jonson and the Language of Prose Comedy* [Cambridge, Mass.,
1960], p. 244). This passage is aptly cited in its entirety in Stephen Orgel's *The
Jonsonian Masque* (Cambridge, Mass., 1965), p. 108.

8. Arthur Brown has already called attention to some of the differences between
these plays as "citizen comedies" in his "Citizen Comedy and Domestic Drama,"
in *Jacobean Theatre,* ed. John Russell Brown and Bernard Harris (London, 1960),
pp. 63–83.

9. The play's pattern of separation and reunification, in which each of the fair's
visitors meets his likeness in the opposing party, is dealt with in Richard Levin's
"The Structure of *Bartholomew Fair,*" *PMLA,* LXXX (1965), 172–179, by far the
best work yet on Jonson's intricate plotting.

mutes some of the shoddier earthbound processes that bring this reorganization about, taking for granted their legitimacy in a good cause, Jonson withholds hearty endorsement to examine the processes themselves, and he encourages us to do likewise. In *Bartholomew Fair* the same skepticism towards extravagant energy and mimesis that appears in both *Volpone* and *The Alchemist* is brought to bear upon the roaring spirit of Smithfield, revealing a grotesque turbulence that coarsens as it liberates, creating tumult and heightening antagonisms while moving characters towards a reconciliation at the level of flesh and blood, where all are united by a common participation in human folly.

I

In spite of the sprawling impression *Bartholomew Fair* usually makes, the play's scaffolding is remarkably intricate and symmetrical. Jonson's plot, the fair's separation and regrouping of its visitors, is carefully worked out along one of the thematic lines of the late morality plays—like will to like—as each member of the Littlewit party eventually confronts his mirror image in the Cokes group.[10] We can also observe an elaborate regularity in the play's handling of pacing and tempo, underscored by Jonson's division of each act into a standard six scenes.[11] Rhythmically, *Bartholomew Fair* consists of a succession of verbal and physical explosions in which the energy of Smithfield imposes itself upon the fair's visitors, aggravating their absurdities and provoking clashes that increase in frequency and violence as the play gathers momentum.[12] In

10. *Ibid.*

11. These scene divisions are original with the 1631 folio printed by John Beale for Robert Allot. This is the only authoritative edition of *Bartholomew Fair*, and although Beale was notoriously careless in particulars we have no reason to suspect the authenticity of the scenes as they stand, especially as they are marked off by authorial "massed" entries as well as by numerical designations.

12. This rhythmic organization in a number of Jonson's most successful plays has been discussed in Freudian terms by Edmund Wilson. See "Morose Ben Jonson," in *The Triple Thinkers*, rev. ed. (New York, 1948), pp. 213–232. Wilson relates Jonson's "cumulative" dramatic techniques to the "hoarding and withholding instinct" of Freud's anal erotic. Whether or not we admit the validity of his terminology, Wilson's description of this phenomenon in the plays as a pattern

the opening three acts this acceleration of noise and confusion takes the form of a double crescendo, first building towards a climax at the close of scene v, then condensing and repeating the entire movement, with a new set of characters, in scene vi. Act I takes place at John Littlewit's house, where the fair's visitors initially meet. As characters accumulate the tempo of these initial scenes rises, until Barthol'mew Cokes states his intention to visit the fair (I.v.59–60) and the gathering is set into momentary confusion. The proctor's guests then file out, and the business of going to Smithfield is repeated in scene vi with Dame Purecraft and her suitor, Zeal-of-the-Land Busy, a Puritan rabbi capable of raising a greater uproar than the entire crowd of scene v. This pattern asserts itself more fervidly at the fair. Act II opens with the solitary figure of Justice Overdo and builds to the general brawl in scene v, in which Ursula, the fair's greasy pig woman, scalds herself with a hot pan. After she is carried back into her booth, the commotion of these scenes is repeated in scene vi with Wasp, Cokes, and Mrs. Overdo. The Justice, disguised as "mad *Arthur of Bradley*," is accused of assisting the cutpurses and is pummeled mercilessly as the act closes:

They speake all together: and Waspe *beats the* Iustice.	COK. *Numps, Numps.* [MRS.] OVER. Good Mʳ *Humphrey.* WAS. You are the *Patrico!* are you? the Patriarch of the cutpurses? you share, Sir, they	IVS. Hold thy hand, childe of wrath, and heyre of anger, make it not Childermasse day in thy fury, or the feast of the French *Bartholomew*, Parent of the Massacre.

say, let them share this with you. Are you i' your hot fit of preaching againe? I'le coole you.
IVS. Murther, murther, murther.[13]

(II.vi.146–154)

In Act III frenetic activity again pulses through the earlier scenes, breaking forth anew in scene v when Overdo is suspected of stealing Cokes's second purse. Scene vi then introduces a new turmoil more intense than the preceding confusion; Busy hurls down Trash's ginger-

---

of accumulation followed by sudden bursts of language and energy is, I think, basically sound, and it is unfortunate that his essay has suffered as a critical oddity because of its Freudian bias. For a more recent treatment of this subject, see John T. French, "Ben Jonson: His Aesthetic of Relief," *TSLL,* X (1968), 161–175.

13. All citations from *Bartholomew Fair* are to Ben Jonson, *Works,* ed. C. H. Herford and Percy and Evelyn Simpson, 11 vols. (Oxford, 1925–1952), VI.

bread stand with the finality of the Last Judgment, filling Smithfield with a "sanctified noise . . . a loud and most strong noise" as he is apprehended and led off to the stocks. By the close of Act III Jonson has established the disruptive mode of his fair firmly enough to abandon this pattern for a more extreme type of discord. Act IV is filled with machine-gun bursts of spasmodic violence that follow in alternate scenes; in scene ii we have Cokes's "musse" with the pear vendor, in scene iv the game of vapors, and in scene vi the free-for-all at the stocks. Moreover, as the insanity of Smithfield soars to a fever pitch, Jonson drops a real madman into his fair to question the actions of sharpers and customers alike.[14] The striking denouement of Act V centers about Leatherhead's puppet booth, introducing a world of wooden "babies" more perverse in its pointless belligerency than anything the fair's flesh-and-blood creatures can offer.[15] Yet here, as some of the more salutary effects of Smithfield emerge and we begin to see a way out of the fair, there is a partial return to the pattern of the earlier acts. The "treble creeking" of the puppets is twice challenged: first in scene v by the "base noyse" of Rabbi Busy, and then by Justice Overdo's more general indictment (V.v–vi). But now, appropriately, these moments of confusion lead to the disabuse of both characters, as the comedy moves towards its concluding feast.

At the level of plot this accumulation of noise and clamor is essential to the commercial success of Jonson's fair. The inhabitants of Smithfield —or any fair for that matter—not only use spontaneous tumult to take advantage of their customers but also create confusion to serve their purposes more efficiently. Thus Edgeworth and Nightingale engineer Cokes's encounter with the pear vendor to make off with his cloak, hat, and sword, while Knockem and Whit set up the game of vapors to rob Wasp and two minor characters, Puppy and Nordern. Smithfield, in fact, is presented as something of an ecological unit that thrives only when its visitors arrive to complete a natural cycle of predator and prey. Yet the fair's disorder has a thematic and dramaturgic meaning beyond its

14. See Ray L. Heffner, Jr., "Unifying Symbols in the Comedy of Ben Jonson," in *English Stage Comedy*, ed. W. K. Wimsatt, Jr. (New York, 1955), pp. 74–97 for a discussion of Trouble-All's thematic significance in the play.

15. See Jonas A. Barish, *"Bartholomew Fair* and Its Puppets," *MLQ*, XX (1959), 3–17.

simple profit motive. In a recent article Jackson I. Cope has shed light upon an important part of this significance, identifying Ursula, the presiding spirit of the fair, as an iconographic representation of *Discordia,* transforming her "from a mere exemplum of the angry woman into a symbol" with far-reaching ramifications.[16] We might also note that the pig woman sweating out her existence in a booth to which "Hell's a kind of cold cellar" has something of the infernal about her as well.[17] If, however, Ursula is a variation on a kind of angry woman or mad devil, with Mooncalf serving as her "errant *Incubee,*" she is at the same time a figure of abundant flesh and compulsive vitality, able to do "forty . . . things in an houre . . . for her recreation, if the toy take her i' the greasie kerchiefe"—a roaring ursuline devil, like the comic bear-demons in *Like Will to Like* or *Mucedorus,*[18] particularly at home in Jonson's Hope

16. *"Bartholomew Fair* as Blasphemy," *Ren D,* VIII (1965), 143–145.

17. Ursula's hot pan, which is cited by Cope in his discussion of the pig woman as an emblem of discord, is perhaps closer to the frying pan or dripping pan carried by Beelzebub in some early folk plays. At Lockinge the devil is even replaced by an "Old Mother Alezeebub" (E. K. Chambers, *The English Folk-Play* [London, 1933], pp. 65–69). This half-humorous identification of cooks with hell-fire and things hellish is traditional, and for obvious reasons. In the mystery cycles presented at Beverley and Chester the guilds of cooks, innkeepers, and tapsters were assigned the pageant of the harrowing of hell, and we might note with particular interest the tapstress in the Chester play who is confined to hell for practices similar to Ursula's. See *The Chester Plays,* ed. H. Deimling and G. W. Matthews, EETS extra series 62, 115 (London, 1893, 1916), pp. 329–331. For Jonson's use of this identification elsewhere, see *The Alchemist,* III.i.18–21.

18. Nicholas Newfangle, the vice in *Like Will to Like,* mistakes his father, Lucifer, for a "dancing bear." See *The Dramatic Works of Ulpian Fulwell,* ed. John S. Farmer (London, 1906). In *Mucedorus* the clown, Mouse, thinks that the bear that frightens him rather resembles "some Diuell in a Beares Doublet." See *The Shakespeare Apocrypha,* ed. C. F. Tucker Brooke (London, 1908), p. 107. George F. Reynolds has suggested that the substitution of a real bear in *Mucedorus* around 1610 accounts for the play's renewed popularity in that year, yet Reynolds admits that such a novel effect would depend upon a popular tradition of actors in bear suits. See *"Mucedorus,* Most Popular Play?" in *Studies in the English Renaissance Drama in Memory of Karl Holzknecht,* ed. J. W. Bennett et al. (New York, 1959), pp. 248–268. Perhaps such a heritage also supplies us with the grotesquely comic bear that pursues and devours Antigonus in *The Winter's Tale* at the moment when the world of that play dissolves in supernatural disorder.

Theater used on alternate days for stage plays and bear baitings.[19] In
any event, there is another and more pleasant side to her incessant activity, one that assumes an existential worth, making Ursula more than
Cope's simple agent of disorder, litigiousness, and license. She is, to be
sure, all of these things, but like the fair around her Ursula creates her
own holiday dispensation that makes stone-faced censure almost as foolish and irrelevant as hearty approval. Neither response can adequately
come to terms with the complex experience of Smithfield, where vitality
is made synonymous with obscenity and corruption.

II

This essential ambiguity in the operation of the fair reveals itself in
the way Smithfield deals with those realms of human endeavor that fall
within its province. Three overlapping areas of experience are thematically central to *Bartholomew Fair*—appetite, law, and art, represented by
the play's three prominent stage properties: the pig booth, the stocks,
and the puppet stand [20]—and each by its contact with the fair is driven
back to a primal state, becoming crude, vulgar, and abusive in the process, but also partaking of a new vigor and potency. In counterpoint to
the tidy banquet at which Justice Overdo expects to unravel the day's
enormities, the fair offers us a world of lusty tastes and smells, mingling
its general stench with the odors of roast pig, gingerbread, fresh fruit,
ale, beer, and tobacco. Even Win Littlewit with her *"Strawbery-*breath,
Chery lips, *Apricot-*cheekes, and a soft veluet head, like a *Melicotton"*
must pale in comparison. The Littlewits are drawn to Smithfield by the

19. For a discussion of bear baiting at the Hope Theater, or Bear Garden as it
was alternately known, see G. E. Bentley, *The Jacobean and Caroline Stage* (London, 1941–1968), VI, 200 ff.; and C. L. Kingsford, "Paris Garden and the Bearbait-
ing," *Archaeologia,* 2d ser., XX (1920), 155–178.

20. For this division of the fair into the related realms of appetite, law, and art,
as well as for the use of John Littlewit as a fourth authority figure, I am indebted
to my friend and former tutor Brian Parker of the University of Toronto. In a
forthcoming article—"The Themes and Staging of *Bartholomew Fair,*" shortly to
appear in *UTQ*—Professor Parker treats both phenomena in greater detail and
comes to some very different conclusions about them.

scent of piping hot pig, while Cokes, the simpleton of the Overdo group, who is said to "beg puddings, and cake-bread, of his tennants," goes to the fair as a great "Rauener after fruite"—a role that anticipates his clash with the pearmonger. Yet, as one of the play's recurring puns will have it, there is foul in the fair, and many of its enticements prove less than wholesome. Joan Trash's gingerbread consists of "stale bread, rotten egges, musty ginger, [and] dead honey," while a potential newt lurks in each bottle of Barthol'mew ale and a spider in each pipeful of fair tobacco. The provender of the fair, however, is not only corrupt in its own right but also a means of provocation to the fair's visitors, either serving as an object of contention (as in Act III, scene iv, and Act IV, scene ii) or more often as an agent of such violence. Here Jonson's most crucial statement on appetite lies in his handling of Ursula and her pig booth.

Justice Overdo speaks more wisely than he knows when he attributes the various modes of roaring behavior to "bottle-ale, and tabacco!" (II.vi). At her stall Ursula dispenses both items, and the combination of steam and smoke that billows out of the pig stand seems symbolic of the fair's pervasive "vapors,"[21] the senseless quarreling that motivates much of the play's action. On a more literal plane we may see this influence in the effect Ursula has on any number of the fair's customers. Busy's behavior in the third act most immediately comes to mind: he first seeks the pig booth "religiously wise . . . by way of steeme," snuffing it out *"like a Hound,"* then emerges a few scenes later thoroughly confirmed in his folly with a zeal that "falls a railing and kicking" at the fair with renewed energy—a passion that carries him first to the gingerbread stand and then to the stocks (III. vi). Knockem, who observes this progress, searches out Ursula to tell her "how her pigge works." The contest of vapors in Act IV provides another instance, as Knockem prepares his dupes by plying them with Ursula's ale. Their ensuing "game" is even referred to as a "beltching of quarrell" (IV. iv). Yet Ursula does not simply reduce appetite to animal ferocity. She is a purveyor of punk as well as pig, capable of driving appetite to lust and prostitution. In one sense this is related to her function as tapster. Ale provokes urine, and it is

21. Cope, *"Bartholomew Fair* as Blasphemy," pp. 145–146. For a more psychological interpretation of the comedy's "vapors," see James E. Robinson, *"Bartholomew Fair:* Comedy of Vapors," *SEL,* I (1961), 65–80.

when Win Littlewit and Mrs. Overdo return to the pig booth to use Ursula's "common pot" that they are converted to whoredom. The progression from pig-eater and ale-drinker to punk is a logical one here, completing a process of corruption that begins with simple involvement with the fair. Indeed, when Quarlous sees Dame Purecraft enter the pig booth in Act III, scene ii, he encourages Winwife "to lay aboard [his] widdow . . . [for] shee that will venture her selfe into the *Fayre,* and a pig-boxe, will admit any assault."

If we use appetite in a wider and more metaphoric sense, we see that Smithfield not only lures Win and Mrs. Overdo into prostitution with promises of material goods—coaches, wires, tires, green gowns, and velvet petticoats—but also encourages such disparate actions as Cokes's mindless accumulation of fairings and Tom Quarlous' mercenary wooing of Dame Purecraft. This final instance, moreover, shows how the charged atmosphere of the fair can give a new bent to conventional morality. The frenzied rhetoric that Quarlous commands throughout the play implies his basic sympathy with a fair that can translate such compulsive speech into madcap behavior.[22] At Smithfield Quarlous is completely in his element, roaring, brawling, and baiting the pig woman as bravely as any of the fair's permanent inhabitants. More important, this affinity for the fair enables Quarlous to use its madness for his own profit, much as the professional Barthol'mew birds do. This ability places him in a unique and superior position in the play midway between Smithfield and its visitors—a position Justice Overdo tries in vain to fill. Thus Quarlous uses Edgeworth, a Smithfield cutpurse, to lift Cokes's marriage license and, disguising himself as Trouble-All, the fair's actual madman, obtains Overdo's blank warrant; one brings him Dame Purecraft's fortune, the other Grace Wellborn's dowry. And largely because his behavior so resembles the method of the fair, Quarlous' actions demand the same type of complex consideration that we must give to Smithfield.[23] Quarlous'

22. Barish, *Ben Jonson and the Language of Prose Comedy,* pp. 189–195. I agree with Barish that Quarlous' language reflects "the increasingly close identification of the satiric commentator with the world on which he comments" but disagree with his conclusion that Quarlous therefore forfeits his special position in the work.

23. Calvin G. Thayer, who sees the fair as a fertility rite, sets Quarlous in stark opposition to its processes, viewing him as "almost the antithesis of fertility" (*Ben Jonson: Studies in the Plays* [Norman, Okla., 1963], p. 141). But Thayer's identi-

motives in pursuing Dame Purecraft are essentially the same as Winwife's in Act I. But while the emphasis in the earlier episode falls upon
the greasy implications of visiting widows "so old, as no chast or married
pleasure can euer become 'hem," Quarlous' own holiday wooing is treated
as part of a general windfall rewarding his resourceful madness. The difference is one of perspective rather than substance, but it is no less real,
for Quarlous, like the fair in which he thrives, transforms an unsavory
situation into one that maintains a careful balance between putrescence
and vitality.

III

Ordinarily we might expect the more disciplined spheres of law and art
to stand in at least nominal opposition to the unrestrained voracity of
the fair, yet these realms are also subject to the peculiar influences of
Smithfield. Here too the fair aggravates the follies of its visitors, revealing the absurdity of their legal and aesthetic formulae. And again the
results are ambivalent: law is corrupted, art vulgarized, but in the process self-righteous posturing gives way to more pragmatic procedures
that recognize human frailty as a natural condition and are thus able
to deal with it. In the area of law this progress can be traced in the comic
discomfiture suffered by the play's three "authority" figures—Humphrey
Wasp, Rabbi Busy, and Justice Overdo. Each of these characters tyran-
nizes others with a form of legal sanction that accounts for his own blind
opposition to the fair. As regent over Barthol'mew Cokes, Wasp is leader
of the Overdo party and significantly is entrusted with one of the comedy's critical legal props, Cokes's marriage license. Rabbi Busy, defying
all civil authority, rides herd over the Littlewit group with the warrant
of a spiritual law he embraces with "a most *lunatique* conscience." Adam
Overdo, the most complex of the three, is a legal figure in a number of
respects. He is first of all the self-appointed scourge of Smithfield who

fication rests upon a misreading of the text. It is Winwife, not Quarlous, who
Ursula claims was "engendred on a she-beggar, in a barne, when the bald Thrasher,
[his] Sire, was scarce warme" (II.v.136–137). In striking contrast, Ursula thinks
that Quarlous looks as if he "were begotten a'top of a Cart in haruest-time, when
the whelp was hot and eager" (II.v.124–125).

seeks out the fair's enormities; he is also the irate Pie-powders Justice described in Act IV, scene i who has been responsible for Trouble-All's misfortunes, and who dispenses a blank warrant to Quarlous in Act V, scene ii in a mistaken attempt to set things right; and finally he is the legal guardian of Grace Wellborn and in this capacity has arranged an inequitable but profitable match for his brother-in-law, Cokes. At Smithfield the designs of all three figures are utterly frustrated, and they meet in common failure in the stocks, the fair's "legal" means of dealing with such creatures.[24]

What makes Wasp, Busy, and Overdo ludicrous is not that they view the fair as a force to be reckoned with—in this they are surely correct—but that they are so consistently off center in their attacks upon it. Moreover, because each strikes out with such immense energy he is thrown off balance by his own momentum when he misses his target. Wasp's opposition to the fair, for example, is undercut by its indiscriminate nature. He denounces everything he sees, thus diminishing the effectiveness of his attack on anything in particular.[25] Wasp is, with the possible exception of Trouble-All, the closest character in the play to an automaton. His authority is a simple spring mechanism with a single response, and he is the first of the three to capitulate to the fair. Rabbi Busy, in sharp contrast, selects his targets with care. He is a conscious hypocrite who attacks not things but a set of fixed and highly charged symbols—idols, high places, Satan, the Old Law, Antichrist, the Beast of Revelations—and is able to use these tags at will, hanging any or all of them on the nearest or most convenient object. This scriptural promiscuity is apparent from Busy's very first scene in which he sanctions the eating of pork to ingratiate himself with Dame Purecraft, maintaining all the while that "the publike eating of Swines flesh" will enable him

24. This use of the stocks may be Jonson's ironic variation on one of the common stage traditions of the earlier moral interludes, the shutting of Justice in the stocks. See T. W. Craik, *The Tudor Interlude* (Leicester, 1958), pp. 94–95. Brian Parker cites a number of additional examples in "The Themes and Staging of *Bartholomew Fair*" (see n. 20).

25. Eugene Waith compares Wasp's opposition to the fair to Cokes's indiscriminate "bulldozing" of values; one accepts all things, the other rejects all. See the introduction to the Yale edition of *Bartholomew Fair* (New Haven, Conn., 1963), pp. 11–12.

to display his "hate, and loathing of *Iudaisme*." Yet the very irrelevance
of Busy's symbols to what he attacks has the same ultimate effect as
Wasp's all-inclusive indictments. When Busy finds a worthy correlative
for his epithets, as he does in Ursula in Act III, scene vi, the proper align-
ment of object and symbol seems merest coincidence, and the force of
his assault evaporates.

As Justice of the fair's Pie-powders session, Adam Overdo has a more
valid claim than either Wasp or Busy to oppose what he terms the "enormities" of Smithfield. Yet the phrase itself suggests the gap between the
Justice's proper function and his self-appointed task. Early in the play
Overdo resolves to pattern himself after a certain "worthy worshipfull
man," a past mirror for local magistrates who sought out injustices by
stalking the streets of his city as a porter, carman, dog killer, or seller of
tinder boxes. Overdo's praise may be a bit excessive, but the point is well
taken. His own variation on such conduct, however, is totally ludicrous.
Overdo rejects the humbler disguises of his model to become a roaring
preacher in a guarded coat. The role, of course, brings out the Justice's
own propensity for overdoing things, as does the ostentatious rhetoric
that accompanies it.[26] Both underscore Overdo's inflated view of his own
person and of his function as regulator and corrector of morals. Yet in
spite of his aspiring tropes and metaphors, Overdo's mind remains behind
on the Pie-powders level. He is able to spot much of the incidental cheating that goes on at the fair but is not up to the task of uncovering Smithfield's greater crimes or the true scope of its enormity. His sensational
apparatus catches trifles, while outright villainy goes unchecked before
his very eyes.

The fair not only eludes the narrow legalism of its opponents but turns
their own objections against them. As each of these figures raises his
voice in protest, he unwittingly contributes to the melee at Smithfield,
aiding the fair in its systematic flouting of law for profit. The same
belligerence that motivates Wasp's assault on the fair involves him in
Knockem's game of vapors, where he loses Cokes's marriage license as
well as his own cloak and is clapped in the stocks for disturbing the
peace. Busy falls victim to his own world of diabolic symbols. He too is

---

26. See Barish, *Ben Jonson and the Language of Prose Comedy*, pp. 204–213,
for a comprehensive treatment of Overdo's language, both in and out of disguise.

thrown in the stocks for his attack on Trash's gingerbread "Idolls" and is completely deflated in Act V when he debates a puppet *"Dagon."* Overdo, as we have already seen, rises to the lure of the fair by selecting a holiday disguise designed to display his most telling limitations as well as aid the fair's cutpurses. Moreover, while the fair abuses these three figures it also nullifies the documents and relationships on which their power depends. Cokes's license is stolen and Overdo's warrant given to the wrong madman, freeing Grace Wellborn from her legal obligations to Cokes and Justice Overdo. Wasp is put out of authority when Cokes learns of his sojourn in the stocks, and the basis for Busy's influence with Dame Purecraft and the Littlewits is undermined when his widow gives herself and her fortune to Quarlous, disguised as Trouble-All. Thus in the arena of law, as in that of appetite, the fair becomes both a corrupting and rejuvenating force. It operates by stealth and misrepresentation, by lifting and altering documents, by madly imposing upon the comparatively naïve opportunism of its visitors, but the results are in the end more satisfactory than the legalism pursued by the play's "authorities." The personal hegemonies of Wasp, Busy, and Overdo are broken up, and Quarlous, who speaks for the ambivalent ways of the fair, replaces these figures as the instructor of a renovated, if not reformed, society.

IV

Discussions of *Bartholomew Fair* have tended to overlook a fourth center of usurped power in the play, partially, one suspects, because John Littlewit so thoroughly enjoys Smithfield and partially because his chosen realm is art, not law. Yet John Littlewit is, as he himself reminds us, *Proctor* John Littlewit, and draws upon his legal training to bolster his role as aesthetic judge. He watches for quirks and quiblins, ready to "apprehend" any striking figure of speech and "bring it afore the Constable of conceit." More specifically, Littlewit sets himself up as a *"Iustice of Wit"* who can "giue the law to all the *Poets,* and *Poet-suckers* i' Towne," including, ironically enough, the *"Mermaid* men" who frequented one of Jonson's favorite taverns. To sustain this pose Littlewit's aesthetic opinions, which are as flagrantly defective as the legal opinions of Wasp, Busy, and Overdo, take the form of innumerable devices, visual and verbal conceits that enable him to flaunt his artistic tastes. In the former class is Win Littlewit's velvet cap, selected by her husband to grace himself with a wife "as fine as the Players, and as well drest." The second category accounts for the proctor's myriad puns which display his wit at the expense of his judgment, his ability to see superficial resemblances at the expense of his capacity to discern material differences. Littlewit's promiscuous word play reduces meaning to mere sound jingles, much as the fair at its worst lowers all pursuits to the level of simple noise, and readies the way for his puppet show where these aesthetic practices will be carried to their logical conclusions.

The fair itself is a world of debased art as well as one of rampant appetite and corrupt law. Art either appears as sensational entertainment or falls into disreputable employment, as in Nightingale's use of song to set up victims for the cutpurses. If, however, a single figure comes to embody this decayed state of art it is Lantern Leatherhead. Leatherhead, "parcell-poet, and . . . Inginer," [27] first takes his place in the fair's triumvirate of art, appetite, and law in Act II, scenes i–ii, when he sets up his "stable of hobby-horses" dispensing "Rattles, Drums, Halberts, Horses, Babies [i.e., dolls or puppets] o' the best . . . [and] Fiddles o' th' finest" alongside Trash's stand of foodstuffs, while Justice Overdo delivers the first of his soliloquies on law and order.[28] This identification is further strengthened when Cokes asks Leatherhead and Trash to furnish respectively his wedding masque and banquet. We also learn that Leatherhead is an accomplished jester who has been "sought out . . . at your great citty-suppers, to put downe *Coriat,* and *Cokeley*" and has been a participant in the mock bear baitings of the period, a role that relates Leatherhead to the baiting of Ursula throughout the play, as well as to the initial staging of Jonson's comedy in a converted bear pit. Above all,

27. This association with bad art is one of the reasons for the traditional identification of Leatherhead with Inigo Jones. In "An Expostulacon wth Inigo Iones" Jonson laughs at Jones's "ffeat / Of Lanterne-lerry" as the production "of some puppet play" is contemplated (ll. 72–76). In the same poem, though, Jones is also compared to "Adam ouerdooe" searching out enormities to use in his entertainments (ll. 79–84). See Jonson, *Works,* ed. Herford and Simpson, VIII, 402–406.

28. Waith suggests an overlapping of scenes here, which would have Leatherhead and Trash set up their stands while Overdo is still talking. This seems both sensible and dramatically sound. See Appendix II to Waith's edition; also his "The Staging of *Bartholomew Fair*," SEL, II (1962), 181–195.

Leatherhead is an accomplished puppeteer, who has "giuen light to" representations of *The Gunpowder Plot, Jerusalem, Nineveh, The City of Norwich,* and appropriately *Sodom and Gomorrah,* and it is in this specific capacity that he is entrusted with Littlewit's "motion" of *Hero and Leander.*

Jonson himself had little but contempt for the puppets. He held them to be both "foolish" and "rude" [29] and resented their successful competition with the legitimate companies. But not even a full knowledge of these attitudes prepares us for the depravity of Littlewit's show. The proctor has "reduced" Marlowe's poem "to a more familiar straine," combining it with a Damon-and-Pythias plot that parodies an earlier piece by Richard Edwards, Master of the Chapel Children during the 1560's. The puppet play brutalizes both legends, turning their virtues of love and friendship into exercises in obscenity and violence. Marlowe's positive irony and Edwards' simple didacticism are simultaneously submerged as Littlewit's entertainment becomes a mirror of the fair. His world is one in which affection can only be shown by finding a common outlet for animosity as Damon and Pythias display their *"friendships true tryall"* by attacking their puppet master in concert, and in which the fate of fair Hero resembles that of Win Littlewit and Mrs. Overdo at Ursula's brothel. Cupid, who is disguised as "Ionas *the Drawer,"* even resembles the pig woman in being both tapster and bawd to Hero, putting *"loue in her Sacke . . . From vnder his apron, where his lechery lurkes."* The two plots are tied together by verbal and physical obscenities. Damon and Pythias denounce Hero as a slut, and when they are required to *"Kisse the whore o' the arse"* in penance bite her there instead.[30] The melee that follows wakes the Ghost of Dionysius, a puppet schoolmaster attired as a scrivener. Art and appetite have had their say in this microcosm; now it is presumably the turn of puppet law. Yet before the play

29. "Discoveries," Jonson, *Works,* VIII, 582.

30. Waith adopts Gifford's stage direction "they kick her," as do Horsman and Partridge, but Hero shrieks *"O my hanches, O my hanches"* just after Damon and Pythias are required to kiss her arse. Biting would seem both simpler and appropriately cruder. This action, moreover, would be easier to accomplish with Leatherhead's glove puppets. See George Speaight, *The History of the English Puppet Theatre* (London, 1955), pp. 65–67, for a discussion of the type of puppets probably used in *Bartholomew Fair.*

can proceed Busy bursts into the booth, armed with all of the standing Puritan arguments against the theater, which he now hurls at Leatherhead's puppets: they are profane vanities licensed by Satan, "The Master of ⟨the⟩ *Rebells,*" and in violation of Old Testament stricture take upon themselves the clothing and identity of the opposite sex. Surely there is no defense for the play's profanity aside from Dionysius' stubborn reiteration *"It is not prophane!"* which fights Busy to a standstill, but when the stage scrivener pulls up his garment to reveal the sexlessness of his species and Busy's cause falls about him in ruins, we begin to realize that (wonder upon wonder) this ludicrous and coarse spectacle has performed the two primary functions of Renaissance art. It has delighted its audience all along, and now in its confrontation with Busy it shows its power to educate and persuade. We can, in brief, draw the same conclusion about the fair's treatment of art as we drew about its handling of appetite and law. Smithfield's corruption and depravity are obvious, but are part of an over-all process of revitalization in which rampant energy may be viewed existentially, law made to operate with an extenuating knowledge of human frailty, and art reminded of its true and proper end.

V

The complexity of response required in *Bartholomew Fair* extends to the playwright's attitude towards his own audience. In *The Shoemakers' Holiday* Dekker's world of merry craftsmen expands to include his spectators and readers, who become *"Professors of the Gentle Craft; of what degree soeuer,"* uncritical subjects of Simon Eyre's charmed kingdom.[31] Jonson's spectators are also treated much as he treats his stage citizens, but in *Bartholomew Fair* this means that they too become visitors to a bewildering and abusive festival. If Leatherhead's puppet booth serves as a microcosm of Smithfield, the Hope Theater or Bear Garden in which the piece was first performed is its macrocosm, and it is in the play's In-

31. In a similar vein Thomas Heywood addresses the reading audience of his *Foure Prentises of London* as "Honest and High-spirited Prentises." Like Dekker, Heywood is here concerned with establishing a magical relationship between his spectators and subject matter and uses metaphor as a type of sympathetic charm to accomplish this.

duction, specifically set in the Hope, that Jonson makes this most explicit. Here, as in the play proper, he presents a central paradox, tempting his audience with situations that seem to call for absolute judgments even as he exposes the folly of such certainty. The Induction opens with a stage sweeper and bookholder who express contradictory views about the nature of drama. The sweeper claims that Jonson has not responded to popular expectations, while the prompter reviles the playwright for pandering to vulgar tastes. These smug opinions not only cancel one another out but in doing so effectively disarm similar censure from Jonson's audience. Those of us who take sides in the quarrel end up appearing as foolish as the figures in his Induction. This dispute is followed by the reading of formal Articles of Agreement between the play's author and audience by a scrivener who functions as Jonson's legal spokesman much as Leatherhead is served by Dionysius, his puppet scrivener. The articles seem equitable enough on the surface, yet each section of the agreement contains within itself a qualifying clause that invalidates its portion of the contract. The play promises "to delight all, and to offend none. *Prouided* [italics added throughout] they haue either, the wit, or the honesty to thinke well of themselues"; each spectator may exercise his judgment in proportion to the admission he had paid "*Prouided* alwaies his place get not aboue his wit"; each member of the audience is encouraged to remain "fixt and settled in his censure," but such a course leads men to "sweare, *Ieronimo,* or *Andronicus* are the best playes, yet," a profession of ignorance so flagrant that it "shall passe vnexcepted at, heere"; stage devices and cheap spectacles such as servant-monsters, nests of antics, drolleries, jigs, and dances are forsworn, "*yet* if the *Puppets* will please any body, they shall be entreated to come in." The clinching qualification is saved for last. By paying in advance Jonson's spectators have literally put their seals to the document "preposterously" and thus have had no real choice in approving or rejecting his previous conditions. In brief, Jonson's Induction treats his audience much as the fair will treat them; provoking them to simple judgments and then nullifying their choices with complex qualifications. The closing paragraph of the Induction sums up this attitude, placing us completely at the playwright's mercy. After remarking on the "speciall *Decorum*" of using the dirty, stinking Hope for presenting a play about Smithfield, the scrivener informs us that his author "prayes [us] to beleeue, his *Ware* is still the same, else

[we] will make him iustly suspect that hee that is so loth to looke on a *Baby,* or an *Hobby-horse,* heere, would bee glad to take up a *Commodity* of them, at any laughter, or losse, in another place" (ll. 161–165). Jonson is here baiting the moralists in his audience in the same way that the fair baits the authority figures in its midst. This is an open challenge to the Busy elements in all of us, and unless we can keep ourselves from over-simplifying the moral issues raised by the play—unless we can sit still and let Jonson's comedy have its way—we lay ourselves open to the same charges that are leveled against the rabbi when he holds forth at Leather-head's booth. Thomas D'Urfey, the Restoration satirist and playwright, seems to have understood this point better than some of Jonson's more recent critics. It is certainly foolish to accept the fair as uncritically as Cokes does, but it is equally dangerous to swing to the other extreme, approaching the provocations of the play as Busy approaches the vul-garity of its puppet show. In *Collin's Walk through London and West-minster* D'Urfey sets up a burlesque situation in which the implications of such a response are made plain. Collin, a country Puritan visiting Lon-don, mistakes a playhouse for a meeting hall and finds himself attending a performance of *Bartholomew Fair.* He bristles at the play's "Carnal Mo-tion" and, losing his temper entirely when Busy is clapped in the stocks, leaps to the stage to exclaim against the degeneracy of the play and its au-dience. A near riot ensues in which Collin, like his stage counterpart, unwittingly contributes to the tumult he denounces, ultimately sacrificing himself too for a commodity of laughter.[32]

32. *Collin's Walk through London and Westminster, A Poem in Burlesque,* Canto iv, "Wednesdays Walk to the Play House," cited in Jonson, *Works,* XI, 329–331.

Myth and Psychology in
The Changeling

ROBERT JORDAN

COMMENTATORS on Middleton and Rowley's *The Changeling* seem to be close to agreement on at least one point, the psychological subtlety of the play.[1] Critic after critic comments on this feature, and many of them concentrate their energies on a depth analysis of the characters. In the present article I would like to challenge this standard critical perspective by suggesting that in the very place where so many critics see complexity of character there can also be found operating something vastly different—a mythic and poetic pattern that may do more to build the play's haunting power than any amount of psychology.

Talk of the play's richness of character inevitably concentrates on two

1. For example, Richard Hindry Barker, *Thomas Middleton* (New York, 1958), p. 124; Una Ellis-Fermor, *The Jacobean Drama* (London, 1961), p. 149; and Samuel Schoenbaum, *Middleton's Tragedies* (New York, 1955), pp. 137–140. Even critics whose interest lies in other aspects of the play frequently begin by acknowledging this strength of characterization—for example, Muriel Bradbrook, *Themes and Conventions of Elizabethan Tragedy* (Cambridge, Eng., 1960), pp. 213–214; and T. B. Tomlinson, *A Study of Elizabethan and Jacobean Tragedy* (Cambridge, Eng., 1964), pp. 185–188.

figures. Apart from Beatrice and De Flores the persons in the play are the palest of stock types, most of them having no more character than the walking gentlemen of Victorian melodrama. In Beatrice and De Flores, however, we have an intensity of emotion coupled with a perversity of behavior that has normally been construed as psychological complexity rather than as the maladroit inconsistency of character to which so many Jacobean playwrights (notably Fletcher) are prone. It is true, of course, that the love felt by De Flores is so brooding that it often seems a morbid obsession, and the selfishness shown by Beatrice is so total that it sometimes appears pathological, but this is usually interpreted not as evidence that Middleton is clumsy but rather as proof that he is sophisticated enough to handle abnormal psychological states.

But Beatrice and De Flores can be looked at from another point of view. We are all familiar with the way in which many studies of the Othello-Iago relationship have moved away from Bradley or Leavis-like character analyses of the two men towards a view of the relationship as the struggle between opposed instinctive forces or fundamental values. The best known example of this is probably G. Wilson Knight's reading of Othello as a symbolization of heroic idealism and Iago as an embodiment of cynicism,[2] but an even more striking, though related, example is provided by J. I. M. Stewart's view of the relationship as expressive of the conflict that exists in any human mind between idealizing and cynical impulses.[3] Othello and Iago, that is, are facets of the one consciousness. Now *The Changeling* is a play that is in some ways similar to *Othello* —in its concentration on the two-person struggle and in the simple clear line of action which leads remorselessly on from a first weakness to a final catastrophe. I would suggest that it is also like *Othello* in that the central characterizations are likewise susceptible to an analysis in abstract terms, though in this case the terms are those of myth or folklore rather than those of differing value systems.

Thus, if De Flores can be regarded as a figure of great psychological sophistication he can also be seen as an extremely simple character construct. Basically he is composed of two qualities, each realized so intensely as to take on monolithic proportions. These two qualities, more-

2. G. Wilson Knight, *The Wheel of Fire* (London, 1960), pp. 97–119.
3. J. I. M. Stewart, *Character and Motive in Shakespeare* (London, 1949), pp. 107–110.

over, are so incongruous that their enforced conjunction generates even more the sense of forces that are both stark and massive. On the one hand, there is the softness of love, a romantic infatuation which is so emphasized as to appear an obsession. On the other hand, equally emphasized, is the brutishness of the man, a brutishness that is not only a matter of coarseness and savagery of spirit but also a matter of physical repulsiveness. There are frequent and striking references to the hideousness of De Flores, a hideousness conveyed through references to his hairiness and roughness of skin [4] and also through the use of gross animal images—serpent, toad, dog.[5] This animal baseness is further reinforced by the emphasis on his menial position, and the whole picture is given an extra intensity by the contrast with his partner, Beatrice-Joanna, who is presented in terms of an antithetical set of simple, stark qualities— aristocratic where he is lowly, beautiful where he is gross, hysterically repelled where he is morbidly doting. In the center of the play, then, standing out all the more because of the pallid quality of the other characters, are two figures locked in a relationship, figures simplified down to a few qualities apiece so that the relationship itself takes on a monumental simplicity—brutishness and love at the feet of beauty and revulsion. With the animality of De Flores emphasized not only through his coarse and savage nature but also through his physical appearance, and through the animal imagery that clusters about him, it seems to me that Middleton is here hovering on the verge of one of the more potent of mythic confrontations, that of beauty and the beast, the princess and the frog. I believe that the dramatic power that the De Flores–Beatrice relationship undoubtedly generates owes much to the way it reverberates with the echoes of this traditional pattern.

Claims of the kind I have just made for a mythic substratum to a dramatic situation usually face an enormous difficulty. The presence of the myth can be asserted but not in any sense demonstrated. What makes the example in *The Changeling* especially interesting, however, is that one can trace the situation in the play back to earlier literary models which actually overlap the primitive forms of this myth.

4. Thomas Middleton and William Rowley, *The Changeling,* ed. N. W. Bawcutt, The Revels Plays (London, 1958), pp. 27 (ll. 35–45), 35 (ll. 43–45), 37 (ll. 73–75), 40 (ll. 147–150). All references in the text are to this edition.

5 *Ibid.,* pp. 9 (l. 115), 14 (l. 225), 29 (l. 80), 40 (l. 146).

A starting point for this analysis is a feature of the play that has been noted by Professor Ornstein.[6] In the first three acts of *The Changeling* the De Flores–Beatrice relationship is quite consciously and systematically developed as a perverted and mordantly ironic variant on a courtly love relationship. Every significant step in this phase of the story seems conceived in these terms. Thus the opening situation is a travesty of the doting lovesick knight being spurned by his cruel and haughty mistress. This is followed by the first sign of grace—the lady drops a glove which the ever attentive knight recovers for her and which the lady allows him to keep as a favor. After this comes the longed-for occasion when the lady, in peril, needs a champion to defend her. And so we find De Flores literally kneeling before Beatrice, begging the service and being granted it. He becomes her champion, kills the threatening enemy, is given a further token (the ring) as a sign of favor, presses his suit, and wins the lady. As an example of the way the travesty works and of the savagery of it, one has only to consider one of these incidents, one not noted by Professor Ornstein. De Flores may actually speak of the dropped glove as a favor (I.i.231), but if the lady allows him to keep it it is not out of a nascent affection but out of revulsion. Once he has touched it she is so disgusted by the object that she refuses to have anything to do with it. As if this were not a sufficient degradation of the romantic image of the glove, it receives a further defilement when De Flores, talking of it, turns it into an image of gross sexuality:

> Here's a favour come, with a mischief! Now I know
> She had rather wear my pelt tann'd in a pair
> Of dancing pumps, than I should thrust my fingers
> Into her sockets here. . . .

                                        (I.i.231–234)

The same sexual defilement, incidentally, is involved in the other love token, the ring, in Act III, scene iv. It is a ghastly enough perversion of elegant romance that this ring should have the murdered owner's finger still in it. It is an extra twist that the finger in the ring is a very sleazy sexual image—one that occurs, moreover, in the subplot (I.ii.27).

But it is more than the broad pattern of incident that reflects the

6. Robert Ornstein, *The Moral Vision of Jacobean Tragedy* (Madison and Milwaukee, Wis., 1965), pp. 179–190.

courtly conventions. Much of the detailing of the story is similarly conceived in terms of the inverted or travestied courtly affair. Thus the killing of the villain knight who threatens the lady here becomes the murder of the innocent Piraquo. This murder is presented on stage with a striking amount of circumstantial detail, and to the casual glance this might look like the accumulation of small facts to give an air of solid realism to the events. Actually these details seem to have been selected to stress the nature of the action as a complete reversal of the courtly contest. In this contest what one normally has is an open challenge and then the face-to-face armed combat, something that by Middleton's time had ossified into the code of the duel, complete with seconds. But instead of the formal challenge and the fight with equal weapons, we are shown De Flores presenting himself to Piraquo as a friend, tricking him into putting aside his weapons, luring him into a deserted part of the fortress, persuading him to admire the view through an embrasure, and then, while he looks out, stabbing him, presumably in the back. The choice of words and many of the turns of language are similarly inspired by the courtly code (for example, II.i.26–35).

Professor Ornstein, as I have said, makes the basic point that there is inversion of the courtly love convention in the Beatrice–De Flores relationship. Nevertheless, he continues to speak of the psychological reality of these characters[7] and to concentrate on the analysis of motive and personality. It would seem to me that where characters are so systematically conceived in terms of a literary convention, albeit one turned on its head, there are at least some grounds for being cautious in one's psychological analyses and some possibilities that the relationship may operate on levels other than the psychological.

But there is more to be said than that. Professor Ornstein finds the inspiration for the courtly love travesty in the use of such techniques in *The Maid's Tragedy*.[8] Perhaps Fletcher's play may have given Middleton the idea, but it seems to me that in choosing to present his travesty suitor as a coarse brute (unlike Fletcher) he may in fact be harking back to a much earlier and more widespread variation on the normal courtly love relationship. What I am suggesting is an echo of that very popular

7. *Ibid.,* p. 181.
8. *Ibid.,* p. 179.

medieval and Renaissance motif, the wild man and the maiden. And if on one side this motif impinges on the courtly love relationship, on the other side it merges into the legendary pattern I spoke of earlier—beauty and the beast.

The wild man, or wodewose, who has been described in great detail by Professor R. Bernheimer,[9] is a shaggy and uncouth creature who lives the life of a primitive huntsman in the depths of the woods. He is a standard figure of European folk tales and folk rituals and from there has moved across into the iconography of late medieval and Renaissance art, literature, and ceremonial, where he is often merged with the classical satyr. More than anything else he is an embodiment of the bestial side of man's nature—man as the savage creature without culture giving free rein to his brute appetites. A figure such as this, of course, is the complete antithesis of the chivalrous ideal, and so he sometimes appears among the evil creatures overcome by questing knights on their peregrinations.[10] However, as a figure of folklore and of sophisticated iconography the wild man is capable of all sorts of subtle modifications, and it is with some of these that I am chiefly concerned. Thus the primary role of the wild man in relation to woman would seem to be that of the ravisher and kidnapper who bears her off into the forests. But even in some of the folk rituals the pattern one finds is that of the woman "capturing" the wild man—leading him on a ribbon or luring him with a ring [11]—and the same reversal of roles can occur in the courtly use of the material. The wild man can be "tamed" by the highborn lady and can even become her servant. When this tendency is exploited to the full, what we seem to have is an icon for the traditional power of the beauteous lady, the power of taming the savage impulses in man and bringing him to gentleness and civility—one of the central motifs of the courtly code.[12]

Elizabethan and Jacobean dramatic entertainments provide a few examples of such wild-man–lady relationships. In *Mucedorus* Bremo the wild man first views the heroine simply as a good meal but is suddenly smitten by her beauty:

9. Richard Bernheimer, *Wild Men in the Middle Ages* (Cambridge, Mass., 1952).
10. *Ibid.*, pp. 121–122.
11. *Ibid.*, p. 136.
12. *Ibid.*, pp. 124–125, 135–136.

> I cannot wield my weapons in my hand;
> Methinks I should not strike so fair a one,
> I think her beauty hath bewitch'd my force,
> Or else within me altered nature's course.
> Ay, woman, wilt thou live in woods with me? [13]

Thereafter he dotes on the lady, while remaining in every other respect the cannibal savage, a De Flores of the woods. Similarly transfigured in an instant of time is the satyr in Fletcher's *The Faithful Shepherdess,* though in this case it is the radiant chastity of the lady rather than her beauty that effects the change.[14] The satyr, moreover, seems less savage than Bremo to begin with, and in his case the lady's powers seem to have led to a general reformation of manners. Many decades earlier George Gascoigne had turned this idea to a courtly compliment in *The Princely Pleasures at Kenelworth Castle* where he has his Savage Man transfigured by the sight of the beautiful and highborn female guests at the entertainment, and particularly by the Queen, whom he begs to serve:

> . . . I, which live at large,
>   a wilde and savadge man:
> And have ronne out a wilfull race,
>   since first my lyfe began:
> Doe here submit my selfe,
>   beseeching you to serve:
> And that you take in worth my will,
>   which can but well deserve.[15]

In this transformation by love, and in this desire to serve, the wild man is beginning to impinge on the functions of the courtly knight, and part of Professor Bernheimer's concern in Chapter Five of his book is to demonstrate the ways in which the wild man develops as parody, subversion or outright replacement of the traditional courtly lover. Earlier in his book (pp. 18–19) he has remarked on a number of occasions on which the savage man appears as a full-fledged courtly knight. The best example of this in Renaissance England is provided by that happy hunting ground

13. *A Select Collection of Old English Plays,* ed. W. Carew Hazlitt, comp. Robert Dodsley, 4th ed., 15 vols. (London, 1874–1876), VII, 233.

14. *The Works of Francis Beaumont and John Fletcher,* ed. Arnold Glover and A. R. Waller, 10 vols. (Cambridge, Eng., 1906), II, 373–375.

15. *The Complete Works of George Gascoigne,* ed. John W. Cunliffe, 2 vols. (Cambridge, Eng., 1910), II, 100.

for wild men, Spenser's *The Faerie Queene,* where Sir Satyrane, who "ever lov'd to fight for Ladies right" (I.vi.20) rescues Una from his less cultivated brethren, the satyrs.

There are grounds, then, for seeing De Flores as a shadowy evocation of the wild man tradition in the area where that tradition interpenetrates with the courtly love convention. The matter could be left at that point, but I would like to argue the further extension, that through the wild man and the lady pattern the De Flores–Beatrice relationship impinges on the even more potent beauty-and-the-beast legends. The relationship is, in fact, a very simple one. In folklore there is plenty of evidence for confusions between the shaggy wild man and the brute beast. Thus a ritual pattern that in one part of the countryside calls for a wild man in another area will make use of a bear.[16] Similarly, in the courtly love stories the beauty and virtue of the woman is often shown as taming not only wild men but also wild beasts—Una's lion, for example, in *The Faerie Queene,* I.iii.5–6. Into the context I have been describing then, the beauty-and-the-beast story pattern fits without difficulty. Some of the folk tales based on the beauty-and-the-beast motif, moreover, involve not only the basic beauty-beast opposition that is my main concern but also details of narrative and character that are analogous to those in the type of courtly love story that lies behind *The Changeling.* In the version of "The Princess and The Frog" given by the brothers Grimm [17] the frog certainly lacks the threatening power of a bear or other shaggy beast, but on the other hand the tale contains the haughty lady, the service performed, and the efforts to evade payment. In this folk tale, of course, the climactic event is the transformation of the beast into a handsome prince, and it is easy enough to see this as symbolic of savagery transformed by the lady's kindness into gentleness and civility, a parallel with the "taming" of the wild man.

In my analysis I have concentrated on the primary image that the De Flores–Beatrice relationship generates—that of the shaggy beast fawning on the beautiful lady. But of course the outcome of the relationship as it is shown in the play is hardly the conventional one. De Flores may observe the formal stages of the courtly wooing, but the forms are hollow

16. Bernheimer, *Wild Men in the Middle Ages,* pp. 53–55.

17. "The Frog King, or Iron Henry," in *The Grimms' German Folk Tales,* trans. Francis P. Magoun, Jr., and Alexander H. Krappe (Carbondale, Ill., 1960), pp. 3–6.

ones. They are drained of idealism, purity, and selflessness and exist only as the vehicles for gross lust, brutal selfishness, and crude cynicism. The wild man may do obeisance before the fair lady but this lady's glance does not purify. The wild man is a wild man still. Indeed, with this lady it could not be otherwise, for in her also one has only the forms of the courtly mode and not the essence—the beauty, the birth, the virginity, but not the inner purity. The fairy-tale ending is subject to a bitter reversal. Instead of the beast being revealed as a prince, the process of this story is to reveal that the princess is in fact a beast.

Ford's "Waste Land":
The Broken Heart

R. J. KAUFMANN

> Thinking of the key, each confirms a prison.
> > T. S. Eliot, *The Waste Land*

> And long we try in vain to speak and act
> Our hidden self, and what we say and do
> Is eloquent, is well—but 'tis not true.
> > Matthew Arnold, "The Buried Life"

THERE HAVE BEEN a number of sensible and effective discussions of Ford's *The Broken Heart* in recent years.[1] The authors of these essays have used the established techniques of modern formal and structural

1. Although I have duly consulted the standard books on Ford by S. Blaine Ewing, *Melancholy in the Plays of John Ford* (New York, 1940); George F. Sensabaugh, *The Tragic Muse of John Ford* (New York, 1944); H. J. Oliver, *The Problem of John Ford* (Melbourne, 1955); and Clifford Leech, *John Ford and the Drama of His Time* (London, 1957); as well as appropriate sections of Robert Ornstein, *The Moral Vision of Jacobean Tragedy* (New York, 1960); and Irving Ribner, *Jacobean Tragedy* (London, 1962), I am responding more particularly to several recent studies in the periodical literature. These studies have a common denominator in their particular style of deploying imagistic evidence in the interest of larger judgments about Ford's intellectual commitments. The studies in question are: Donald K. Anderson, "The Heart and the Banquet: Imagery in Ford's *'Tis Pity* and *The Broken Heart*," *SEL*, II (1962), 209–217; Glenn H. Blayney, "Convention, Plot and Structure in *The Broken Heart*," *MP*, LVI (1958), 1–9; Charles O. McDonald, "The Design of John Ford's *The Broken Heart*," *SP* (1962), 141–161; and Mark Stavig's new book, *John Ford and the Moral Order* (Madison, Wis., 1968). All textual citations are from John Ford, *The Broken Heart*, ed. Donald K. Anderson, Regent's Renaissance Drama Series (Lincoln, Nebr., 1968).

analysis to defend Ford against the strictures of earlier critics—most notably T. S. Eliot—who found his plays moving enough, but dramaturgically
inept and lacking in metaphorical integrity. The implication, where the
accusation was not insultingly direct, was that Ford's mind was deficient
in visionary power and that in consequence—however insidious the muted
cadence of his blank verse and despite his gift for annotating the more
fugitive ranges of human sensibility—his plays are poetically *superficial,*
making their appeal to detachable sentiments rather than to those deep,
congested feelings at our common human core. Shakespeare as usual and,
sometimes, Webster, Jonson, and Chapman are cited as positive instances
of capacities for which Ford by facile comparison is a deprived negative.
Blayney, McDonald, Anderson, Stavig and, to some extent, Sensabaugh
in his later work have struggled to rescue Ford from this critical con-
descension which can be more damaging to a just perception of an
artist's quality than brutal forms of denigration. Recent Ford critics argue
his case mainly by showing that his plays have a higher quotient of itera-
tive imagery of a Shakespearean sort than Eliot and others detected. Their
work goes almost exclusively to the issue of verbal coherency and a correlative *ordonnance* of essentially conventional moral perspective. The
new Ford is saner, more purposive, less guilty of Fletcherian opportunism
and altogether more conscious of his artistic duties than the antinomian,
romantic stereotype they set out to correct. Their work has been done
well insofar as it is merely revisionist. But in terms of a more adequate
—as opposed to a merely more coherent—reading of Ford's artistic par-
ticularity, there remain some serious doubts. If their Ford is less superficial, he is also more mechanical; if he is less quixotic in his moral vision, and less fragile, he is also unduly normalized, to the point where
he seems well on his way to a Popean domestication of tragic feelings,
a kind of sober archivist of the Jacobean dramatic ethos. I believe that a
somewhat different conception of Ford's attitude towards his materials
and a more circumspect critical approach to his use of language can advance our understanding of his art.

I

The Broken Heart is imaginatively organic. It springs and takes dramatic force from one complex and essentially botanical metaphor by means of which the dramatist's vision has been, in G. Wilson Knight's phrase, "projected into forms roughly correspondent with actuality."[2] I am concerned with establishing the main aspects of this governing image of forestalled growth and with the means by which it unifies and energizes Ford's drama. An entrance to the play's poetic ground plan can be opened by examining this governing image as it appears in and radiates from four central passages: Orgilus' use of the Phaeton myth at the time of Ithocles' death (IV.iv); Nearchus' perception of the effect of tyranny on human lives (IV.ii); Tecnicus' warning to Orgilus when he leaves the scholar's life (III.i); and the oracle of the fate of Sparta (IV.iii).

Stated in analytical form, the governing image argues that life and growth cannot continue to exist where the means of sustenance, the fertilizing energies, are cut off or diverted from their normal course. The process is one of truncation and severing; it is followed by the frustration which normally accompanies unfulfilled desires. Further, failure to control or convert the energies thus deprived of their normal function results in their release for destructive purposes, in desiccation and desolation. The inevitable end of the process is death, the final burning-out of the energy itself. The atmosphere of the play is controlled by images of truncation, frustration, and desiccation which reach their culmination in the powerfully realized death scenes in the last acts. This articulation can be traced as it is worked out within the play.

The Phaeton myth is at the core of the image plan. We will need the story itself, for it is not fully invoked in its modern applications. As told by Ovid, Phaeton, son of Clymene and the Sun, sought to take his father's place for one day, to guide the Sun's chariot on its dangerous course rising to the height of the sky and descending into the sea. Proud, ambitious, and undaunted by fear, Phaeton chose to override his father's wise counsel on the limitations his mortality would impose. After a brief moment of joy in his power Phaeton found that he was in fact

2. "Shakespeare Interpretation," in *The Wheel of Fire* (London, 1930).

trapped in the chariot with no power at all, having entirely lost control of the horses carrying him on an everwidening course of destruction. In their reckless plunge back to earth the whole world is set ablaze, living growth is burned away, and the world left desiccated. Phaeton, horrified by the consequences of his action, is granted his one last wish, death, when earth's cry of pain is answered by Jove's thunderbolt.

The allusion to the myth is already quite full in Orgilus' charge against Ithocles at the scene of Penthea's death. "Caught! You are caught, Young master," cries Orgilus, as the engine traps Ithocles in his throne of death beside his sister.

> . . . 'tis thy throne of coronation,
> Thou fool of greatness. See, I take this veil off;
> Survey a beauty *wither'd by the flames*
> Of *an insulting Phaeton,* her brother.

He taunts:

> You dreamt of kingdoms, did 'ee?
> . . . .
> whiles Penthea's groans and tortures,
> Her agonies, her miseries, afflictions
> Ne'er touch'd upon your thought.
>
> (IV.iv.22–36; italics added)

Simply in terms of the action, Ithocles, infused with pride and ambition, like Phaeton, usurped his father's position, breaking the betrothal vow between Penthea and Orgilus, which his father had sanctioned, by arbitrarily giving his sister to Bassanes in marriage. Indeed, Penthea charges him with

> forfeiting the last will of the dead,
> From whom you had your being.
>
> (III.ii.41–42)

We remember that Ithocles, conscious of his betrayal, has rationalized his act, saying that it was performed in the *"heat* of an unsteady youth," without knowledge of the "secrets of commanding love" (II.ii.44–51). Like the "seeled dove," he mounted upward to "perch on clouds," and the action of the play is, in part, the process of his tumbling "headlong down with heavier ruin" (II.ii.3–5). His selfish choice has interposed an insuperable barrier between his sister and her "commanding love" in the form of a marriage which has "withered" her life and cast "clouds" over the "pure firmament" of her beauty (II.i.87–88). He has blighted her as a female element by marrying her to an old and, by implication, impotent man; he has scorched and withered the "earth." The ravaging effects of his choice extend to nearly the whole world of the play. Penthea, Orgilus, Calantha—in a sense, Sparta—and he, inevitably must die. In his lengthened day Ithocles has had to face the "horror" his actions have wrought, the "rape" on his sister's purity, the "ruin" on Orgilus. He has had occasion to wish, as Phaeton did, for release from the diminished life in which he has entrapped himself along with the others. The temporal relationship of the action, then, is brought swiftly and dramatically into focus by means of this graphic allusion at a crucial moment in this play. Ford encloses the play within the boundaries of this action by means of an image which is spatial, presentational, and synoptic.

There is another and more nearly symbolic sense in which the myth is incorporated into Ford's metaphorical substratum. Phoebus is accorded qualities of splendor and brilliance in Ovid's myth, in addition to the life-giving forces of heat and light. In the course of Phaeton's journey, beauty is distorted by overrunning its proper bounds, and the life-giving forces are perverted into flames of destruction. Ford makes significant use of this metaphor of conversion from life to death throughout *The Broken Heart.* Nearchus' simple admission that

> Calantha's bosom
> Is warm'd with other fires than such as can
> Take strength from any fuel of the love
> I might address to her.
>
> (IV.ii.196–199)

is in fact an important image of a large family which correlates strength and fuel with love, at the same time it traces the course of the play as a moving away from the source of life. The motif is established at the beginning of the play in Orgilus' apostrophe to love:

> Love, thou art full of mystery! The deities
> Themselves are not secure in searching out
> The secrets of those flames, which hidden waste
> A breast made tributary to the laws
> Of beauty;
>
> (I.iii.36–40)

When diverted from their proper course, the fires of love lay "waste" that which they normally would sustain and strengthen. Penthea gives passionate testimony to the power of the fire of love to scorch, to frustrate, "With desires infinite but hopes impossible!" (III.ii.49). This is the worst fate she can envision for the man who betrayed her so cruelly; but, owing to her consequent inner desiccation, she is the central instrument of the destruction she foresees.

The image is impressed on the imagination in another way in Bassanes' lament for Penthea's bereaved condition and ensuing death:

> Let the sun first
> Be *wrapp'd up* in an everlasting darkness,
> Before the light of nature, chiefly form'd
> For the whole world's delight, feel *an eclipse*
> So universal.
>
> (IV.II.81–85; italics added)

Penthea, of course, has long been so shrouded in spirit and has expressed her desire for the covering of the grave, the "winding-sheet," "a fold of lead" (III.v.32). Her literal eclipse in death parallels and documents Ithocles' earlier act which severed her love and beauty from organic fulfillment. She is both the victim of the misused "sun" of life and herself a "sun" of beauty eclipsed. The image pressures, though intense, are highly coordinated, for both Penthea and the physical sun are nurturing sources if respected.

As I indicated at the outset, Ford's central conception is complex. The process metaphor of truncation, frustration, and desiccation is full and rich. Through it Ford reaches progressively further into the psyches of his characters. Nearchus' refusal to force Calantha's marriage provides another gateway to Ford's metaphorical base. Nearchus explains to Amelus that he can, he must, allow himself to be rivaled for Calantha's hand by a man unequal in birth,

> for affections injur'd
> By tyranny or rigour of compulsion,
> Like tempest-threaten'd trees unfirmly rooted,
> Ne'er spring to timely growth.
>
> (IV.ii.205–208)

The speech has deserved impact. His wisdom forms a sharp contrast to Ithocles' folly. Again, it comes at a crucial point in the drama, just before the death of Penthea speeds the action on to its foreordained conclusion. It underlines a host of images dealing with the cessation or abortion of organic growth caused by disease or failure at the roots. Further, it illustrates the power of one being to compel another to do its will with the force of a tempest.

In the first scene Orgilus presents his embittering plight to Crotolon and the audience by means of this image of ravaged growth. A peace between their families was sealed by "an interchange of holy and chaste love" between Penthea and Orgilus, which "fix'd" their souls

> In *a firm growth* of union that no time
> Can *eat into* the pledge.
>
> (I.i.30–32; italics added)

This is the core psychological situation of the play: an absolute pledge has been made of the sort that cannot be consumed by time in the way that the canker "eats" the plant's firm growth. But neither can their love achieve full growth. For, with the death of Penthea's father

> sprouted up that poisonous stalk
> Of aconite, whose ripened fruit hath ravish'd
> All health, all comfort of a happy life.
>
> (I.i.36–38)

Nourishing his pride and desire for revenge, Ithocles poisoned the lovers. The "ripened fruit" is the "monster love" of Bassanes, which has produced only fear and jealousy. Penthea's ravings, releasing all that has been buried deepest in her thwarted soul, make the total deflection of all growth, spiritual and actual, pathetically evident. Her piteous lament that she literally has borne no child, having been blighted by Ithocles' Phaeton career,

> Since I was first a wife, I might have been
> Mother to many pretty prattling babes.
> They would have smil'd when I smil'd; and, for certain,
> I should have cried when they cried; truly, brother,
> My father would have pick'd me out a husband,
> And then my little ones had been no bastards.
> But 'tis too late for me to marry now,
> I am past child-bearing; 'tis not my fault.
>
> (IV.ii.87–94)

is an aria of frustration poignantly expressing what it is not to fulfill one's most important function. No child but a bastard is possible when the wife is forced to become a whore. For her not even this is possible—no births are imaginable in the world of this play.

A similar frustration is prefigured for Ithocles in Armostes' use of the myth of Ixion (IV.i.69–73). Instead of gaining a "real, visible, material happiness," Ithocles will embrace only a "cloud" and beget only a "prodigy." In turn, Calantha will embrace only the "shadow" of her lover at her coronation (V.iii.62).

Ithocles' act has destroyed his world. It has severed the love between brother and sister; in Ithocles' own horrible, sterilizing image, ambition has gnawed "a passage through the womb that gave it motion" (II.ii.2). The ripped womb is imagistically homologous to the burnt earth—each a matrix violated. Penthea can be reconciled with Ithocles only when she insures that his position will parallel hers exactly (III.ii). Her intermediation in her brother's suit with Calantha is not a charitable act—such an interpretation would offend the spirit of the play and crassly sentimentalize it. It is an act of vengeful contagion. Theirs is a world in which only sadness can grow, only silence is hoarded (II.iii). Orgilus' portrayal of his own agony fully expresses this aspect of the atmosphere Ford creates. "All pleasures are but mere imagination," he says,

> Feeding the hungry appetite with steam
> And sight of banquet, whilst the body pines,
> Not relishing the real taste of food.
> Such is the leanness of a heart divided
> From intercourse of troth-contracted loves.
>
> (II.iii.34–39)

The banquet is finally denied Ithocles (V.i). Bassanes must be satisfied with gazing at beauty and wishing for love, since he lacks the means truly to possess either.[3]

The outlines of the governing image and the atmosphere it creates

---

3. The banquet imagery, isolated and interpreted by Donald K. Anderson in the essay cited earlier, is an objective correlative for the deeper, more pervasive image stratum having to do with deprivation of sustenance, psychic as well as physical, just as the imagery of "desubstantialization" or sublimation of solid "food" into gaseous form is a variant of the comprehensive imagery of perversion of normal growth and regulated natural process. The play's image matrix is very firm.

should be sufficiently clear by now to counter any statement, such as Professor Bradbrook's, that the "structure is not assisted by any pattern in the language." [4]

What happens psychologically and spatially in *The Broken Heart* is this: each character is boxed in, entrapped, by the other characters; the area of the boxes keeps getting smaller and smaller until there is no choice but to break it open by force. In this sense the play very much resembles Strindberg's *The Father,* and in this sense the "engine" in which Ithocles is entrapped, like Strindberg's strait jacket, is appropriate as a symbol for the whole play. The image of "the box" itself is used in several ways, two of which illuminate my point. Ithocles can become a tragic figure, can be terribly affected by the situation he has created, precisely because "his heart / Is crept into the *cabinet* of the princess (IV.iii.117–118; italics added). Once his naïve egotism is penetrated by his own socially unjustifiable love for the Princess, comprehension of his sister's pain and Orgilus' agony is born and oppresses his imagination. In a masterly synoptic image Ford adds both scope and depth to his central metaphor. At the beginning of Act III, after Orgilus' crucial encounter with Penthea in the grove, Armostes enters carrying a "casket," saying:

> It is the health of Sparta, the king's life,
> Sinews and safety of the commonwealth:
>
> (III.i.66–67)

It is this final box, the casket, and this only, which will bring health and safety to the diseased state.

This process of moral intensification through constricting pressure is tellingly worked out in Ford's handling of the unpromising stereotype of the jealous husband, Bassanes. Bassanes' jealousy is superficially of the casebook variety, but it works symbolically in the world of *The Broken Heart.* Rather like the Gloucester subplot in *King Lear* or the madhouse sequence in *The Changeling,* it provides a more palpable or accessible version of the main action. One of the distinguishing features of tragedy in the later stages of an epoch is the inflection of stereotype. Bassanes, in contradiction to Anderson's contention, is not another failure at comic lightness on the part of Ford, for he is not, save perhaps margin-

4. M. C. Bradbrook, *Themes and Conventions of Elizabethan Tragedy* (Cambridge, Eng., 1935), p. 260.

ally, ever so intended. He "begins" in stereotype, but he is developed by Ford. He too suffers. Whatever his faults, he is excluded painfully from Penthea's feelings, exiled and rejected by her self-absorption as surely as by his own disqualifications. He is another exemplar of the disease of frustration, and his "cure" from jealousy comes at the total cost of his hopes. He does not gain the partial remedy of a large dignity in the end. He is wedged so tightly into his self-constructed role that he is as lonely in his penitence as he had been in his jealous imaginings. If one forgets Burton's diagrams of love melancholies and rejects facile knowledge of stage stereotypes, one can see the effectiveness of Ford's development of Bassanes' structural role. The other characters are also prey to jealousy of various kinds appropriate to themselves. Through Ford's multiform analysis, jealousy can be seen as a deep-reaching accompaniment of the prevention of the growth of the characters' needs. Jealousy is the result of deprivation in fact or imagination of what one believes to be his by right or superior need. There is "role" jealousy just as there is "object or possession" jealousy, a circumstance Ford understood almost as well as Shakespeare. Orgilus, Ithocles, Penthea, even Calantha are prey to such jealousy. It breaks out first in words at points of high emotional tension (Penthea's "mad scene," Orgilus' interview with his father, Ithocles' irrational speeches in the episode about Calantha's ring) and then in the violence and masochistic justice of their final deeds. Bassanes and Nearchus are the only ones able to control their jealousy at the end.

The play is full, but it is not "overloaded" as Eliot would have it, and there is no part which is not an organic contribution to the whole. My claim can be made clearer by a brief look at the oracle which contains the fate of Sparta:

> *The plot in which the vine takes root*
> *Begins to dry from head to foot;*
> *The stock soon withering, want of sap*
> *Doth cause to quail the budding grape.*
> *But from the neighboring elm a dew*
> *Shall drop and feed the plot anew.*
>
> (IV.iii.11–16)

The play depends upon a familiar mythic pattern—the vegetative myth of the dying king. It begins with the reinvigoration of the aged king Amyclas through the conquering sword of Ithocles. The king quite explicitly places his hopes for the state in the persons of Ithocles and Calantha, thus binding the main action of the play inextricably to the health of the state (III.iii; IV.iii). But the "languishing disease of time" has already had an effect, and no "physic" can "restore" it to its former youth and vigor. The "plot" once dried cannot sustain the season's fruit. The marriage proceedings of Euphranea and Prophilus—who are non-public characters—have more than a casual place in this scene. The king is able to insure their marriage, whereas he can do nothing in the case of Penthea and Orgilus. The "dried plot" of that earlier failure to act has not produced the fruit which could now nourish the state of Sparta. There is need for the "learning" and "knowledge" of the "*nursery* of Greece," for the "herbs" of Apollo, for the "dew of the neighboring elm" to compensate for the "opinion" which has infected the roots of Sparta, so as to check the age and disease which have left it languishing and withered and therefore incapable of supporting growth from its own stock (V.i.1–5). Ford does not create "problems" which call for "solutions." He creates fully imagined "situations" which are "resolved" organically. The largest enclosing—and constricting—image usage is a special kind of "situation." We refer to the play's setting in Sparta.

II

The fact that Ford, as Havelock Ellis put it long ago, "curiously" chose to set *The Broken Heart* in Sparta is only of passing interest to most critics; they insist he meant only to evoke a remote and dreamlike atmosphere reminiscent of Sidney's *Arcadia*. But Ford's use is far more particularized than this. As is well known, the ideal Spartan exemplified traits very close to the Stoic cardinal virtues of courage, justice, moral insight, and self-control or temperance. Its hero-lawgiver, Lycurgus, according to Plutarch's standard account, decreed that no laws should be recorded; they were rather instilled as the substance of a Spartan education and were effectively internalized by means of public censure and derision. Having established his design, Lycurgus, extracting a promise from the citizens to retain the laws in his absence, traveled to Delphi to ask Apollo's approval of his work. When he had received the divine blessing, he took his own life *by starving himself*.

These basic assumptions of the historical Sparta are vitally relevant to Ford's Sparta. In both communities, sanctioned human emotion has been radically circumscribed and individual desires subordinated to communal ends. There is an unremitting preoccupation with public virtues: honor, duty, truth, reputation, and moderation. But in the world of *The Broken Heart,* there is a strong countercurrent which threatens to upset the delicate balance of restraints imposed from within and without. The characters are troubled by thoughts of sickness and death, with frustration, compulsion, and division. Images of secrecy, shadows, and shrouding weave an atmosphere of moral density, and this is deepened by allusions to stealth and counterfeiting. Since, according to the Spartan scheme, virtue has been converted into the only potential which one possesses, people begin to speak of human relationships and actions in commercial terms. For in Ford's Sparta, there is a deep fissure between public standards and individual needs. Since the society allows too few constructive outlets for the passions, these are transformed into destructive energy; but, because the characters never question the premises of their culture, their destructiveness assumes the peculiarly Spartan (or Stoic, or Calvinist) form of self-deprivation. Ford's Spartans continually invoke the vocabulary of recognized virtues in order to repress the residual, unsocialized self.

Ultimately, however, they are compelled to express their deepest impulses through symbolic gesture. Perhaps it is this quality above all that has made the drama seem dreamlike to so many readers: Ford's characters seldom express their deepest feelings directly, so these feelings must be inferred by means of image, cadence, emphasis, and action. It is a world of displacement and substitution, a carefully edited version of the actual world of dreams. Ford has created a boundary situation, in which communal values are still powerfully operative but essentially irrelevant to these particular individuals. The destructive forces which are released cannot be counteracted by anything within the play, since Tecnicus, the only figure with both insight and foresight, is neutralized by old age and fatalism; and King Amylas hovers like a tattered pennant of lost authority. He is a wounded Fisher King, impotent and ineffectual in life as in his death late in the play—not a character but an environmental index.

The role of Orgilus, the vengeful lover, is more often misunderstood than any of the others. In this dramatic world where public roles are so important, he can never be fully identified with one. There is no indication of how he could usefully occupy his time, given other circumstances. In this respect, he resembles those disinherited men, such as Vindice or Bosola, who figure prominently in Jacobean tragedy. He is obliged to try to live a "leftover life," and all his actions are displaced expressions of the residuum of selfhood he seeks to reinstate but cannot. Hence, the ventriloqual and disembodied impression he makes upon himself as well as us.

Orgilus is a well-conditioned product of Spartan society in that, for him, contracts assume the validity of laws, which in turn acquire the status of literal facts. Thus, when his vows of love and devotion to Penthea are thwarted by her marriage, he is pathetically balked. So intense is the reality of his vow to him that he insists upon reciprocal recognition of it. Complicating his dedication to Penthea is a very human physical passion for her, which his language vibrantly records. Since intense passion is not an approved emotion in this rational, restrained society, Orgilus camouflages his true emotions by doggedly reiterating his *legal* rights to his betrothed. The extent of his commitment to his vow, as well as the confusion of motive in his own mind, is sharply defined during his stolen interview with Penthea:

ORGILUS
I would possess my wife; the equity
Of very reason bids me.
PENTHEA
Is that all?
ORGILUS
Why, 'tis the all of me, myself.

(II.iii.71–73)

Penthea's apparent devaluation of his faith reduces him to poignant simplicity, but ordinarily he speaks in legalistic and priggish terms about his vow. By releasing him from further obligation to her, Penthea gives Orgilus a freedom which he is incapable of using. Failing to gain her recognition of his claims, he subsequently directs all of his energies toward public acknowledgement of his vow, by committing revenge in its name.

From the first scene onwards, Orgilus seeks to convert private commitments into civil terms—diplomatic and legal images abound. This is especially true of his love for Penthea: he complains that he is

> made tributary to the laws
> Of beauty
>
> (I.iii.39–40)

and begs her to

> Be just, . . .
> In thy commands. When thou send'st forth a doom
> Of banishment, know first on whom it lights.
>
> (II.iii.46–48)

Not only is his love a "contract"; even his friendships are treaties. The betrothal was to confirm "a lasting league" (I.i.24) between the families of Thrasus and Crotolon; when it fails, he pretends to "undertake a voluntary exile" (I.i.77). A marriage between Prophilus and Euphranea would "inleague our blood" (III.iv.12), and in the last act he invites Bassanes to "accept a league of amity" (V.i.23).[5]

His wounded nature is deeply divided against itself, and, without fully understanding this fact, Orgilus recognizes that he can no longer act effectively through his own person. In desperation he undertakes a series of disguises, therefore, to achieve some sort of artificial integration of his personality. His first disguise as the scholar Aplotes is a superficial one, as its meaning, "simplicity," implies, but it allows him access to Penthea in the best Spartan tradition of the stolen tryst. When, however, she exclaims

> Go thou, fit only for disguise, and walks,
> To hide thy shame.
>
> (II.iii.117–118)

he is propelled toward a deeper subterfuge—that of appearing in his own person while counterfeiting his motives. She has unwittingly tutored him by her own claim that

> I can turn affection into vengeance;
>
> (II.iii.110)

The rest of Orgilus' movements consist of a search for his true enemy. Bassanes is the obvious target for his envy; but despite his bitter railing at

5. I am indebted to my former student, Barbara McEachron Hole, for a number of telling observations about Ford's structural use of his Spartan setting.

the old man, he never considers him as the source of his injury, a point to which I shall return. The logical source of his difficulty is Ithocles, who arranged his sister's marriage to aid his own political advancement. While maneuvering for position, however, Orgilus, like Vindice in *The Revenger's Tragedy,* grows captivated by his unsuspected histrionic ability. Always a master of rhetoric, he is never more brilliant than in his tests of Ithocles' credulity:

> O, my good lord, your favors flow towards
> A too unworthy worm. But as you please;
> I am what you will shape me.
>
> (III.iv.92–94)

Ithocles is almost too good an audience to lose. The trauma of Penthea's madness reactivates the circuit which converted frustrated passion into wrath, inspiring him to arrange a "new device," wherein

> Lord Ithocles and he himself are actors.
>
> (V.ii.5)

And, they are both just that—actors, for once his supposed enemy is dead, Orgilus discovers that the Spartan sense of honor he thought he had purged from his constitution revives, as he recognizes that he has destroyed a "fair spring of manhood"! (IV.iv.71) His stagy murder of Ithocles proves emotionally irrelevant. It utterly fails to satisfy him, and he cannot relinquish his role until he has successfully staged his own destruction. The conditioning he has undergone obliges him to "recognize," however dimly, that in killing this "spring of manhood" he has effectively struck at his basic self. The murder is a form of spiritual castration.

When confronted with Tecnicus' riddles, Orgilus had protested, "I am not Oedipus" (IV.i.141). But ironically he, like Oedipus, finds that his true enemy lies within. Although Orgilus implies a symbolic or subconscious awareness of this fact in choosing to die by letting his own blood, the source of his passion, there is no larger recognition. Publicly he is still convinced of the justice of his revenge and, characteristically, he treats his death as a legal penalty rather than as a resolution of incompatible tensions. Maintaining his heroic disguise, he takes full advantage of his final opportunity for stage-managing by acting out in meticulous detail, with all the appropriate verbal accessories, a suicide in the Stoic format. It is left to the audience to recognize the tragic nature of Orgilus' drive to narrow the terms of his life to the point where he destroys himself with apparent deliberation but with no clarifying vision:

> A mist hangs o'er mine eyes; the sun's bright splendor
> Is clouded in an everlasting shadow.

(V.ii.152–153)

Bassanes should be taken more seriously than he usually is, for in him the dramatist makes available an otherwise fragmented anatomization of Orgilus' mind. Bassanes is, in short, a kind of alter ego or reductive analogue to Orgilus. When he first appears, he is threatening to have a window dammed up in order to remove his wife from temptation, acting out projectively and literally the attempts of other Spartans to dam up uneducated passions. Like Orgilus', his language has a vital immediacy; it is filled with bestial and disease imagery, reflecting the ascendancy of envious passion in his mind. He resembles his rival also in that he idolizes Penthea, imagining her in celestial and sacred terms; yet he lacks a saving faith in the object of his adoration. Passions have made "a desperate wound" (III.ii.162) in his nature, leading him to counterfeit in public as, for example, in his ecstatic praise of the joys of marriage, punctuated by bitter asides about the faithlessness of woman (II.ii). Despite their extravagant love for Penthea, both Orgilus and Bassanes are too firmly imprisoned by their internal confusions to have any real sensitivity to her separate selfhood. In their minds, her virtues become pawns to prove their own merit, rather than qualities which make a woman good and beautiful.

As long as his private anguish is not brought into open conflict with received traditions, Bassanes can function adequately. But when his suspicions bring him into the public sphere, as they do when he bursts in upon Penthea and Ithocles, the consequences are sufficiently serious to stimulate a conversion. It is the force of public ridicule which most effectively acts upon the jealous husband:

> Rumor will voice me the contempt of manhood,
> Should I run on thus. Some way I must try
> To outdo art, and cry a jealousy.

(III.ii.204–206)

The pattern upon which Bassanes chooses to model his new character is, appropriately, one of Stoic moderation:

> No tempest of commotion shall disquiet
> The calms of my composure.
>
> (IV.ii.38–39)

This gives the playwright an opportunity to dramatize the inadequacy of such an ideal, for Penthea's madness, which immediately ensues, obviously requires deep concern: Stoic moderation here means moral blindness. Although the fear of ridicule from Orgilus remains with Bassanes, his composure gives way as he pathetically searches for "a help for nature" (V.i.8). The final frustration of Penthea's death, however, causes him to follow the example of his peers: since passion is unacceptable, and moderation impracticable, he defines his entire future by means of a vow:

> . . . I have seal'd a covenant with sadness,
> And enter'd into bonds without condition,
> To stand these tempests calmly. Mark me, nobles,
> I do not shed a tear, not for Penthea.
> Excellent misery!
>
> (V.ii.62–66)

In this histrionic ceremony of renunciation, Bassanes chooses to annul large areas of normal human sensitivity in order to render himself less vulnerable to the encroachments of remorseful passion.

Whereas Orgilus, Penthea, and Calantha have already traveled far on the path of self-deprivation before the action begins, Bassanes passes before our eyes from unassimilable passion to a Stoic conversion which, in practice, requires renunciation. He performs, then, two useful dramaturgical functions: that of exposing many of the qualities which Orgilus largely disguises in himself, and that of embodying in his personal development the general pattern of the action. His "plot" functions like the Gloucester subplot in *King Lear,* which by its comparative absence of heroic drive and by its grossness of structure assists the audience in understanding the subtler main action.

Ithocles and Calantha dramatize most obviously the Spartan assumptions under which all the characters operate. Ford uses the short scenes at court effectively, providing a framework for the whole play. He establishes the Spartan ideal very early, in the second scene of the first act. It is here that we are shown a warrior who is seen as "a star fixed," a model of moderation who is motivated only by a strong concept of duty. Calantha

gives Ithocles a victory wreath which, she says, is "Deserved, not pur-
chased," and he responds with the Spartan creed that all owe

> out of gratitude for life
> A debt of service, in what kind soever
> Safety or counsel of the commonwealth
> Requires, for payment.
>
> (I.ii.76–79)

The persistent use of commercial metaphors quickly qualifies the nature
of this apparently disinterested code. In fact, actions have become capital
in their eyes, and, for all his fine abstractions, Ithocles does expect to be
rewarded for his successful generalship.

Calantha is less a dramatic character than the aesthetic embodiment of
Spartan virtues. In her destruction lies the most simplified criticism of the
code of renunciation, for the fissure in her nature is a result of incom-
patibility between Spartan ideals and her irreducible womanhood. She
suppresses the stirrings of human emotion with almost complete success,
and it is fitting that her betrothal to Ithocles (which precedes her father's
gift of him to her) should take place off stage, in great secrecy. She
develops in the final act the full potential of the aesthetics of renunciation,
first by ordering her kingdom and then in the ritual expression of passion
in her symbolic marriage to the dead Ithocles. But the moment that her
womanly emotions are expressed verbally, she is destroyed. It is dramatically appropriate that she, the perfected Spartan, the one most nearly
able to live under the rule of abstractions, should die without the assist-
ance of any empirical agency. While Calantha is the only character who
dies with a full recognition of what it is that destroys her, even she does
not question the basic premises which cause the fatal division in her
nature, a division which is literalized in the controlling image of the
broken heart.

In the world of *The Broken Heart,* the characters are doomed by
tragically narrow, nonorganic identifications of their own natures; thus,
Orgilus comes to see himself as an avenger, Penthea plays the role of a
wronged woman, and Calantha is nothing if not a Spartan. They are
forced to preserve the validity of their choices by stabilizing their roles in
death. For them, death is not merely passive suffering. In a culture where
renunciation is a fully structured ethic, death is a public *action,* deliberately organized to provide an opportunity for demonstrating one's heroic

stature. Even the mad Penthea arranges to die sitting in a chair, behind the ritual privacy of a veil, surrounded by women who provide an appropriate musical accompaniment.

The Broken Heart builds up its quiet but nearly unbearable tension from the fact that, in its world of stylized manners and repressed feelings, all the characters are "guessing about" each other; they use their energies to determine to what degree their fixed notions about the world are confirmed by the cues they seek to read in others' behavior. The play is an inquest into the resources of the self, and, because of the beleaguered egotism of the principal characters, they are (in the phrase from Eliot's "The Waste Land" I have used as an epigraph) always "thinking of the key" which is to release them from their prison of shame, or ambition, or grief, or deprivation, and, thus thinking, "each confirms a prison."

III

The Broken Heart is a "tragedy of manners." This is more than a play on words. No play in the English Renaissance canon is more preoccupied with specific problems of behavior, with social codes, with how one should act. Nowhere is there the same degree of attention to the problems of constructing and maintaining one's persona, nor the same obsessive regard for the direction and control of the self. In consequence, the characters of the play often divide themselves inwardly into that part which directs and that part which acts. Sanctions for behavioral choices are specified, evaluations are made of the resulting presentation of self. The play is unlike any other of the period in this almost relentless concern. And this is not all. A number of sequences are devoted to the kind of direct commentary on etiquette which we normally associate with comedy —*The Broken Heart* even concludes with a "proviso" scene, an element virtually obligatory in manners comedy in its mature Restoration form. It could be said that Ford's endeavor is to raise maxims of social prudence to the level of commanding moral obligations. In doing this the play is very much in tune with the intellectual climate of the mid-seventeenth century. The dominant monument to this concern is Hobbes's *Leviathan* which is only the most searching of numerous efforts to derive a philosophy of obligation or, more technically, a deontology which provides a

unitary theory of obedience and duty. In common language, Hobbes—
and, I believe, Ford along with others—set out to answer the questions:
to whom must man listen? (for "obedience" is radically a form of responsible "hearing"), and how, in consequence, ought he to behave? Few
tragedies are concerned with prescribing behavior; instead most explore
the eccentric ramifications of personality or work negatively to show
behavior that is dysfunctional no matter how glamorously it is embodied.
The Broken Heart—surely one of the least comical of plays—subscribes
to a philosophy of manners, endorses a theory of obedience, and subsides
finally into a condition of social entropy in which none of the major
characters has an iota of latitude in the face of his vision of duty. *The
Broken Heart* is a deontological argument; it is a tragedy of manners.

In the cursus of modern literature, perhaps, Henry James's late novels
and particularly *The Wings of the Dove* best exemplify the ethical pre-
suppositions and moral imperatives of "the tragedy of manners," though
Ibsen's later plays—*Hedda Gabler* or *Little Eyolf*, for example—could
serve equally well. What are the distinguishing characteristics of this
mode? First, the principals have already suffered the losses which pre-
scribe their goals before the action begins. The past confiscates the present
and denies normal evolutionary options to the principals. Self-reverence
(variously called honor, fidelity, pride, principle, etc.) displaces centrifugal
emotions. In the "tragedy of manners" no one "learns" anything, no new
choices are made, no one "falls" in love, though many are shackled to old
loves. We watch a world of characters who are sadder to be sure but not
wiser. The limits of ethical value shrink to obedience to past imperatives.
Suicide is the common denominator. The loci of allegiance are beyond
the physical and temporal precincts of each characters' realm of confidence. The mood is one of renunciation which becomes a positive virtue.
Renunciation comprises not merely silent surrender of what one wanted
or wants, but the destruction of anyone who might arguably gain possession of what one cannot have one's self. Thus the dark motor of the
"tragedy of manners" is jealousy, and this may be presented in many
guises. Logical derivatives of this circumambient jealousy, arbitrary
prohibitions and negative sanctions, replace positive ones. As a result—
and this gives the "tragedy of manners" its peculiar tone—virtue depends
upon how one behaves in losing and how one interprets his carefully
composed behavior more than in what, judged by positive standards, he

has done to others. Thus *Othello* is the nearest to a "tragedy of manners" in the Shakespearean canon: not only in its "An honorable murderer if you will," but in its understanding of the displacing power of jealousy, so that we sense the play in two irreconcilable manifolds of judgment: the wholly "wrong" construction of events that rises in Othello's mind and finally becomes coterminous with it, and the empirical procession of events which this displaces. The power of *Othello* depends upon our capacity to preserve both constructions in ironic parallel. We see Othello made victim to his less than adequate but not unshapely notion of how he is obliged to behave in the face of what he "knows." Without Othello's reverence for his duty, his priestly decorum or more flatly his "good manners," the play would become sordid and unbearable. Othello's savage treatment of Desdemona in the "brothel scene" is doubly shocking, because it is enacted against a background of stately, somnambulistic acceptance of mannerly duty. The murder is also an act of renunciation, as Othello's large, anterior delight in possessing Desdemona requires. But *Othello,* though no tidy parable of damnation, is thrown up against what is at least a memory of God's jurisdiction, and the oppositions of dark and light are clear and firm enough to leave the play near the center of our normal, constitutive ethic. *The Broken Heart* is not like this. In this beautifully sustained play an unassimilable theory of happiness maintains a fugitive existence within a format of repression severe and efficacious enough to make a blighting and blighted Sparta the inevitable symbolic setting for the play's action. This "tragedy of manners" is the resultant of these unusual intersections of belief in the divided consciousness of its author.

"Actors" and "Play Acting" in the Morality Tradition

ANN WIERUM

T HE MEDIEVAL ALLEGORY of the Psychomachia, or war between good and evil in man's soul, is most characteristically presented in the Tudor morality plays as a theatrical plot of deception. Vice masquerading as virtue tempts Mankind by sophistical argument into believing that evil is good. Like all archetypes, the play-acting metaphor reflects simultaneously a religious (or mythological) and a simple but profound psychological truth. Theologically it is of course rooted in the idea of Satan, the Protean archdeceiver. Lucifer in *Wisdom Who Is Christ* (1450–1500),[1] the earliest morality to make use of physical disguise, demonstrates in its archetypal dramatic form the reason why "the devil hath power / To assume a pleasing shape." Wearing a devil's dress over the costume of a "gallant," he explains in stark terms the purpose behind his subsequent disguising:

1. Approximate dates of composition for this and all other moralities cited are taken from Alfred Harbage, *Annals of English Drama 975–1700*, rev. S. Schoenbaum (London, 1964).

189

> . . . to tempte man in my lyknes,
> yt wolde brynge hym to grett feerfullness,
> I wyll change me in-to bryghtnes,
>   & so hym to be-gy [le],
> Sen I xall schew hym perfyghtnes,
> And wertu provyt yt wykkydnes;
> Thus wndyr colors all thynge perverse;
>   I xall neuer rest tyll the soule I defyle. [2]

(ll. 373–380)

(Even here one may note the association of "bryghtnes" and "colors" with disguised evil, a theme reiterated in many later plays.) Lucifer then removes the devil's array he has worn to lecture the audience and reappears as a "goodly galont" to his victims.

Psychologically speaking, however, deception is impossible unless the victim is ready to deceive himself; and the play-acting metaphor describes both situations equally well. Man, endowed with free will, nonetheless seldom chooses evil with full consciousness but seeks ways to "rationalize" his wrongdoings and to dress them in a more palatable name and guise. The vice Pride in *Nature,* who takes the euphemistic alias of "Worship"; Wrath, who "putteth on the coate of Manlynesse" (*The Life and Repentance of Mary Magdalene*); Covetous in *Enough is as Good as a Feast,* who disguises himself as "Policy" complete with respectable garment: these vices, and many more, naturally employ the actor's basic tools in order to enact the double-edged allegory.

But just as stage name and costume are only the beginning for the actor, so the morality masquerade often extends beyond these rudimentary devices. In his most effective role as tempter and psychological persuader, the Vice must excel as performing "actor." He must be able to assume a false face or "mask" of affection, grief, kindliness, piety, respectability, simplicity, honesty, or "innocent merriment" as occasion

---

2. *Wisdom Who Is Christ,* or *Mind, Will, and Understanding,* in *The Macro Plays,* ed. F. J. Furnivall and Alfred W. Pollard, EETS (London, 1904).

In quoting from the morality plays, I have expanded contractions and have substituted *th* for the thorn and *y* for ʒ. In quoting passages of dialogue, I have standardized the position and spelling of speech prefixes. I have also modernized the spelling of play titles and of most character names, except within quoted material.

demands; and he often describes his own talents in theatrical terms. "To hold all thynges vp, I play my part now & than" (*King John,* 1538–ca. 1562); "he can playe too partes the foole and the K. [knave]" (*The Conflict of Conscience,* ca. 1572); ". . . now will I goe playe will sommer agayne" (*Misogonus,* ca. 1570). "Farewel my masters our partes we haue playd," says Covetous at the end of *Enough is as Good as a Feast* (ca. 1560); and he has indeed played his part superbly, for he has sent his victim to Hell.[3]

From these basic theatrical motifs, certain repeated patterns emerge which it will be the purpose of this paper to examine. Several critics have discussed the Vice as "actor," particularly in connection with the influence of morality themes on Shakespeare's treatment of villainy and false appearances. But in each case the emphasis is on the later drama, and the play-acting theme in the moralities has not been the primary topic. The major contribution is Bernard Spivack's *Shakespeare and the Allegory of Evil,* which traces the emergence and history of the Vice, the development of the morality intrigue plot, and the Vice's "hybrid" image in Iago and other Elizabethan stage villains. Spivack also draws attention to the play-acting connotations of the Vice's false name, false garment, and false face.[4] But his primary concern with the allegorical motives of " 'motiveless malignity' " prevents a detailed examination of certain broader "theatrical" and social connotations of the Vice's false role, to be discussed later. Anne Righter and Sidney Thomas discuss more briefly the association of Vice and "actor" as background to Shakespearean themes, although these critics seem to stress the secular and comic aspects of the

3. John Bale, *King John,* ed. J. H. P. Pafford and W. W. Greg, Malone Society Reprints (Oxford, 1931), l. 676; Nathaniel Woodes, *The Conflict of Conscience,* Malone Society Reprints (Oxford, 1952), l. 391; "Laurentius Barjona," *Misogonus,* in *Early Plays from the Italian,* ed. R. W. Bond (Oxford, 1911), II.iii.79; W. Wager, *Enough is as Good as a Feast,* Henry E. Huntington Facsimile Reprints (San Marino, Calif., 1920), sig. G⸵. These plays contain many such theatrical references, of which those quoted are only a few examples.

Future quotations from these plays will be from the above texts.

4. *Shakespeare and the Allegory of Evil: The History of a Metaphor in Relation to His Major Villains* (New York, 1958); see esp. pp. 151–205. This study is greatly indebted to Spivack's work for its discussion of conventions associated with the Vice.

All references to Spivack will be to the above work.

Vice rather than his allegorical significance.[5] Anne Righter describes the
consistent use of self-consciously theatrical references in the speech of the
later vices, but she relates this theme to the nature of theatrical illusion
rather than to the special function of play acting in the morality tradition.
Two studies of the use of disguise in Elizabethan drama take note of the
morality influence in its comic and tragic dimensions. Victor O. Freeburg
discusses the morality background of the comic Elizabethan "rogue in
multi-disguise."[6] Defining disguise in its larger sense of assumed personality, M. C. Bradbrook points out that it is the archetypal "disguise of
the serpent" in the moralities which "lends such strength to Shakespeare's
concept of the false appearance or *seeming*."[7]

By recognizing the dramatic vitality of the Vice as "actor" or disguiser
and the importance of this theme in Elizabethan drama, all of these
studies thus provide a needed counterbalance to earlier critical condemna-
tions of the morality plays as "poor and thin," "unprogressive," "mori-
bund," possessed of "the aridity and mortal dullness proper to merely
transitional and abortive products."[8] Yet there would seem to be room
for a more detailed examination of the theatrical metaphor in the moralities themselves, taking the above works as a point of departure. The
central allegory of evil as masquerade leads frequently to short and extended play-acting scenes in which the Vice "rehearses" and demonstrates
as well as describes the "acting" abilities linked with his metaphorical
masks. In some cases, the traditional sequence of conspiracy (or "rehearsal"), followed by the skillfully "acted" temptation scene, takes on
the aura of a rudimentary play-within-a-play. As the moralities become
more secular in content, the Vices often practice the more literal social

5. Anne Righter, *Shakespeare and the Idea of the Play* (London, 1962), pp. 68–
73, 95–100; Sidney Thomas, *The Antic Hamlet and Richard III* (New York, 1943),
pp. 11–32 and *passim*.

6. *Disguise Plots in Elizabethan Drama* (New York, 1915), pp. 121–137.

7. "Shakespeare and the Use of Disguise in Elizabethan Drama," *EIC*, II (1952),
160–161.

8. C. F. Tucker Brooke, *The Tudor Drama* (Boston, Mass., 1911), pp. 48, 110–
111, and *passim;* John A. Symonds, *Shakspere's Predecessors in the English Drama*,
rev. ed. (London, 1900), p. 118. For similar opinions, see Katharine Lee Bates, *The
English Religious Drama* (New York and London, 1893), pp. 201–203; Charles W.
Wallace, *The Evolution of the English Drama up to Shakespeare* (Berlin, 1912),
p. 86.

frauds of the flattering courtier, social upstart, coneycatcher, and other natural-born "actors" who at the same time take added dramatic dimension from their allegorical roots. Although the following discussion does not aim at exhaustive coverage of so large a theme, a roughly chronological examination of some individual "actors" and play-acting scenes may throw some further light on the nature of the morality tradition.

It will be noted that the deliberately theatrical speeches cited earlier seem to be a relatively late development in the morality genre. Anne Righter argues that the disguise motif does not appear until the moralities have taken on a more secular aspect during the sixteenth century.[9] This statement ignores the theological background of disguise exemplified by the figure of Lucifer in *Wisdom,* although admittedly his disguising does not go much beyond the strictly symbolic change of garment. But if we adopt M. C. Bradbrook's definition of disguise as assumed personality, we may look to another fifteenth-century play for the dramatic archetype of the Vice as performing "actor." *The Castle of Perseverance* (1405–1425) is dramatically unique in presenting the Psychomachia as epic warfare, the form originally used by Prudentius in his fourth-century allegorical poem of *The Psychomachia.* But even here, deception wins where open assault has failed. Prudentius makes this point in two minor episodes where vice disguises itself as virtue; but deception is far more interesting dramatically if Mankind himself is the victim.[10] In *Perseverance,* after Mankind's army of virtues has repulsed the open attack of vice, his "old friend" Covetise is sent to lure him from the safety of his castle:

> Cum & speke with thi best frende,
> Syr Coueytyse! thou knowyst me of olde.
>
> . . . .
>
> how, Mankynde! I thee say,
> com to Coueytyse, I thee prey;
>
> . . . .

9. Righter, *Idea of the Play,* p. 69.

10. Mankind does not appear in Prudentius' poem. Hardin Craig, *English Religious Drama of the Middle Ages* (Oxford, 1955), pp. 352–353, notes that the Continental medieval moralities (if one excepts the debatable case of *Everyman-Elckerlijc*) also contain no central Mankind hero. By contrast, it would thus seem that the English moralities contained from the beginning a greater dramatic potential.

Coueytyse is a frend ryth fre,
thi sorwe, man, to slake & ses.[11]

(ll. 2430–2474)

Although Covetise does not change his name or garment, one can with a
little imagination hear and picture his wheedling accents and winning
smile as he acts out the Vice's most typical false role of affectionate
friendship.

The necessity for the reader to "make imaginary puissance" of such
scenes is so important both to the following discussion and to a general
understanding of the moralities, that a brief digression seems warranted
here. Most moralities take a good deal of perseverance to read. Written
in a period when English prosody was for the most part in a season of
doldrums and uncertainty, they can rarely be read for their poetry alone.
Allegorical character names set up a further barrier although, as Arnold
Williams suggests, the spectator would be less blinded by them than the
reader who is constantly confronted with allegorical speech prefixes on the
printed page.[12] They are in fact plays for acting. Richard Southern in his
reconstruction of staging and stage action in *The Castle of Perseverance*
demonstrates convincingly that even this lengthy play would "go" as
live theater.[13] In his study of Tudor stage conventions, T. W. Craik
constantly reminds us that the Tudor plays "were far more effective
when acted than we can guess when we merely read them. . . . so much
of the meaning . . . is conveyed by the significant use of action and
costume that unless this is borne in mind they cannot be appreciated or
even properly understood." [14] By applying these precepts to the thematic
and structural use of the play-acting metaphor, one can more clearly
visualize its dramatic effectiveness. The actor playing the part of an
"actor" must be doubly interesting to his audience. The traditional disguise of evil, presented most elementally in *Wisdom* and *Perseverance*,

11. *The Castle of Perseverance,* in *Macro Plays,* EETS.

12. "The English Moral Play before 1500," *Annuale Medievale,* IV (1963), 18.
This comment refers specifically to *Mankind* but could readily be applied to many
other moralities.

13. *The Medieval Theatre in the Round: A Study of the Staging of "The Castle
of Perseverance" and Related Matters* (London, 1957); see esp. pp. 145–216.

14. *The Tudor Interlude: Stage, Costume, and Acting* (Leicester, 1958), p. 2.

contains an inherent potentiality for "theatrical" elaboration which would achieve its strongest impact in actual stage performances.

Within any traditional genre, individual authors may exploit its conventions more or less dynamically according to their own skill and artistry. It is therefore not surprising that among the extant plays the earliest imaginative expansions of the theatrical metaphor appear in *Nature* (ca. 1495) by Henry Medwall and *Magnificence* (ca. 1515) by John Skelton, both educated literary men known for their artistic originality in other works.[15] Medwall's euphemistic aliases for the Seven Deadly Sins represent the first functional dramatic use of this convention.[16] Skelton's Cloaked Collusion ("Sober Sadness") is the first after Lucifer in *Wisdom* to adopt a physical disguise, although the same allegorical meaning lies behind the devices of the devil Titivillus in *Mankind* (1465–1470), who makes himself invisible and tempts the hero with false dreams. More important, although in terms of Spivack's study the figure of the leading Vice as chief intriguer and literal star actor has not yet emerged, both authors make dynamic use of the character's "acting" capacity.

Among the array of Deadly Sins and worldly intriguers in *Nature,* who tempt Man from his initial innocence, Pride ("Worship") is the most skilled "actor": a position equally fitting for his allegorical status as the Cardinal Sin and his social status as flashily dressed "gallant" and counterfeit gentleman who boasts that his father is a knight and his mother "callyd madame." He describes in detail his fashionable garments: a scarlet cloak, laced doublet with satin stomacher, and short gown with wide sleeves. His role as social upstart is also revealed in an interesting colloquy with Sensuality: "Syr I vnderstand that this gentylman is borne to great fortunes and intendeth to inhabyt herein the contrary. And I am

15. Skelton's reputation needs no defense. Medwall is known to have written one other play, *Fulgens and Lucrece,* notable as the first extant secular drama in English. He may also have written a "lost" morality entitled *The Finding of Truth,* although since the source of information is John Payne Collier, it cannot be regarded as highly reliable (see Spivack, notes, pp. 472–473).

16. Pride becomes "Worship"; Envy, "Disdain"; Wrath, "Manhood"; Covetousness, "Worldly Policy"; Gluttony, "Good Fellowship"; Lechery, "Lust"; and Sloth, "Ease." The false-naming device, as Spivack has documented its use (pp. 155–160), is almost universal in the sixteenth-century moralities.

a gentylman that alway hath be brought vp wyth great estatys and affeed
wyth them and yf I myght be in lyke fauour wyth this gentylman I wold
be glad therof and do you a pleasure" (Pt. I, following l. 836).[17] This
speech gives a vivid impression of the spurious gentleman attaching himself to the household of a rich young man newly arrived in London.

It also sets the stage for the little "drama" in which Sensuality earns his
bribe by insinuating Pride into Man's service. While the newcomer
lingers modestly in the background, Sensuality begs leave to introduce
him:

> Syr yf yt please you here ys come a straunger
> That neuer was aquaynted wyth you ere
> Somwhat shamefast and halfe in fere
>
> (Pt. I, ll. 895–897)

His pride touched, Man graciously assents. Pride apologizes for his
"trespace," adding that he but wished to see for himself the man whom
all were praising so highly, and now he could see that they told no lies.
"But ye may say that I am bold" (Pt. I, l. 935). Overwhelmed with
pride, Man protests that he is worth his weight in gold and begs to employ him as his valued advisor, although his chief counselor Reason must
be "fyrst in auctoryte." Alarmed at such backsliding, Pride exerts all his
"acting" skill in registering disappointment in his new friend's character:

> PRIDE
>
> Alas alas man ye be mad
> I se well ye be but a very lad
> On my fayth I was very glad
> Of your fyrst acquayntaunce
> And now I forthynk yt vtterly
>
> . . . .
>
> MAN
>
> Wurshyp for goddys sake greue ye not
>
> (Pt. I, ll. 987–1003)

Thus softened, Man is now forced to agree that Reason is but a "karle"
and a "straw" who is forever ordering him about and never lets him

17. Henry Medwall, *Nature*, in *Quellen des weltlichen Dramas in England vor
Shakespeare*, ed. Alois Brandl (Strassburg, 1898).

The figures of New-Gyse in *Mankind*, Courtly Abusion in *Magnificence*, and
Nichol Newfangle in Ulpian Fulwell's *Like Will to Like* are three further examples of the vice as fashionably dressed social upstart.

alone; and soon afterwards, in a tavern brawl vividly described but unfortunately not enacted, he banishes his interfering counselor altogether. Later, when Man has repented of his first downfall and (temporarily) returned to Reason, Sensuality employs the same "acting" technique as he rebukes the hero for deserting his old comrades the Seven Deadly Sins:

[*Then he wepyth*]

MAN

Why wepe ye so

SENSUALITY

Let me alone
It wyll none other wyse be
and ye saw the sorowfull countenaunce
Of my cumpany your old acquayntaunce
that they make
For your sake
I dare say ye wold mone theym in your mynde
They be so louyng and so kynde

(Pt. II, ll. 81–90)

The Vice's ability to produce instant hypocritical tears in pretense of grief or affection for his victim is one of his outstanding attributes.[18] These carefully matched scenes from a relatively early play suggest the author's recognition of its theatrical effectiveness.

Although the estate of Man in *Nature* is too generalized to be clearly identified as a court setting, Pride has all the attributes of the Vice as flattering courtier who makes his first formal appearance in *Magnificence*. Medwall as chaplain to Henry VII's Cardinal Morton and Skelton as tutor to the young Henry VIII would both have had ample opportunity to observe courtly intrigue, and they could hardly have ignored its play-acting qualities. Sir Thomas Elyot, another shrewd observer of the Tudor court, continually stresses the flatterer's skill as "actor":

Of this peruerse and cursed people be sondry kyndes, some which apparauntly do flatter, praysinge and extollinge euery thinge that is done by their superior. . . . And if they perceyue any parte of their tale misstrusted, than they sette furthe sodaynly an heuie and sorowfull countenaunce, as if they were abiecte and brought in to extreme desperation. . . . Semblably

18. Spivack (pp. 161–163) notes the frequent use of this device as a standard motif.

there be some that by dissimulation can ostent or shewe a highe grauitie, mixte with a sturdy entretaynement and facion . . . naminge them selfes therfore playne men. . . . And in this wyse pytchinge their nette of adulation they intrappe the noble and vertuous harte, which onely beholdeth their fayned seueritie and counterfayte wisedome. . . .[19]

From the "sorowfull countenaunce" of Man's temporarily deserted companions in *Nature* to the "Sober Sadness" of Cloaked Collusion to "Honest Iago, that look'st dead with grieving," Elyot perfectly describes the false face of the flattering Vice. Man, the Prince Magnificence, and the princely born Othello may each, in his initial innocence, be described as a "noble and vertuous harte."

Elyot's lines hint at the deadly purpose behind the disguising of evil. But in the moralities its introduction often takes a comic turn. In *Magnificence,* when the courtier-vice Cloaked Collusion first enters, his fellow conspirators mock at him and pretend not to recognize him because he is dressed in priest's robes. Counterfeit Countenance provokes his wrath by calling him "syr Iohn double cloke" (sig. B4ᵛ).[20] "Sir John" is of course the contemptuous term for the illiterate, roistering village priest mocked by Catholics and Protestants alike in a wide range of Tudor plays. This lively interlude of satirical comedy is a long way from the stark symbolic disguising of Lucifer in *Wisdom,* but the more sinister aspects of "Sober Sadness' " guise of piety soon emerge. The immediate object of his intrigue is the Prince's counselor Measure who (like Reason in *Nature*) must be banished before the vices can achieve their ends. In a complex and powerful scene of false piety, almost amounting to a play-within-a-play, Cloaked Collusion brings about the banishment of Measure while pretending to intercede for him. By separating himself both from good counsel and from the allegorical better part of his nature, Magnificence thus consents to his own downfall which leads him to despair and attempted suicide— the ultimate sin of pride in Catholic theology.

The scene is carefully prepared. The court fool Fancy paves the way, as is proposed by Crafty Conveyance:

> what and I frame suche a slyght
> That fansy with his fonde consayte

19. *The Boke Named the Governour* (1531), ed. Foster Watson (New York and London, 1907), pp. 190–193.
20. John Skelton, *Magnificence,* Tudor Facsimile Texts (Oxford, 1910).

Put magnyfycence in suche a madnesse
That he shall haue you in the stede of sadnesse [i.e., Measure]
And sober sadness shalbe your name

(sig. C')

Cloaked Collusion tells the audience what to expect as he boasts of his skill as "actor" and psychologist:

I can dyssemble I can bothe laughe and grone

. . . .

whan other men laughe than study I and muse
Deuysynge the meanes and wayes that I can
Howe I may hurte and hynder euery man

. . . .

Paynte to a purpose good countenaunce I can.
And craftely can I grope howe euery man is mynded.

(sig. C'–C')

The actual scene in which Measure falls from favor is only reported; but it would seem that he has been provoked into a quarrel with Crafty Conveyance and Fancy (". . . they fell a-chydynge . . . by a praty slyght," sig. C3') and will soon be deposed altogether.

   When Magnificence next appears on stage his mind is already corrupted, and "Sober Sadness" in his pretended intercession does not need further to deceive him. The Vice's primary dupe in this scene is Measure himself, for whom he enacts an extended "play" of the grieving friend. Cleverly stationing his "audience" at a safe distance, he kneels before the Prince in a show of pious humility:

Please it your grace at the contemplacyon
Of my pore instance and supplycacyon
Tenderly to consyder in your aduertence
Of our blessyd lorde syr at the reuerence
Remembre the good seruyce that mesure hath you done
And that ye wyll not cast hym away so sone

[sig. E3'–E3']

Speaking aside, he readily admits that he is only pretending to intercede in order to collect his bribe; and Magnificence, in his corrupted state, applauds his cleverness and reluctantly agrees to let Measure approach him. While Cloaked Collusion goes to fetch him, Courtly Abusion praises his colleague as a "wyse man," and the irony of the Prince's reply would

not be lost on the audience: "An honest person I tell you and a sad."
Even more ironic is the exchange between Cloaked Collusion and
Measure:

> CLOAKED COLLUSION
> By the masse I haue done that I can
> And more than euer I dyd for ony man
> I trowe ye herde yourselfe what I sayd
>
> MEASURE
> Nay in dede but I sawe howe ye prayed
> And made instance for me be lykelyhod
>
> . . . .
> The holy goost be with your grace
>
> [sig. E4ʳ]

Measure then attempts to plead his own case but his efforts only arouse
the Prince's wrath, and he is banished out of hand.

Magnificence then falls into a violent and helpless fit of rage and is
physically ill, while "Sober Sadness" ministers to him and holds his head.

The once-trusted officer provoked into a brawl which leads to his
banishment; his replacement by the vice figure; the pretended intercession; the fit of rage: the parallel to Iago's role in procuring the banishment of Cassio, if not exact in all details, is nonetheless striking, although
curiously enough no critic has noted the connection with this particular
episode.[21] Iago himself sums up the theological purpose behind such a
play-acting scene:

> When devils will their blackest sins put on,
> They do suggest at first with heavenly shows,
> As I do now . . .
>
> (*Othello*, II.iii.340–342)

As Spivack demonstrates throughout his work, these lines may be said
to epitomize Iago's morality heritage. But such imagery in Shakespeare
is not restricted to descendants of the Vice. Polonius unwittingly makes
the same point:

---

21. Spivack does, of course, discuss Cloaked Collusion as a typical vice and notes
the importance of the banishment of Measure (pp. 153, 161–162, 193, 383). Thomas
L. Watson, "The Detractor-Backbiter: Iago and the Tradition," *TSLL,* V (1964),
546–554, discusses the general similarity of Iago, Cloaked Collusion, and other vices
as slanderers but does not note the specific parallel.

> . . . that with devotion's visage
> And pious action we do sugar o'er
> The devil himself.
>
> (*Hamlet*, III.i.46-48)

Medwall, Skelton, Elyot, and Shakespeare all present in various modes the theme of courtly intrigue and corruption hidden beneath a fair appearance. To the Tudor audience, the man who corrupts a prince or a person of high rank would seem to strike at the heart of their society; and their vital social concern with this theme would gain added urgency from its religious implications.

The application of morality themes to affairs of state takes an interesting new turn in two "estates moralities" written in polemical support of the Reformation. *A Satire of the Three Estates* (1540-1554) by Sir David Lindsay treats events of the Reformation in Scotland. In *King John,* John Bale takes the revolutionary step of applying the Psychomachia plot to historical chronicle. The vices are corrupt priests and friars as well as flattering courtiers, roles which were often combined in the court life of the time. Charges of fraud, avarice, and lechery, hidden beneath the sanctimonious cloak of clerical garments, form a major preoccupation (at times amounting to an obsession) of Reformation propagandists.[22] Sedition, the leading Vice of *King John,* sums up the matter in a long speech full of deliberately theatrical references in which he reels off a comprehensive survey of Catholic orders and vestments:

> In euery estate, of the clargye, I playe a part
> sumtyme I can be, a monke in a long syd cowle
> sumtyme I can be, a none & loke lyke an owle
>
> . . . .
>
> sumtyme I can playe, the whyght monke, sumtyme the fryer
> the purgatory prist, & euery mans wyffe desyer
>
> . . . .
>
> yea sumtyme a pope, & than am I lord [of] ouer all
>
> (ll. 196-210)

But Sedition's role as "actor" is on the whole more verbal than organic. The monk Dissimulation who calls himself Simon of Swinsett ("Monasti-

---

22. Rainer Pineas, "The English Morality Play as a Weapon of Religious Controversy," *SEL*, II (1962), 166, argues that a major purpose of these playwright-propagandists was to expose the deceptive nature of Catholicism to their audiences.

cal Devotion" in an earlier version) [23] is a more accomplished performer. In his plot to poison the King, he naturally approaches his victim under a guise of piety; and the following exchange between the monk, the King, and the "widow" England carefully stresses the falsity of his "seeming":

KING

Who is that Englande, I praye the stepp fourth [sic] and see

ENGLAND

He doth seme a farre, some relygyouse man to be

DISSIMULATION

Now Iesus preserue, your worthye and excellent grace
for doubtlesse there is, a very Angelyck face

· · · · · · · · · · · · · ·

KING

A louynge [gentle] persone, thu mayest seme for to be

(ll. 2044–2051)

The scene which follows builds up considerable tension and ironic force as Dissimulation presses the poisoned cup on the King under a guise of kindly concern for his weariness and thirst, tries at first to evade John's request that he drink half as a toast to him, then accedes and dies a "martyr's" death along with his victim.

In *A Satire of the Three Estates,* Lindsay turns the topical attack on the false-seeming of clerical garments into an extended comic "rehearsal" sequence in which the vices Flatterie, Falset, and Dissait assume clerical disguises and take the names of "Devotion," "Sapience," and "Discretion." The lively mock-baptism scene in which they change their names presents obvious play-acting possibilities in its parody of Catholic ritual. The change of garments, in which the Vices apparently receive their disguises from a confederate in the audience, involves a dynamic interplay between actors and spectators. Flatterie begs for the loan of "Clarkis cleathing" and a "portouns" (portable breviary), while Falset appeals to "sum gude

23. In a cancelled addition to the A text of the manuscript in the Malone Society edition, the monk introduces himself under the allegorical alias (l. 146 of addition following l. 1682). But in the final B version, he uses the historical name, retaining the other only as an epithet: "Simon of Swynsett, my very name is per dee / I am taken of men, for monastycall deuocyon" (ll. 2054–2055). This is a fascinating example of the open fusion of allegory and realism in the false-naming convention which reaches its dramatic perfection in the epithet of "honest Iago."

fallow" to lend him a hood (ll. 722–770).[24] Dissait struts and poses in his new costume; and the suggestion of the actor rehearsing his role is reinforced by the theatrical term "buskit" (or "dressed for a part"):

> Now am I buskit and quha can spy,
> The Deuill stik me, gif this be I?
> If this be I, or not, I can not weill say,
> Or hes the Feind or Farie-folk borne me away?
>
> (ll. 729–732)

The stage is now set for their introduction to Rex Humanitas. But perhaps inevitably, the author discovers the comic possibilities inherent in making the blundering "actors" forget their parts. The rudiments of this device may be seen briefly in *Nature,* when Sloth rebukes Pride for calling him by his true name but then relents and says the alias is only necessary when Man is present. Avarice ("Policy"), the leading Vice of *Respublica* (1553), is more of a perfectionist and shows himself as a Stanislavsky-like "actor-manager" when he tries to make his subordinates use their stage names even among themselves. Throughout their subsequent duping of the Lady Respublica, Avarice's concern for the blunders of his fellow conspirators who frequently slip out of their roles, lends a strong impression that he is metaphorically stage-managing a play-within-a-play. In *Magnificence,* Counterfeit Countenance almost gives the show away by entering before his "cue" and calling Fancy by name while the latter frantically motions him to silence. Fancy evades suspicion by a piece of fast talking and later curses him for his stupidity. Lindsay in *A Satire* extends the comic possibilities even further. Falset forgets his alias when presented to the King and stands tongue-tied, while Dissait in a sharp aside rebukes him for being "not weill-wittit." Flatterie is finally forced to make the introduction himself. When the King asks "Sapience" why he could not have told his own name, he adds an ingenious touch to his characterization:

> I am sa full of Sapience,
> That sumtyme I will take ane trance:

24. *A Satire of the Three Estates,* in *The Works of Sir David Lindsay,* ed. D. Hamer, Scottish Text Society (Edinburgh, 1931–1936), Vol. II. All quotations are from Version III in this text.

> My spreit wes reft fra my bodie,
> Now heich abone the Trinitie.
>
> (ll. 864–867)

Lindsay economically combines a comic interval with a satirical stab at monkish mystical trances.

As in the scene already discussed in *Magnificence,* the initial effect of the disguising of evil seems purely comic. But its darker implications are made clear in the ironic welcoming words of the King whose downfall is the object of the comedy:

> Ye ar welcum gude freind [i]s be the Rude:
> Appeirandlie ye seime sum men of gude.
>
> .   .   .   .
>
> Ye ar richt welcum be the Rude,
> Ye seime to be thrie men of gude.
>
> (ll. 841–927)

Like Bale, Lindsay carefully stresses Man's capacity to be gulled by outward "seeming": a matter of particular urgency when the gull is also a king. In the long sequence which follows, the three Vices support one another in a more tragic vein as they play out their carefully prepared roles as "men of gude." As in *Magnificence,* the result is the slandering of the King's virtuous counselors and (temporary) disaster for his kingdom.

The theme of human gullibility moves to a lower social level in two popular plays of the mid-century: the anonymous *Impatient Poverty* (ca. 1547) and *Lusty Juventus* (ca. 1550) by R. Wever. In both these plays the figure of the leading Vice is well developed; and his chief "acting" talent lies in the ingenious maneuvers by which he works his way into the acquaintance of his dupe. As in the earlier plays, the object of the intrigue is to separate the hero from his virtuous counselor and thus prepare for his downfall. But another object, most strongly emphasized in *Impatient Poverty* although it also appears in earlier moralities, is to bring him to a state of desperation and despair by fleecing him of his money. The Vice's relationship with his victim is therefore that of coneycatcher to his gull: a relationship always inherent in the morality situation but in these two plays additionally linked with the social theme of gambling.

Like the flattering courtier and the corrupt cleric, the coneycatcher must excel as "actor" in the sense that he may deliberately assume a false role or personality. Thomas Harman in his coneycatching pamphlet, *A Caveat for Common Cursitors,* not infrequently describes the rogue in terms of his skill at impersonation. An object of his special horror, whom he favors with several woodcuts as well as two strikingly inept poems, is one Nicolas Jennings, a "counterfet cranke" (or beggar who feigns epilepsy) who is also a master at several other disguises. The first of these poems, accompanying a woodcut showing Nicolas in two of his roles, is worth quoting in full:

> These two pyctures, lyuely set out,
> One bodye and soule, god send him more grace.
> This mounstrous desembelar, a Cranke all about.
> Vncomly coueting, of eche to imbrace,
>   Money or wares, as he made his race.
> And sometyme a marynar, and a saruinge man,
>   Or els an artificer, as he would fayne than.
> Such shyftes he vsed, beinge well tryed,
>   A bandoninge labour, tyll he was espyed.
> Conding punishment, for his dissimulation,
> He sewerly receaued with much declination.[25]

"Thowgh I seme a shepe, I can play the suttle foxe." These words of the Vice Dissimulation in *King John* (l. 708) might well have been spoken by Nicolas as Harman depicts him. Or as the Vice Haphazard puts it: "By the Gods, I know not how best to deuise, / My name or my property, well to disguise." [26] In the figure of Nicolas, Victor Freeburg's "rogue in multi-disguise" takes on a real-life identity.

Both in real life and in the moralities, the coneycatcher's victim is often the gullible young prodigal newly arrived in London or the unwise parvenu who ostentatiously displays his wealth. The newly rich Prosperity of *Impatient Poverty* and the prodigal Juventus both are lured to taverns, dicing, and evil companions by merry "good fellows" who accost them on the street and offer friendship and good counsel. R, the young "raw courtier" in Gilbert Walker's *A Manifest Detection of Dice-Play,* relates to his mentor M a similar tale of how he was introduced to gaming and dicing by a pleasant and well-dressed stranger who offered

25. *A Caueat or Warening, for Commen Cursetors* (1567), ed. Edward Viles and F. J. Furnivall, EETS (London, 1869), p. 50.
26. "R.B.," *Apius and Virginia* (ca. 1564), Tudor Facsimile Texts (Oxford, 1908), sig. B^r.

to teach him the ways of London. In an effort to undeceive the young gull, M exposes to him the "sleights and falsehoods" of gamblers. Among the more elaborate devices which he describes is one called "the barnard's law," which requires an association of conspirators, "each of them to play a long several part by himself." These skilled "actors" include the "taker-up," who has learned "a hundred reasons to insinuate himself into a man's acquaintance"; the "verser," noted for his respectable and gentlemanly appearance; and the "barnard," who instigates the game often by acting the part of a country bumpkin or drunkard.[27]

The family resemblance to the methods of the insinuating vices seems unmistakable. In his dedication, Walker explains that he wishes to expose "such naughty practices" only because "under colour and cloak of friendship, many young gentlemen be drawn to their undoing." In *Lusty Juventus,* the Vice Hypocrisy takes not only the "colour and cloak" but the alias of "Friendship" in order to draw the hero away from his mentor Good Counsel and introduce him to the familiar vices of the roistering prodigal. Encountering Juventus on his sober way to the Protestant "preaching," Hypocrisy professes great astonishment at meeting the old friend of his youth who had even now been in his words and thoughts. When Juventus politely disclaims the acquaintance, Hypocrisy acts out a little scene of injured humility and sententious moralizing:

> A poore mans tale cannot nowe be heard
> As in tymes past.
> I cry you mercy, I was somewhat bolde
> Thinking that your mastershyp would
> Not haue byne so straunge:
> But now I perceue, that promocion
> Causeth both men, maners and fashion,
> Greatly for to chaunge.[28]

[sig. C3ʳ]

Suitably chastened, Juventus persuades himself that he must indeed be an old friend and apologizes for his lapse of memory.

27. *A Manifest Detection of the most vyle and detestable vse of Dice-play* (1552), in *The Elizabethan Underworld,* ed. A. V. Judges (London, 1930), pp. 47–48. Judges (pp. 492, 494) marks the suspicious similarity between Walker's earlier account of "the barnard's law" and certain famous passages in Greene's *A Notable Discovery of Cozenage.*

28. R. Wever, *Lusty Juventus,* Tudor Facsimile Texts (Oxford, 1907).

In *Impatient Poverty,* the Vice Envy ("Charity") uses much the same technique in approaching his victim Prosperity, although he varies the pattern by calling himself "cosin" as well as friend. Here too he shows his kinship with Walker's taker-up. "Yea, and it shall escape him hard," warns M, "but that ere your talk break off, he will be your countryman at least, and, peradventure, either of kin, or ally, or some sole sib unto you. . . ." (*Dice-Play,* p. 47). At first Prosperity brusquely denies all knowledge of his accoster under the suspicion that he is a sponging poor relation. But he rapidly changes his mind when "Charity" remarks that he is going on a pilgrimage to Jerusalem and had hoped to find a custodian for the bags of gold locked in his chest at home. Prosperity is now all-eagerness to oblige his "cosin," but the Vice adds a final touch of verisimilitude to his role by putting on a show of injured dignity:

> What, arc ye nowe in that moode
> Nowe I am youre kyngman [*sic*] because of my good
> Before of me he hadde dysdayne [29]
>
> > (sig. C2ᵛ)

Like Hypocrisy, Envy cements his psychological hold by forcing his victim to apologize.

But before the Vice can introduce Prosperity to his merry associates, who will rook him of two thousand pounds in a game of dice, he must first get rid of his Conscience. The play-acting scene, in which "Charity" persuades Conscience to flee the land by telling him that a warrant is out for his arrest, functionally resembles the scene in *Magnificence* discussed earlier. It also illustrates most economically the Vice's lightning-fast change of personality as he turns from deluded victim to conscious audience.[30] After gulling Conscience under the familiar guise of kindly concern, "Charity" speeds him with pious tears and then triumphantly invites the audience to share the joke:

> I shall pray for you, praye ye for me.
> Thys is an heauy departynge   [*Et plora*]
> I can in no wyse forbeare wepynge
> yet kysse me or ye go
> For sorowe my harte wyll breke in two.

29. *Impatient Poverty,* Tudor Facsimile Texts (Oxford, 1907).

30. As Spivack points out (p. 161), the contrast between the Vice's weeping and laughter is a striking example of his "virtuosity in the art of false faces."

Is he gone, then haue at laughynge
A syr is not thys a ioly game
That conscience doeth not knowe my name
Enuy in fayth I am the same
what nedeth me for to lye
I hate conscience, peace loue and reste
Debate and stryfe that loue I beste
Accordyng to my properte

(sig. Cᵛ)

The ironic juxtaposition of false piety and true hatred strongly recalls the theological background of disguise even in this apparently secular play.

Envy, Cloaked Collusion, Pride, and the vices of *A Satire* all display outstanding "acting" talents in securing the banishment of Virtue. The leading Vice, Covetous, in W. Wager's *Enough is as Good as a Feast* performs an extended play-acting scene to the same purpose, preceded by a well-developed "rehearsal"; the total sequence virtually amounts to a play-within-a-play. Both Spivack and Craik have analyzed the temptation scene in detail: the former to show the Vice in his most typical role as boastful intriguer, and the latter as part of a case study of the entire play in order to demonstrate the theatrical effectiveness of the Tudor interlude.[31] In many ways, this play may be described as the dramatic culmination of the "pure" morality form. Working within the confines of a traditional genre, Wager exploits with great skill and imagination its literal and metaphorical theatrical possibilities.

Covetousness needs some ingenuity to make itself socially acceptable, and Covetous sets the stage with care. On hearing that the Worldly Man has repented and forsaken him, he hurriedly sends Precipitation for his gown, cap, and chain so that he may dress for his part as "Policy." As Craik suggests, these properties convey the idea of a respectable "wealthy burgess." [32] True to the tradition of the blundering subordinate, Precipitation first mistakenly brings a cloak—entirely too sinister a costume—and is cursed for his stupidity. Like Dissait in *A Satire,* Covetous struts and poses in his respectable robes and evokes Inconsideration's admiring comment that he looks "worthy to be Mayor of a town" (sig. Cʳ).

31. Spivack, pp. 171–174; Craik, *Tudor Interlude,* pp. 99–110.
32. *Tudor Interlude,* p. 90.

The Vice also rehearses an appropriate false face. ". . . how like you this countenaunce?" he demands of Precipitation, who gives his approval: "Very comely and like a person of great gouernaunce" (sig. C^r). This insistence on a suitable "mask," sometimes merged with the blundering-actor device, has also by now become conventional. In Lewis Wager's *Mary Magdalene* (ca. 1558), when the Vice Infidelity asks his fellow conspirators how they like him in his new role, they tease him about his face being unsuitable to his respectable garment, and he obligingly composes his expression. Politick Persuasion in *Patient and Meek Grissill* (ca. 1559) promises that his countenance shall be "graue, sad and demure." Private Wealth in *King John* curses Sedition for an untimely outburst of triumphant laughter and warns him to "Kepe a sadde countenaunce. . . ." (l. 1713). One is reminded of Macbeth and Lady Macbeth, who also instruct one another in the play-acting art: ". . . look like th' innocent flower, / But be the serpent under't" (I.v.62–63); "Away, and mock the time with fairest show; / False face must hide what the false heart doth know" (I.vii.81–82). In the moralities, such passages are often comic in tone, but their implications are equally serious.

In *Enough,* the sinister purpose behind Covetous' disguise gradually emerges in the carefully "staged" temptation scene. Encountering the Worldly Man humbly attired in company with "poorly arrayed" Enough, the Vice first maneuvers the good counselor to one side by politely requesting a private word with his companion. But before proceeding, he arouses his victim's astonishment and curiosity by pretending to be speechless with grief:

> Oh Sir, oh good Sir, oh, oh, oh my hart wil breke:
> Oh, oh, for sorow God wot I cannot speak.

> (sig. D^r)

When the Worldly Man asks what is the matter, "Ready Wit" (Precipitation) supports the role:

> Pure looue causeth him, Sir I wus.
> I am sure that he looues you at the hart.

> (sig. D^r)

During this scene of the "play," stage directions call for the Vice to "weep" at three points which culminate in a peroration of tears and "great lamentation." Having thoroughly captured his "audience," Covetous now further plays on his curiosity:

I cannot chuse, oh, oh, I cannot chuse:
Whow! I cannot chuse if my life I shuld loose.
To hear that I hear, oh wel it is no matter:
Oh, oh, oh, I am not he that any man wil flatter.

(sig. D^r)

When finally persuaded to reveal the cause of his grief, Covetous blurts
out with supreme irony that the Worldly Man is accused of covetousness
and of deserting his old comrades, whom he used to entertain so lavishly
(a stratagem which was used to good effect in *Nature*). Considerably
shaken but still wavering, the hero protests that he cannot please everyone and steps toward Enough, who is still standing aside. The Vice
quickly plucks him back. He then plays a trump card by simultaneously
slandering Enough and appealing to his victim's social snobbery:

Nay hear you, this greeveth me worst so God me saue:
They say you keep company with euery beggerly knaue

(sig. D^v)

The victim hesitates, and "Policy" further outmaneuvers Enough by
scoffing at his mean attire and by offering as more respectable company
himself and "Ready Wit": both old friends of his father and more "fit"
for his acquaintance. The hero admits that he had heard his father speak
of "one Policy" a hundred times; and as in the earlier plays, such an ac-
knowledgment is the first allegorical sign pointing to his downfall.

During the rest of the temptation scene "Policy," supported by "Ready
Wit," persuades the Worldly Man to heap up riches as his divinely
ordained "vocation" in life, by which means he can give charity to his
"poor breethern." Enough, who has apparently been watching the "play"
first in bewilderment and then with growing suspicion, tries to warn the
hero of his blindness. But he is no match for such sophistry and soon is
driven away. The Worldly Man appoints "Policy" and his associates as
stewards of his estate and, by cheating his tenants and creditors, amasses a
great fortune. But he dies unable to pronounce the name of God in an attempt to dictate his will and is carried off to Hell.

No Tudor play after this one presents the traditional Psychomachia
intrigue plot in a form so extended and dramatically mature. By the
early years of Elizabeth's reign, the external forms of allegory have become increasingly fragmented by the impulse toward literal realism; and

those playwrights who employ morality conventions must struggle with new dramatic problems of integration. But since by this time the traditional form has developed to a high point, certain conclusions may be drawn concerning the significance of the play-acting theme in the major moralities previously discussed. These conclusions may be summarized in terms of the Vice's individual role as "actor" and the dramatic function of the play-acting scenes in which he performs.

As Anne Righter points out, the association of Vice and "actor" is perhaps inevitable, since both in a sense are dissimulators who assume "names and costumes not their own." [33] But the resemblance goes beyond these externals, since the Vice may also play a short or extended false role. In a social context, his roles blend flexibly and naturally with such real-life hypocrites and pretenders as the flattering courtier, social upstart, sanctimonious corrupt cleric, or coneycatcher, all of whom may mask their true natures in order to further their ends. Although still presented as types rather than individuals, these figures would be instantly recognized by their audiences. In a theatrical context, the Vice's two-faced role can achieve considerable dramatic sophistication. The actor impersonating an "actor" takes on a double theatrical identity. He can also play two different characters on the stage. To the gullible Mankind hero in the play, he is what he pretends to be, while Mankind's conscious counterpart in the audience enjoys the irony as he sees the evil intriguer behind the "mask." In his typical part as "guide, philosopher, and friend," the Vice plays his most extended and consistent false role.

It is also important to remember the religious and psychological implications which give to the play-acting theme its elemental vitality. The passage cited from *Wisdom* (p. 190) embodies an early dramatic expression of the reason why, to the Tudor audience, pretense and disguise are linked with evil. Among many possible nondramatic expressions of this theme, Sir Thomas Elyot gives perhaps the most lucid prose exposition. In a passage from *The Governour,* he explains that although "iniurie apparaunt and with powar inforced" (in other words, the Psychomachia as open conflict) may be resisted with like power or avoided by wisdom, neither strength nor wisdom can escape evil as dissimulation. He goes on to say:

33. *Idea of the Play,* p. 68.

Wherfore of all iniuries that which is done by fraude is moste horrible and detestable, nat in the opinion of man onely but also in the sight and iugement of god. . . . *And the deuill is called a lyer, and the father of leasinges. Wherfore all thinge, which in visage or apparaunce pretendeth to be any other than verely it is, may be named a leasinge.* . . . For fraude is . . . an euill disceyte, craftely imagined and deuised, whiche, under a colour of trouthe and simplicitie, indomageth him that nothing mistrusteth.

(Book III, chap. 4, p. 207; italics added)

Iago, referring to Cassio, tells Othello that "certain men should be what they seem" (III.iii.132): a double irony which Shakespeare's audience would have been quick to appreciate. Whether as the vice on stage or in the social life of the time, the man who pretends to be what he is not would appear to many as a tool of Satan.

Iago's role as slanderer, already mentioned in relation to *Magnificence,* brings up an important plot function of the play-acting scenes. In the preceding discussion we have seen that these scenes frequently lead to the banishment of Virtue. The rudimentary plot of slander is perhaps always implicit in the attempt to separate the hero from his virtuous counselor. Inherent in making evil appear to be good is the mirror image of making good appear evil. "Fair is foul, and foul is fair." Or, to paraphrase Lucifer's less equivocal words in *Wisdom,* part of his end is to prove that virtue is wickedness. Even in so crude a play as *Mankind,* the hero is deluded into believing that Mercy has been hanged as a horse thief. The banishment of Reason, Measure, Conscience, and Enough is accomplished with more finesse, but its theological purpose remains the same. Shakespeare's audience would probably have recognized the same religious implications behind the slandering or banishment of Virtue in *Othello* and *King Lear.* The association of the allegorical play-acting metaphor with the realistic theme of slander, so easily applied to situations of everyday life at all social levels, indicates once again the flexibility and expansiveness of the morality tradition.

Moving from specific plot motif to dramatic structure, the play-acting theme has an interesting effect on the over-all shape of the moralities. In the plays discussed we have seen that the initial conspiracy scene, with its frequent connotations of "rehearsal," is always comic or even farcical in tone. But its purpose is also to inform the audience of the deceptions to come in the temptation scene, where the Vice uses his skill as "actor" and psychologist to attract the attention of his victim, to gain his confidence, and to separate him from Virtue. In *Enough is as Good as a Feast,* where the pattern of "theatrical" connotations seems most highly developed, the sequence of conspiracy followed by temptation gives a distinct, though rudimentary, impression of a play-within-a-play. To a somewhat lesser degree, *Respublica* and *A Satire of the Three Estates* reveal a similar pattern, in that the vices support one another in acting out the false roles which they have to some extent "rehearsed" beforehand. The pretended intercession in *Magnificence,* although outside the traditional temptation pattern, also may be seen as a separate "drama" within the play. Although the authors may not have consciously aimed at this effect, the idea of the play-within-a-play seems inherent in the morality situation and ready to emerge in the hands of the more gifted playwrights.

The ultimate purpose of the temptation is of course the damnation of Man's soul. We are reminded of this fact particularly in *Enough,* where for the first time in the moralities Satan accomplishes his desire as announced in *Wisdom* and carries off to Hell the deluded and unrepentant Mankind hero with no chance for his redemption after death. Thus, in the morality tradition, comedy and the seeds of tragedy are inextricably blended: a condition which may throw some light on the ancient controversy over whether the Vice is an evil or a comic figure. In fact he is both. But his comedy is not mere buffoonery for its own sake, since the conspiracy scene is vital to the morality structure as a means of enforcing the recognition of evil. If we regard the conspiracy as a comic "rehearsal" for the potential "tragedy" to come, the comedy of the Vice takes on additional structural validity.

"For then Sathan being a disguised person . . . in the likenesse of a merry ieaster acted a Comoedie, but shortly ensued a wofull Tragedie." [34] This passage from a sixteenth-century nondramatic work does not refer

34. This passage from Simon Patericke's "Epistle Dedicatory" to his translation of Innocent Gentillet's attack on Machiavelli is ironically cited by Tucker Brooke (*Tudor Drama,* p. 213) in discussing the revolutionary impact of the "Machiavellian villain" on Elizabethan drama. He does not appear to notice that Patericke, by arguing in terms of a miniature morality play plot, may also show the influence of the theological idea behind the moralities in framing the Elizabethan reaction to Machiavelli.

explicitly to the morality plays, but for this very reason it is significant in suggesting the organic association of play acting with disguised evil which was part of the theological inheritance from the Middle Ages. Substitute the Vice for Satan, and these words may serve as an abstract for the typical morality play.

The Horatians and the Curiatians in the Dramatic and Political-Moralist Literature before Corneille

LIENHARD BERGEL

I T IS COMMON KNOWLEDGE that the drama of the Renaissance and the Baroque is largely historical in the sense that the authors of the time preferred classical and oriental history as sources for their plots.[1] Yet within these groupings of historical material are important subdivisions which reflect significant cultural trends. It is not accidental that in the period of political absolutism dramatists drew on Roman imperial history, while the earlier humanistic theater had favored fables from pre-Caesarian times. These predilections in dramatic literature find a parallel in the field of political-moralistic writing, which included history. The shift from Livy, the preferred historian of the humanists and their disciples, to Tacitus, is accompanied by a corresponding switch on the part of the dramatists.[2] This parallelism is not accidental. Though the poetical treatises of the time stress the distinction of "genres," these divisions often remain purely formal and external and do not affect the substance. The

---

1. Historical drama of the Renaissance and the Baroque differs greatly from that written during, and influenced by, the Romantic period; discussing these differences would require a special investigation.

2. Important observations on this change can be found, among others, in Giuseppe Toffanin, *Machiavelli e il Tacitismo* (Padua, 1921).

reason for this is that the principle of *utile et dulce,* of *prodesse et delectare,* applies to all genres and is therefore an invitation to disregard the boundary between drama and political-moralistic literature: both genres wish to instruct and to present their instruction in pleasing, "literary," form.[3] Furthermore, in Greek and Roman literature as well as in that of the Renaissance and the Baroque, no clear distinction is drawn between the purposes of historiography and the various branches of philosophy: both disciplines desire to make man "wiser," to teach him how to face reality and how to act.[4]

It was therefore natural for the playwrights of the Renaissance and the Baroque to read widely in fields so closely related to their own, though they were not necessarily "learned" in the academic sense of the term. Because they possessed this broad background, one must assume that when they chose a historical episode or a historical character as the basis for a play, they were to some extent familiar with the interpretations these personages and events had received before them, both in dramatic and in expository form; the dramatists of the time worked not only in a tradition of genre, but also of content. They did not feel strictly bound to the latter, but they must have been aware of it, even though in each case explicit documentary confirmation may be lacking. It is with these multiple circumstances in mind that an effort will be made in the following paper to present the history of an episode from Livy that has been treated in

3. See Lienhard Bergel, "The Rise of Cinquecento Tragedy," *Ren D,* VIII (1965), 197–218, where it is pointed out that the popularity of tragedy at the time was largely based on the fact that drama was considered a useful vehicle for spreading philosophical-political doctrines. In the light of history, Bertold Brecht's famous "new" techniques appear as a rather crude renewal of old practices.

4. These observations do not imply that Renaissance and Baroque historical drama were mere philosophy or historiography in the form of dialogues. A distinction must be made between the "intentions" of the writers of the time, which were largely determined by tradition and theoretical treatises, and the actual results, which fortunately often differed greatly from the intentions. This distinction, which was formulated with particular clarity by Croce and demonstrated in his criticism, seems to me essential for the study of Renaissance and Baroque drama. It is also interesting to note that the classical identification of historiography with large areas of philosophy was renewed by Vico and Croce. Interesting examples of this identification can be found in the Renaissance and Baroque "biographies" of important men; the relevance of moralistic historiography for the drama has, in my opinion, not yet been sufficiently explored.

both dramatic and political-moralistic literature. The episode is a famous one: it deals with the war between Rome and its mother town, Alba, a conflict that was settled by the triple duel of the Horatian brothers, who represented Rome, with the three Curiatians.

For the Roman historian, the legendary events reflect a remote past of semibarbarism. Far from romantically embellishing this fragment of primitive history, Livy presents the conflict between Rome and Alba as a manifestation of *cupido regnandi,* in which the rulers of both sides carefully create conditions that will inevitably lead to war. His sympathies are with the peaceful Numa, not with his successor, the crafty Tullus Hostilius, who engineered the war between two towns related by blood. But Livy's interest lies not in matters of external policy, but in issues of individual conduct in their social context: is the Roman hero who won the battle for his city, justified in killing his sister because she reproached him for slaying her betrothed, an Alban, and if he is not, what is the suitable punishment? The fit of fury in which the murder was committed is obviously not to the taste of the Roman historian who shared many tenets of Stoic philosophy. Yet he must admit that the motive of the murder—an aroused patriotism—provides mitigating circumstances. He finds little comfort in the token punishment that is finally imposed and reports without comment the reasons for this relaxation of justice: the tears of the father of the young Horatian who was originally condemned to death, and admiration for the impassivity that the son exhibited during the trial. All in all, for Livy the episode is permeated with a primitive instinctual patriotism that is not to his liking, though he does not explicitly criticize it. It is also most significant that Livy does not mention at all the benefits that may have accrued to Rome from the victory, as was frequently done by later interpreters of the story. In general, in the opening sections of *De urbe condita,* Livy is extremely sparing and cautious in observations on the "mission" of Rome. Friedrich Klingner is correct in pointing out that the ambiguous attitude of Livy toward the earliest history of Rome, the almost total absence, for example, of the perspective presented by Vergil, has usually been overlooked.[5]

However, the reserve that was so characteristic for Livy, is replaced by

5. *Römische Geisteswelt* (Munich, 1956), pp. 439–440. Livy tells the story in chaps. 22–25 of *De urbe condita.*

unhesitatingly firm judgments in the writings of St. Augustine. He discusses the Horatian episode in a broad context when, in Book III of *De civitate Dei,* he disputes the wisdom of the Romans in enlarging their state by an uninterrupted succession of wars. He bluntly asks the question: "Did the Romans have to break the peace, in order to become great?"[6] The war between the Romans and their mother city seems to him a particularly striking example of senseless *libido regnandi.* He centers his attention on the young Roman woman who was killed by her brother: was her grief over the death of her betrothed "unpatriotic" or not? The Church Father vigorously sides with her: "The pain of this one woman seems to me more humane than the behavior of the whole Roman people." St. Augustine discovers refinements in her humanity that are not found in Livy: perhaps she wept not only over the loss of her betrothed but also over her brother, who was capable of slaying someone whom he knew was dear to his sister. Thus St. Augustine unmistakably subordinates collective, patriotic considerations to the values of private, individual affections. He denies specifically that the Horatian who obtained victory for his country deserves to be called "great," a hero; he was simply an inhuman murderer, ready to kill for the supposed good of his country. A similar view of the incident was held by Orosius, who deals briefly with the episode in his *Historia contra paganos* and agrees essentially with his master, St. Augustine.[7]

A turning point in the evaluation of the legend is represented by Dante. As he explains in the *Convivio,* he originally shared St. Augustine's views on the early history of Rome but later reversed his position and reached the conclusion that a special form of divine providence guided the expansion of the Roman state. According to Dante, this providence was also at work in determining the outcome of duels, and he applied this principle with particular satisfaction to the combat between the Horatians and the Curiatians that settled the war between Alba and Rome in favor of the latter.[8] This interpretation further widens Dante's disagreement with

6. *De civitate Dei* III.10, and *passim.*
7. In Bk. II, chap. 4 of his *History,* Romulus and Tullus Hostilius are mentioned together as bloodthirsty criminals and adventurers, eager to start wars.
8. *De monarchia* II.1.2 "[populum Romanum imperium] nullo jure sed armorum tantum modo violento obtinuisse arbitrabar." But in *Convivio* IV, v, he discerns special divine intervention in the outcome of the triple duel.

the Church Father. For St. Augustine, this triple duel was like a gladiatorial fight that only proved the wretchedness of the pagan gods that, like spectators in an arena, allowed a sixth innocent victim, the Horatian woman killed by her brother, to fall after the performance in the circus was over. Dante finally summarized his legalistic and historical-theological reflections on the history of Rome in the famous sixth canto of the *Paradiso,* the canto of the Roman Eagle, the symbol for the Empire. In this canto, he attaches to Rome's victory over Alba the significance of a second founding of the city: it was the first major demonstration of the specifically Roman, providence-guided *virtù* that led to the establishment of the Empire and thus laid the groundwork for the Christian Church. Dante's indifference to the concerns that were foremost in the mind of St. Augustine is also shown in the lines immediately following the reference to the triple duel: the period of the reign of the seven kings, the first step toward the greatness of Rome, is briefly indicated by two crimes: *dal mal delle Sabine al dolor di Lucrezia.* St. Augustine, on the other hand, had reserved some of his most bitter sarcasm for discussing the rape of the Sabine women and showed deep compassion for the victim of the second crime. He saw a broad divine providence at work in every historical happening, but vigorously denied that any additional special dispensation was at work in the expansion of Rome.

This difference of opinion between St. Augustine and Dante has been the subject of much discussion. Dantists have sometimes felt that to admit this disagreement between two dominant figures threatens to disturb the image of a supposedly homogeneous, harmonious, Christian "Middle Ages" and have therefore tried to minimize the conflict or argue it away.[9] The way out of the difficulty can probably be found in an interpre-

9. A useful survey, based on firsthand knowledge of the sources, is found in Charles Till Davis, *Dante and the Idea of Rome* (Oxford, 1957). See also the reference cited in n. 10. Of great importance is Paul Renaudet, *Dante disciple et juge du monde gréco-latin* (Paris, 1954). These books frankly admit the cleavage between St. Augustine and Dante. E. R. Curtius, *Europäische Literatur und lateinisches Mittelalter* (Bern, 1954), p. 39, speaks of the "silent battle" of Dante against St. Augustine that took the form of disregarding him as much as possible. Etienne Gilson, *Dante et la philosophie* (Paris, 1939), p. 219, observes that St. Augustine would have rejected some of Dante's ideas *avec horreur.* A typical example of glossing over the differences is E. R. Rand's essay: "St. Augustine and Dante," in *Founders of the Middle Ages* (New York, 1928), p. 258 ff. Rocco Montano, "La

tation of Dante that has recently been stressed again by Ugo Limentani.[10] Limentani argues that Dante's political views, which are so closely related to his conception of the mission of Rome, should be considered not as full-fledged political theory but as an expression of the ideals of a poet, a subjective statement using the terms of the political theory of the time, and should therefore not be evaluated in the same manner as ordinary philosophical propositions. If this point of view is adopted, then Dante's interpretation of the Livy story and of early Roman history no longer seems to be lacking in the moral concerns defended by St. Augustine. Instead, the apparent crudity of these views can be understood as an extreme expression of one of Dante's dominant sentiments, the longing for a world organization that would insure justice and peace. Dante the moral dreamer believed that the principal instrument for translating these ideals into practice was the Emperor as the legal successor of the Roman rulers, and his faith in the validity of this succession explains his worship of Roman history and his occasional blindness to its defects. Limentani justly points out that to Dante it is the ideal that matters, and not the means for realizing it.

Views very similar to those of Dante are found in Petrarch. Petrarch deals with the Livy episode in the third chapter of *De viris illustribus*. Actually, the *vir illuster* is not the King Tullus Hostilius for whom the chapter is named, but the victorious Horatian. Petrarch merely presents an abbreviation of Livy's story, but the omissions are significant. By placing the emphasis on the successful stratagem insuring the victory, he illustrates the theme of the chapter—the cleverness that helped to build Rome and thus complemented the daring of Romulus and the piety of Numa. Petrarch, too, is convinced of the divine mission of Rome and therefore does not find it necessary to discuss the moral and legal complexities inherent in the story.

Poesia di Dante: III: *Il Paradiso,*" *Delta,* nos. 20–21 (1959), chap. 4, offers some suggestions for reconciling the conflict.

10. "Dante's Political Thought," in *The Mind of Dante,* ed. Ugo Limentani (Cambridge, Eng., 1965), pp. 113–137. Limentani stresses the loneliness of Dante and his renunciation of practical political activity after many disappointments, circumstances that encouraged a tendency toward utopian thinking and a romanticizing of history. For a different view see P. G. Ricci, *Dante e Roma* (Florence, 1965), pp. 141–145.

Machiavelli's interpretation of the episode differs from both St. Augustine's and Dante's. Machiavelli does not occupy himself with the vices of the early Romans, as did St. Augustine, or with the metaphysics of Roman history, as did Dante and others before and after him: he concentrates on a question of practical statecraft. He is disturbed by the conclusion of the episode, the substitution of a token punishment for the execution of justice, and he remarks dryly: "In a well organized commonwealth, patriotic merit can never be considered an excuse for crime." [11]

It is probable that Pietro Aretino, an avid though not a "learned" reader, was familiar with these interpretations of the Livy story; they were all found in widely known, easily accessible authors. He was therefore faced with a choice between various approaches when he wrote his play *L'Orazia*. At first glance, his own attitude toward the issues of the fable seems to put him on the side of Dante, rather than of St. Augustine. In his dedication of the play to Pope Paul III, Aretino observes a parallel between the Roman victory over Alba and the victories of Charles V over his Lutheran opponents—indeed, the Emperor rendered the head of the Catholic Church the same service as the Horatian did the king of Rome. *L'Orazia* may therefore seem to be merely an adaptation of the events told by Livy to the issues of the Counter Reformation. However, the true critical problem offered by Aretino's play is exactly this: to determine the relationship between his official convictions, as expressed in the dedication, and his true sentiments, which often reveal themselves almost against his will. In this respect, though on a much less complicated level, Aretino's *L'Orazia* anticipates some difficulties of Tasso's poetry and of Baroque literature in general. [12]

11. *Discorsi sopra la prima deca di Tito Livio*, Bk. I, chap. 22.

12. *La Gerusalemme liberata* was intended as an epic poem celebrating the reconquest of the Holy City, but the poetry of the work has little to do with these intentions, and the Mohammedans are often presented in a more sympathetic light than the Christians. If Aretino and Tasso arrive at results that are not always identical with their original plans, this does not imply a lack of sincerity in their official convictions; it simply means that the *furor poeticus* does not allow itself to be strictly controlled. Such is the basis for Croce's much discussed distinction between "poesia" and "non poesia"; this theory demands that the critic atune himself to two different tonalities in the work of literature he has before him: one in which the sentiment of the author objectivizes itself spontaneously, and another in which this inspiration is lacking and "prose," ratiocination or oratory, takes its place. The

The play begins with a clash between two characters—a Roman priest and the father of the Horatians—who discuss the war between Rome and Alba. The priest sees the war as motivated by voracious greed intent on subjugating a neighboring town. But the head of the Horatian family corrects him: it is divine *pietas* that wishes Rome to become the seat of a monarchy, and the first step toward this end is the union between the two cities, which, if necessary, has to be brought about by force of arms. The priest admits that some kind of fate, together with the desire for power (*le superbe ansie del scettro*) may be responsible for the war, but he protests against the stars which force human beings into such an ignoble enterprise. It is not difficult to discern in this difference of opinion the same conflict that distinguishes St. Augustine from Dante. The arguments that the old Horatian offers in support of his views are exactly like those Sallustius had described and St. Augustine had criticized: the thirst for honor, and patriotism are curiously intermingled. The father is immensely proud that the "deity ruling the fatherland" has selected his son as its instrument. The suffering a Roman victory may inflict upon his daughter does not disturb him, because it is her duty to show her constancy and greatness of soul by subordinating her personal feelings to the destiny of her city. The scene leaves the reader with the impression that, though he sides with the old Horatian, Aretino is nevertheless uneasy about the justice of his arguments, and the eloquence with which the priest criticizes *libido regnandi* makes it appear unlikely that the latter is merely a spokesman for erroneous views.[13]

This impression is strengthened in the following act, in which Celia, the daughter, moves into the foreground. This young woman criticizes the ideals that guide her family and her nation with a warmth of feeling and a logical consistency that remind us of St. Augustine. She attacks the

most recent restatement of this view is found in Lucien Goldmann, *Le Dieu caché* (Paris, 1955). The problem of "sincerity" in Baroque literature arises only when writers consciously disguise their true opinions in order to outwit official censorship. As far as Aretino specifically is concerned, the sincerity of his opposition to Luther can hardly be doubted, even if one agrees with G. Petrocchi that this opposition was not motivated by a deep religious sentiment but was based on the practical consideration that a faith of foreign origin is not suited for Italians (G. Petrocchi, *Pietro Aretino tra rinascimento e controriforma* [Milan, 1948], p. 72).

13. Pertinent passages are found in *Il Teatro tragico Italiano,* ed. Federico Doglio (Parma, 1960), pp. 133, 134.

arguments offered by the King and by her father that the external liberty of a country is a treasure that has to be defended at all costs: she is convinced that the striving for political independence is often associated with arrogance. Her attitude corresponds closely to several passages in the Fifth Book of *De civitate Dei,* where St. Augustine comments on Sallustius' observation that for the Romans the desire for freedom, the thirst for glory, and the urge for conquest are intimately linked.[14] Celia's contrast of patriotism and arrogance on the one hand with humility and obedience on the other are also in the spirit of the Church Father: "He who humbly serves merits more praise than he who rules with arrogance." In the eyes of Celia, as in those of St. Augustine, power and arrogance are almost inseparable.[15]

This portrait of Celia is largely Aretino's own creation. For St. Augustine she remained a simple woman who was instinctively guided by her love for her betrothed, and this constituted her humanity; Aretino, however, changes her into a highly articulate spokesman for the complicated reflections of the Church Father. Thus, she defends the rights of her heart with a lucidity that is characteristic for the heroines of Renaissance and Baroque tragedy: "No power on earth can deprive me of the right to my pain. . . . The heart is one's best friend: it never lies and it prevents one from becoming satisfied with oneself." The Augustinian inspiration of this passage is obvious. Celia's speeches combine clarity and precision with a warmth and spontaneity that is in marked contrast with the stiff, tortured, "Baroque" language that is typical for the advocates of the "greatness" of Rome. This justifies the conclusion that Aretino was more in sympathy with the victims of patriotism than he wants to admit, and he therefore returns to more acceptable positions. The official spokesmen for the claims of the state, of the fatherland, condemn Celia for lack of self-control: her insistence on the rights of the heart is criticized as a weakness. The whole apparatus of Aristotelian and Stoical views that is characteristic for the tragedy of the time is brought into play, and Celia is made to appear like the Dido of an earlier play by Alessandro Pazzi: a woman who is "blind," because she is unable to sacrifice passion to duty.

14. *De civitate Dei* V. 12–18.
15. Pertinent passages are found in Doglio, *Il Teatro tragico Italiano,* pp. 140, 141; and *La Tragedia classica,* ed. Giammaria Gasparini (Turin, 1963), pp. 229, 230.

Her death from the hand of her brother is presented as justified, because it corresponds to the ideals of patriotism.

Yet, in spite of this apparent shift of sympathy to the advocates of Rome's greatness, Aretino does not permit Celia's cause to be entirely defeated: it is taken up by the Roman people. Here again Aretino develops some brief suggestions of Livy in his own original way. As in Livy, the citizens are aroused by the murder that has been committed but, beyond that, they openly defend Celia's conduct: "She deserved honor, rather than death, for her laments." [16] If the people do not insist on strict enforcement of the law in punishing her brother, this is not because of the services he rendered Rome, but because they admire certain qualities of his character. Also the young Horatian, her brother, is largely Aretino's own creation. At first glance he seems to be the true son of his father, possessed like him with the glory of Rome and cruel to those who recognize ideals other than those of the most violent patriotism. Actually, however, Celia's brother bears little resemblance to the typical Romans Sallustius described and St. Augustine partly admired, but also severely criticized. In Aretino's play the young Horatian's undeniable devotion to his country is only a minor aspect of his individuality. What is constantly stressed about him are his haughtiness (*alterezza*), his frightening fierceness (*un certo terror fiero*), and his "constancy." As a character he is particularly fascinating because he never reveals himself fully and directly. In contrast to other figures of this play and to Cinquecento tragedy in general, he does not analyze himself on the stage or explain his feelings to others. He is so absolutely sure of himself and so contemptuous of his fellow citizens that he addresses them rarely, and then only in brief outbursts. It is this enormous pride that makes it possible for him to bear calmly the consequences of his rashness in killing his sister—he does not repent nor does he ask for mercy: *"E la vita e la morto non prezzo e sento."*

His only trait of ordinary humanity is his consideration for his father. Only for his father's sake is he willing to appeal the sentence of the *duumviri,* and he tries to prevent the old man from sacrificing himself by pronouncing an abject confession of guilt in which he does not actu-

16. Doglio, *Il Teatro tragico Italiano,* p. 206—a truly Augustinian passage.

ally believe. The people do not understand the real motive for this confession—his complete contempt for the proceedings—nor do they fully grasp the source of the enormous self-control he has shown during the trial—his pride. They misinterpret these qualities which they admire, as greatness of soul, and they therefore commute the death sentence to a token punishment. Only gradually do they begin to realize that this Stoic impassivity is intimately mingled with an enormous self-esteem and complete indifference to their own sense of justice. The young Horatian does not wish to owe his life to mercy and prefers to suffer death with constancy, because humbling himself would hurt his image of himself. It is this ideal of himself as a completely self-sufficient *animo forte* that is his real guiding force, and not the desire for fame won by rendering great service to the fatherland. Even the voice from Heaven that tells Orazio to accept the token punishment is not capable of breaking his pride, which appears to him as something divine. It is in the form of a prayer that he asks permission from his "strong soul" to do what Heaven imposes on him—his own will is superior to that of God. At the same time he assures his inner god that compliance with the demands of men and of the gods of ordinary people is not cowardice, since this submission will require *virtù,* the same kind of courage that he displayed on the battlefield. Aretino's Orazio is probably the first superman of Renaissance literature who is not a brutal, egotistical transgressor of the law as are the standard tyrants of Senecan tragedy. In his self-reliance, his "constancy," he resembles the Stoic heroes of the martyr tragedy of the Baroque, though he differs from them because he is not guided by any religious or altruistic ideal. Perhaps a comparison with Tasso's poetry can again be helpful. Tasso's Mohammedan heroes are also patriots serving their country, but their outstanding characteristic is their pride, their "greatness."

Aretino's play has frequently been criticized for not possessing a unifying theme. But this unity does exist: like so many other Cinquecento tragedies, *L'Orazia* is a study in greatness. If "greatness" means remaining true to oneself, then it is shown in Celia's determination to defend her inner self against the pressures of patriotism, and in her brother's firmness in maintaining a Stoic pride against the claims of ordinary communal justice. Although it is difficult for the modern reader to reconcile these conflicting conceptions of greatness, this difficulty obviously did not exist for Aretino. In his play, the Roman citizens mediate the contrast by honoring the greatness of both Horatians.[17]

Fifty years after the publication of Aretino's *L'Orazia* there appeared in France a play that is based on the same fable. Laudun d'Aigaliers' *Horace trigémine* is an obscure work; it is hardly known and difficult to interpret.[18] Nevertheless, it is a remarkable performance for an author twenty years old and already writing his second tragedy. The play shows no traces of direct influence by Aretino, though there are some feeble indications that the author may have known his predecessor.

The introductory poems, written by admirers of Laudun, direct attention to the historical conditions under which the play was written and provide the clue for its interpretation. These poems were written when France began to enjoy a brief period of relief from the religious civil wars, a relief that was due to the policies of Henri IV, who is celebrated as the physician who cured France from the *tragicas neces fratrum*. Perhaps, seeing the horrors of war again on the stage, the audience will appreciate the newly established peace even more because of the contrast between fiction and reality: they will see *furor non furor, sanguis haud sanguis*.[19] The re-enactment on the stage of the horrors of a fratricidal

17. The literature on *L'Orazia* is highly contradictory and in general not very rewarding. It fluctuates between condemning the play as one of the worst of its kind, and praising it as the best of the Cinquecento; the latter view seems now to be prevailing, though the justification is usually very sketchy. The most pertinent evaluation of the play is still that of Croce, who does not discern any unifying theme but stresses three basic motifs: the patriotic religion of the father, the impetuous femininity of the daughter, and the titanism of the son. Though he opposes the nineteenth-century practice of character analysis, Croce is in practice still strongly influenced by it and therefore neglects dramatic conflicts that transcend character portrayal. To my knowledge, the relationship between *L'Orazia* and St. Augustine has never before been observed.

18. The fullest discussion of the French author is found in the introduction to Pierre Dedieu's critical edition of Laudun d'Aigaliers' *L'Art poétique français* (Toulouse, 1909). The play is briefly mentioned in R. Lébègue, *La Tragédie française de la Renaissance* (Brussels, 1944), but only in connection with questions of play construction. I have not been able to consult Tage Hermann, *Den latinske tradition i det førklassiske franske drama* (Copenhagen, 1941).

19. "Gallia cum pius / Erricus bile caput solveret et febri, / Exturbans furias truces / . . . Quin laetare magis, Gallia, nam jocor; / Spectatumque veni, veni. /

war will teach the French to keep peace in the future. The poems explain why Laudun chose the fable of the Horatians and Curiatians for his play: the strife between Rome and Alba was also a conflict between brothers. Much more insistently than Aretino, but in harmony with St. Augustine, Laudun emphasizes throughout the common origin of Rome and Alba, and the Fury Tisiphone, who in Senecan fashion opens the play, makes it clear that she is determined to set neighbors against neighbors, a way of doing harm that she particularly enjoys. That in the play a brother will kill his sister, has for her symbolic significance. The war between Rome and Alba is unequivocally presented as unjust, and the unfolding of the play makes it clear that this condemnation applies to both sides.

This theme of civil strife is related to another, more general, motif. Mercury, who speaks the first prologue, informs the audience that the play will demonstrate the fall from greatness of a hero who is inflamed with pride and in his moral blindness will kill his sister. Thus, the moral-religious orientation of the author is clear from the beginning: Laudun d'Aigaliers does not share Dante's interpretation of the Livy story but instead sides with St. Augustine. Tullus Hostilius is presented as a ruler possessed by the desire for fame, who wishes to obtain *le sceptre universel de tout l'Empire humain* and is convinced that destiny is on his side. Greatness, as he understands it, is determined by the amount of blood a ruler has managed to shed, and unlimited bloodshed is for him the surest road to peace. His confidant encourages him to cling to these beliefs and assures him that he is greater than his predecessor Numa Pompilius, who wasted his time with prayers and banished the beast of martial fury. In a later context it is implied that Numa behaved in this peaceful manner

---

Horrebit furor hic non furor, entheo / . . . Hic sanguis fluet, haud sanguis . . . / Hic clamor strepet, haud clamor, amabilis / Sed vox Pierii chori . . ." Pierre de Laudun d'Aigaliers, *Les Poésies* (Paris, 1596), p. 31. These passages also provide some insights into the Baroque attitude toward the stage and into the psychology of play viewing: the audience is expected to accept what it sees not as "real" but only as a "play"; for the late sixteenth and for the seventeenth century, life is a stage, and the stage a stage within a stage. To my knowledge, no systematic study has yet been undertaken of the numerous passages in prologues of the dramatic literature of that time, in which the audience is specifically told it should consider what it will see merely as a performance. This is a kind of *Verfremdungseffect avant la lettre.*

because he was not a thoroughbred Roman but a Sabine. Thus, Tullus Hostilius, the "ferocious lion" he likes to call himself, justifies his aggressiveness toward the Albans, whose stock, he feels, is degenerated and who therefore deserve to lose their independence. The Romans are presented in the most unfavorable light possible; though they speak of destiny, they are actually bragging savages possessed with the fury of conquest that Tisiphone stirred up in them.[20]

Compared with the Romans, the Albans appear more humane. Their leader, Metius, has a high respect for the Romans under the rule of Numa Pompilius. The reason for the aggressive behavior of the present generation of Romans is that *"Ils ne sont plus dévots, c'est de tous maux la source."* Metius admits that in the past the Albans did not conduct themselves better than the Romans, but his own ideals are those of Numa and the opposite of those inspiring Tullus Hostilius and his subjects: "I despise honor, I curse the state [as an instrument of conquest], I abhor greatness." It is in this Augustinian spirit that he proposes the triple duel as a means for avoiding further large-scale bloodshed, and he admonishes both sides to disregard considerations of honor or territorial expansion.[21]

Through the contrast between the two rulers the question of "greatness" is established as the central theme of Laudun's play, and, since the issue is presented in the context of a crucial moment in Roman history, an evaluation of the conflicting ideals implies also a judgment on the myth of a Roman destiny guided by providence. The divergence between St. Augustine and Dante provides the ideological background for Laudun's

20. Mercury speaking: "On verra d'un bon-heur enflamber les poulmons / D'un vainqueur. . . . / Qui soudain accablé dépitera son heur / Pour l'éclipse piteuse de son unique soeur." Tullus Hostilius speaking about himself: "[qui] Met pour juste guerdon tout un pay en friche / . . . / Et du sang ennemy fait toute une Mer rouge / Dans le sang espandu fait nager son cheval . . . moy qui justement suis esté racompté / Entre les vrais Romains . . . Les destins ont voulu qu'une telle Cité / Fust régie à jamais par mon humanité." His confidant describes the King as "Escumant de courroux et plein de cruauté" and continues: "Rome vous doit beaucoup plus qu'à l'autre Empereur / . . . [Qui]maintint tout son pays d'une prière seule."

21. Metius speaking: "Mais non point envieux je dépite l'honneur, / Je maudis cet état, j'abhorre la grandeur." His opinion about the Roman claim on Alba: "Ils mettent leur espoir en la légèreté / D'un exécrable droit masqué d'honnèteté." He believes wars should not be started "En espoir vain d'honneur ou de piteux servage."

Horace trigémine, as it does for Aretino's *L'Orazia.* In the second half of
the play, the question of greatness is explored from a different point
of view. The old Horatian has brought up his children in the worship of
the martial glory they will earn by serving their country. But now he
realizes that, if his sons remain faithful to the tenets he inculcated in them,
he may lose them, and his paternal affection rebels against the possibility
of such a loss. Like Aretino's Celia, he experiences a conflict between
private emotions and the public demands of patriotism. But he has been
only too successful in training his offspring in the Roman ideals: one of
his sons tries to console his father by reminding him of the glory he would
earn if one of his children were killed in the service of the country. However, at least for a brief period, the father is unable to accept this comfort
and exclaims: "O fame, too dearly bought by disastrous deeds," and his
awakened humanity makes him doubt that the gods are on the side of
Rome.[22]

Thus Publius, the father, becomes one of the main spokesmen for
Augustinian ideas in the Roman camp,[23] and the role of the daughter is
correspondingly diminished. Even before the catastrophe occurs, Horatia
considers herself a victim of senseless ambition and of war-intoxicated
fury, but her reflections never rise to the height of Aretino's Celia. Neither
does Laudun's character match the Italian heroine in the strength and
simplicity of her emotions. She manages to balance her passion with the
demands of "reason" and "duty" in the manner of Corneille's Chimène:
whether it is her brother or her fiancé who will be killed, the death has to
be revenged. The young Horatian woman, who was one of the main
characters in Aretino's play, is here essentially an instrument for bringing
about the climax—the issues created by her murder.

These scenes contain Laudun's most original contribution to the inter-

22. The old Horatian speaking: "Vous ai-je de mon bras en grandeur élevés, /
Pour être maintenant au carnage immolés? . . . Faut-il qu'un innocent à la faute
du père / Soit immolé soudain à fin de satisfaire [les dieux]?" When his son reminds him: "Les destins sont pour nous. . . . C'est du peuple Latin qu'ils ont le
plus grand soin," he replies "En êtes-vous bien sûr? Quelle folle espérance / Vous
gouverne le coeur? . . . O renom trop vendu, désastrée entreprise."

23. The term "Augustinian ideas" is used here to indicate a specific trend of
thought of which the outstanding representative was the Church Father; the term,
therefore, does not imply direct "influence."

pretation of Livy's fable. The token punishment that the Roman citizens had imposed on the murderer in Aretino's play is for Laudun totally unacceptable, and he introduces a new character, Horatia's confidante, to justify this position. Her convictions are essentially those of Machiavelli: patriotic services cannot be accepted as an excuse for transgressing the law. The King is at first inclined to agree with this principle and to mete out to the sororicide the punishment he deserves. But later he is swayed by the arguments of his counselor, whose reasoning combines, in a remarkable way, Dante's point of view with the crudest maxims of *raison d'état*. The victorious Horatian was, after all, an instrument of a divine providence that wishes Rome's boundaries to be extended—how could one execute an agent chosen by Heaven to do its will? But to this pseudo-theological argument Laudun adds another of an entirely different nature. For the counselor there exists no difference between human beings and animals who have a natural urge to search for prey, and nature should be obeyed. He concludes with cynical advice: if you have a hundred warriors who killed their sisters but who are good soldiers, you should use them to expand your realm. Women like the murdered Horatia can easily be replaced, but one cannot easily find men who possess the prowess of her brother. The King is truly impressed by the practicality of this advice and promotes the Horatian to be a member of his entourage. The token punishment is carried out but is immediately followed by public celebrations in honor of the young victor.[24]

24. Horatia speaking: "De voir mes jeunes ans captiver au servage / D'un temps ambitieux tout bouillonnant de rage." The young Horatian justifying himself: "Une hautaine fureur ne peut être contrainte." The Chorus commenting on the murder: it is just to punish a person "qui présume / De son bras victorieux / Ravager toute la terre / Avec la fureur de guerre / Qu'il prétend venir des Cieux." The counselor speaking: "Quel différent est-il entre nous et les bêtes / Se soutenants toujours ès furtives conquêtes. . . . C'est le désir que j'ai de voir votre couronne / Fleurir en accroissant comme un destin ordonne." (When the counselor mentions in one breath human savagery and divine will working together, he speaks like a Hegelian *avant la lettre,* who believes that the *List der Idee* makes use of human passions to carry out its plans; a rudimentary form of Hegelian philosophy must be assumed to be present in the ideology of the Roman mission represented by Dante.) The young Curiatians do not differ much from the Romans: "Je ne désire rien que d'aggrandir mon nom / Par le fait valeureux d'un acte de renom / . . . Je ferai que Titan cachera tous ses rais / Pour la seule vertu de mes actes épais."

Yet the defender of justice and humanity, the confidante of the murdered woman, is not silenced by the actions of the King. She is speaking
both as a woman and as a Sabine, a person of foreign origin. At first she
stresses the feeling of insecurity, particularly among women, that will
prevail if crime is rewarded, but then, knowing that her cause is lost, she
does not hesitate to reveal her true opinion about the Romans. In her earlier speech she had seen some justification for the expansion of Roman
rule as long as it was accompanied by strict enforcement of the laws of
the state; now this argument can no longer hold. She reminds the King
that Rome has a long record of savagery in dealing with women: there
was the deceit Romulus practiced when he organized the rape of the
Sabine women. In this disregard for women—who are also by nature
opposed to war—she sees a particularly revolting example of Roman barbarism. Here the confidante repeats observations that are also found in
St. Augustine. The Church Father comments sarcastically on Sallustius'
observation that the virtuous behavior of the Romans was due to their
noble character rather than to the fear of punishment: "I presume they
showed their moral goodness by raping the Sabine women and thus disregarding all laws regulating the relationship between cities and states."
In another chapter St. Augustine discusses the Roman propensity to
create situations similar to that in which the young Horatian woman
found herself when she was torn between two loyalties, just as were the
Sabine women who had been forced to marry Romans.[25] The confidante
in Laudun's play considers herself more a Sabine than a Roman and therefore capable of seeing the Romans in their true light. From this insight
she draws the logical consequence and decides to leave Rome in disgust:
the company of wild beasts is preferable to remaining in that city.[26] Thus,

25. *De civitate Dei* II.17;III.13.

26. The confidante addressing the King: "O barbare affamé . . . Tu as rompu
nos lois dérobant nos franchises . . . Que deviendra la femme? . . . Vous ne serez
plus sûre auprès de votre époux. . . . Mais errer je m'en vais toute déchevelée /
Hors l'inique pays de la gent Romulée / Pour vivre en un cachet avec quelque animal." F. K. Dawson points out that in French Renaissance tragedy "Those who
suffer . . . are victims, hapless, helpless, frequently women. They are caught up
in the hatreds that ambition and lust for power so often breed: politics is no arena
for the sensitive and the scrupulous" ("Aspects of the Theatre," in *French Literature and its Background,* ed. John Cruickshank [London, 1968], I, 141). This au-

the two secondary figures that Laudun added to the plot as offered by Livy are neatly balanced—the counselor, convinced of Rome's mission, and the Sabine woman who rejects Rome altogether.

With her magnificent outburst the play has reached a climax, and a continuation would seem superfluous. But Laudun is not yet satisfied—he does not want to leave the slightest doubt about the nature of his convictions. He therefore includes in his play the events that led to the final destruction of Alba, which was ordered by the King as a punishment for its revolt. After the victory over the rebels, Tullus Hostilius is more prideful than ever. Never before was his "greatness" more evident to him than now, and he demonstrates it by ordering an excessively cruel form of execution of the vanquished enemies. These details are taken from Livy, who in this case abandons his usual detachment and makes a significant comment: "This was the first and last time the Romans carried out an execution without sufficiently observing the laws of humanity." [27] For the French author, such behavior appears to be the logical consequence of the cult of martial greatness, and he therefore modifies Livy's account of subsequent events: the King, who believes he has reached the highest point in his career, suddenly feels a weakness overcoming him, and he and his adviser are struck by lightning. Heaven has shown what fate it metes out to overbearing rulers.

Thus, Laudun d'Aigaliers, like St. Augustine, sees war—any war—as a manifestation of *cupido regnandi*. For both, the thirst for power is the supreme expression of a worldliness that has an excessive faith in man's faculties, while actually *"la sûrté du monde, . . . C'est toute légèreté."* Many of Tullus Hostilius' speeches have a ring similar to those of Marlowe's Tamburlaine, an overconfidence that is also the theme of Laudun's first play, *Dioclétien.*[28] What is particularly remarkable is that in his sec-

---

thor also points out the close link that exists between the French theater of the Renaissance and the religious and political events of the time.

27. *De urbe condita,* Bk. I, chap. 28. The following chapter, in which Livy shows his pity for the vanquished Albans with remarkable directness, is also important. One hour of Roman destructiveness wiped out the work of four hundred years, and Livy concludes with the comment: "Roma interim crescit Albae ruinis."

28. H. R. Trevor-Roper, *The Crisis of the Seventeenth Century* (New York, 1968), is useful in many respects for understanding the mood of Laudun's play, written at the end of the sixteenth century. Trevor-Roper stresses the pursuit of

ond play Laudun applies these convictions to a series of wars that were ostensibly fought for religious motives. Although the poet was a confirmed Catholic,[29] he still condemned civil-religious conflict as a sheer struggle for power. There are some indications that Laudun first intended to identify the Catholics with the Romans and the Albans with the Huguenots, but this pairing is not strictly maintained—both sides are presented as being in the wrong, with the Albans occasionally showing greater humanity than the Romans.[30] Obviously, Laudun d'Aigaliers does not accept the myth of the mission of Rome as it is presented by Dante and Petrarch; his attitude toward early Roman history is that of St. Augustine. A partial explanation of this attitude is found in a composition on which Laudun began working while he was finishing his Roman play, an epic poem that bears the same title as that of Ronsard, *La Françiade*. Both poems belong to the tradition, represented earlier in the sixteenth century by Jean Lemaire and others, that created a rival to the myth of Rome as established by Vergil and Dante. This rival myth connects the early history of France with Troy in the same way Vergil had done for Rome. In Ronsard's poem, Francus, Françion, the mythical founder of the French monarchy and the French state, is a son of Hector—Françion is a French Aeneas. Thus, Roman history was divested of the halo of uniqueness that it possessed for Vergil, Dante, and Petrarch, and it became possible to present the early rulers of Rome in an unfavorable light; Ronsard even goes so far as to picture the Romans as the enemies of the budding French state. In Laudun's epic poem, the break with the tradition represented by Vergil and Dante is even more radical than in Ronsard. For Ronsard, Françion is still a Trojan, while Laudun accepts the modifications of the legend, made by Jean de Tillet, Hotman, and oth-

---

"unattainable mirages, heedless of mortal limitations" that was characteristic for that century and produced the crisis of the following. He presents the practical, economic-social consequences of Renaissance "over-reaching."

29. Laudun wrote a sequence of religious poems: *La Communion du vrai Catholique*. (See the introduction to Pierre Dedieu's edition of Laudun's *L'Art poétique français*.)

30. It would go beyond the scope of this article to discuss in every detail the way in which Laudun fluctuates in his identification of Romans and Albans with Catholics and Huguenots. There still remain many puzzling passages to be explained.

ers, who declared Françion to be of Germanic origin.[31] This break with the Vergilian-Dantean tradition made it much easier for Laudun to interpret the legend of the Horatians and the Curiatians in the spirit of St. Augustine. For convinced Catholics like Ronsard and Laudun it was not necessary to accept Dante's vision of an undivided history of Rome— for the French poets, as for St. Augustine, that history had two parts, a pagan and a Christian, and it was possible to adopt only the latter.[32]

The only author of a play using the fable of the Horatians and Curiatians who specifically mentions St. Augustine is Lope de Vega. In the dedication of his play *El honrado hermano* (*The Steadfast Brother*) he calls Livy's story "of such quality that St. Augustine considered it worthy of his comment in the third book of the City of God; there he defended

31. Gustave Allaise, *De Franciadis epica fabula in posteriore XVImi saeculi parte, Praesertim apud Petrum Laudunium ab Aquileriis* (Thesis, Paris, 1891) quotes long passages from Laudun's epic poem, which is also discussed in P. Egger, *L'Hellénisme en France* (Paris, 1869), I, 407–410. Important for understanding the rival myth are also Nathan Edelman, *Attitudes of Seventeenth-Century France toward the Middle Ages* (New York, 1946); and Charles Lenient, *La Poésie patriotique en France dans les temps modernes* (Paris, 1894).

32. It is interesting to note that at the same time that France developed its myth about its national origin and its relations to Rome, Germany did the same, but with different results. It was the purpose of French writers to create a myth that paralleled that of Rome—France was to be a second Italy. The German myth, however, was hostile both to Rome and to Mediterranean civilization in general. For Dante, the medieval theory of the *translatio imperii romani ad Germanicos* was not in conflict with Roman history but assured its uninterrupted continuity. In contrast to Dante, some German humanists, such as Carion, Sleidanus, Hutten, Bebel, and Celtis, transformed that theory into an instrument for nationalistic myth-making. In the writings of these humanists are found the beginnings of a tendency that proclaims the racial and moral superiority of the Germans and the Teutons over the decadent and corrupt Romans, a tendency that received new impetus in Romanticism. (For the way in which these trends affected England, see Samuel Kliger, *The Goths in England* [Boston, Mass., 1952].) Book III of Sebastian Münster's *Cosmographia,* which celebrates the successful resistance of the Teutons to the Romans, also belongs to this tradition. This book served a German dramatist of the time, Jakob Ayrer, as the source for a series of plays on early Roman history, one of which has the story of the Horatians and Curiatians as its subject. The play was published in the same year as Laudun's *Horace trigémine* but, in contrast to the French drama, it is entirely devoid of interest and completely lacking in ideological content. (See Gerald Strauss, *Sixteenth-Century Germany: Its Topography and Topographers* [Madison, Wis., 1959].)

the tears Horatia shed by referring to the examples of Aeneas and Mar-cellus of Sicily." [33] Thus, Lope's play is removed from the sphere of Ro-man patriotism from the beginning; the appeal to St. Augustine seems to be largely intended to justify the poet's concentration on private emo-tions. At the outset the young Horatian woman professes her indiffer-ence to the political implications of the expanding conflict between Rome and Alba, and the process of sentimentalizing and humanizing the heroic story reaches its climax. [34] With its indifference to the heroic-patriotic and its stress on individual relationships, Lope's dramatization of the Livy story resembles the plays dealing with the plight of Romeo and Juliet and the episodes in *La Gerusalemme liberata* in which the lovers belong to nations in conflict. In Lope's play, there are only occa-sional references to Rome's greatness, but these passages are stilted and of a superficial rhetoric, lacking in any personal involvement on the part of the poet. Neither of the warring parties is favored: both the Romans and the Albans present a mixture of good and bad qualities. In Lope's *Steadfast Brother* the terms "honor, fame, patriotism, greatness," ac-quire a special meaning. Thus Julia, the young Horatian woman, wants to acquire fame and prove to be a true Roman by going against the will of her family and sticking to her love for an enemy. [35] In her dedication to Roman valor, as she understands it, she feels justified in dulling the

33. *Obras de Lope de Vega publicadas por la Real Academia Española* (Madrid, 1896), VI, p. 364. Lope's interest in the Church Father is also attested by his play *El divino Africano*, a dramatization of St. Augustine's life.

34. A similar development can also be observed in painting. The fresco series by Giuseppe Cesari in the Sala degli Orazi e Curiazi of the Palazzo dei Conservatori in Rome emphasizes the pathetic, rather than the heroic-patriotic, aspect of the fable—the idyl of the love between the two young people and the cruelty of the death of the Curiatian.

35. Julia fell in love with the young Curiatian when he broke into her country house to steal some tools. She puts up a weak defense: "Y aunque a Horacio y a Romana / Parezca cosa liviana / Que esta casa non resisto, / Franca os la doy, entrad; / Porque de locura pasa / Que defiendese la casa / Quien rindió la voluntad" ("though it will displease my brother and seem unworthy of a Roman woman not to defend myself, come in; for it would be foolish to defend the house when my heart has already yielded"). She invites him to return: "Porque si es valor romano / Hacer una hazaña fuerte, / Qué más que darme a la muerte / Por un enemigo albano?" ("if Roman valor shows itself in bold undertakings, I show mine in risking death for the sake of an Alban enemy").

sword of her brother before the fatal duel. Also her brother's conception of honor differs from the traditional ideal: it is highly personal, a determination to exhibit prowess. In spite of the pleadings of his fiancée not to risk his life, he insists on carrying out his assignment as a participant in the triple duel, not because he wishes to serve his country or do his duty, but because his task, like that of his brothers, is extremely dangerous —thus he will prove to be steadfast and deserve to be called *honrado*. Here Roman virtue assumes a new meaning: it is identical with intensity of emotions and the determination to obey them at all costs. Both brother and sister represent the Spanish variety of "honor" that exhibits itself also in bullfighting: the matador does not wish to serve his country or acquire fame—he wants to prove to himself that he possesses *cojones*.[36] It is an individualism that borders on anarchy. Both brother and sister are daredevils: the charm of Julia consists of having *un cuerpo hermoso que tiene un alma bellicosa*—a formula that would also fit some of Ariosto's and Tasso's heroines—and her brother is inspired neither by the ideals of ancient Rome nor by those of St. Augustine. Yet Lope is capable of treating magnificently complicated issues involving patriotic duty and the relationship between the individual and society. However, in order to deal with these questions, he resorts not to fables of classical Rome but to the history of Spain—the myth of Rome has hardly any significance for him. In this he follows a tradition that, to my knowledge, has not yet been sufficiently explored. Spanish dramatic literature of the sixteenth and seventeenth centuries is rich in plays that glorify Spanish resistance to the Roman conquest. Cervantes' *Numancia* is the most illustrious example; there, Scipio, a representative figure in the history of the myth of Rome's mission, appears in an unfavorable light, and the river Duero, addressing Mother Spain, prophesies that the Spanish will take revenge

---

36. The derivations of the Latin *coleus* (testicle) have an interesting history. Both the Italian *coglioni* and the Spanish *cojones* signify power and boldness, while the French *couillon* and the English "cullion" denote a base person! The old Horatian equates being a Roman with being haughty and fearless, his son with being bold and arrogant. The literature on the Spanish concept of honor is large. Some of the most important publications on the subject are discussed in Gustavo Correa, "El doble aspecto de la honra en el teatro del siglo XVII," *Hispanic Review*, XXVI (1958), 99 ff. Correa discusses fully the physiological basis of one aspect of honor.

on Rome for having repressed them.[37] In a dramatic tradition of this kind, Lope could feel free to discard the associations with the myth of Rome when he wrote his play dealing with one of its most famous episodes.

Yet, by proceeding in this nonchalant manner, Lope may in actuality have been a better historian of early Roman history than he could realize. The weakest parts of the play are those in which Lope writes a standard drama of love intrigue—to the love between Julia and her Curiatian he adds another between the daughter of a Roman senator and the victorious Horatian, and the two women console and assist each other in their troubles. Here a stilted, high-flown language prevails. Those sections of the play that are truly alive are written in a different mood and style and dramatize an episode in the life of a primitive society in which two neighboring communities come into conflict because of continued border violations and the practice of cattle rustling. The atmosphere is reminiscent of the early American West and the plot a kind of cowboy melodrama.[38] With this unconventional approach to the beginnings of Rome

37. Amos Parducci, "Drammi spagnoli d'argomento romano," in *Italia e Spagna,* ed. A. Pavolini (Florence, 1941), pp. 267 ff., lists many plays dealing with Spain's heroic resistance to the Roman invaders.

38. In his "Western" scenes Lope drops all pretenses at artificiality and makes his characters speak in a way that is proper to their situation. When a country girl flees to Julia's house to escape the raiding Albans, Julia tells her: "You were the most precious sheep they were after." When Horacio, carrying on negotiations with the Albans in their city, behaves in an arrogant manner, he is warned: "Watch out, you are not in your own chicken yard." There are many other examples of this kind. The older critics of Lope's play are greatly upset by the freshness (in both meanings of the term) of passages like these. Both the editor of the edition published by the Royal Academy of Spain and Menendez y Pelayo, (*Estudios sobre el teatro de Lope de Vega,* [Madrid, 1921], vol. II, chap. 6) complain bitterly about the anachronisms in the sentiments attributed to heroes of early Rome, about the absence of *couleur locale* and the complete failure to do justice to the greatness of Rome. The discussions of the play concern themselves mostly with the question of its possible influence on Corneille and compare Aretino's play favorably with that of Lope. Probably the best study of the poet, José Montesinos, *Estudios sobre Lope* (Mexico City, 1951), does not discuss the play but makes excellent observations on Lope as a "folk" writer who catches elemental vital impulses, "the pure feeling of existing and acting," "when pure existence seems to be the only possible moral attitude." It is this feeling of pure vitality that is present in the poetic passages of the play and that is there called "Roman."

Lope probably came closer to truth than Dante and Petrarch. It was certainly far from Lope's intentions to "debunk" a venerable tradition, but his marvelous sense for the simple and instinctual aspects of human nature led him to a better understanding of the core of the Livy story than his predecessors. Livy, from the vantage point of his highly sophisticated civilization, has difficulty in concealing his disgust with some details of the episode he relates, and St. Augustine approaches it with the indignation of a religiously inspired moralist; Lope, on the other hand, easily perceives the human, historical truth contained in the fable without the metaphysical superstructure added by Dante.[39] Lope neither condemns early Roman history, as did St. Augustine, nor does he speculate on it, as did Dante. For the Spanish poet, that history is merely a source for interesting plots, but this ideological indifference does not affect in any way his devoted adherence to the second Rome, that of Christianity.

39. It is regrettable that Vico in his *Scienza nuova* gives only slight attention to the story of the Horatians and Curiatians: he discusses only what seem to him possible remnants of primitive poetry in a number of legal phrases found in Livy's account of the episode. Vico's interpretation would probably have come closer to Lope than to any other writer dealing with the fable.

Calderón's Tragedies of Honor: Topoi, *Emblem, and Action in the Popular Theater of the* Siglo de Oro

BRUCE GOLDEN

P EDRO CALDERÓN DE LA BARCA's *dramas de honor, El médico de su honra, El pintor de su deshonra,* and *Á secreto agravio, secreta venganza,*[1] are designed to astonish members of their seventeenth-century audience as well as leave them more than slightly disquieted. At the con-

1. Since Menendez y Pelayo, *Calderón y su teatro* (originally published in Madrid, 1881), saw the three plays as a distinct group, so have Bruce W. Wardropper, "Poetry and Drama in Calderón's *El médico de su honra," RR,* XLIX (1958), 3–11; P. N. Dunn, "Honour and the Christian Background in Calderón," *Bulletin of Hispanic Studies,* XXXVII (1960), 75–105; Irvine A. Watson, "*El pintor de su deshonra* and the Neo-Aristotelian Theory of Tragedy," *Bulletin of Hispanic Studies,* XL (1963), 17–34. See also Calderón de la Barca, *Dramas de honor,* with notes by Angel Valbuena Briones (Madrid, 1956), pp. xxxviii ff. Evert W. Hesse in his edition of *El mayor monstruo los celos* (Madison, Wis., 1955) argues that Calderón's drama about the Tetrarch of Jerusalem should be included with the honor tragedies, but there are important differences between that play and the three studied here. See Maurice J. Valency, *The Tragedies of Herod and Mariamne* (New York, 1940), pp. 159–161. The studies by Dunn and Watson are also available in *Critical Essays on the Theatre of Calderón,* ed. Bruce W. Wardropper (New York, 1962).

clusion of the action, an audience should feel, to use the terms of the
siglo de oro, turbación as well as *admiración*. While helping to assess
Calderón's accomplishment, the traditional Aristotelian approach to
tragedy does not fully describe the impact of Calderón's tragedies on his
audience. To do this one must consider elements from Calderón's own
culture—the Golden Age of Spanish literature. Some of these are certain
commonplaces or *topoi* of the Spanish honor code which relate to the
importance of silence and secrecy, prudent circumspection and intrigue,
and the need to wait patiently for the auspicious occasion before taking
the necessary action that results in a bloody spectacle.

Calderón's *dramas de honor* differ from most *comedias* centered on
honor. Most end happily—marriage, forgiveness, and acts of mercy mark
the final scenes—but the action of Calderón's three plays culminate in
vengeful murder: they are tragedies of honor. Calderón, like everyone
else in the *siglo de oro,* followed Lope's advice: "Subjects concerned with
honor are the best because they move everyone forcefully. . . ."[2] But
in the *Arte nuevo* Lope mentions none of the means by which "subjects
of honor" should be dramatized. Calderón's technique is to utilize certain
topoi from the honor code as constituents of a tragic action as the hero
follows the dictates of the code.

Beginning at least with Homer and the Old Testament, these *topoi*
echo familiar ideas embodied in the classical tradition of Mediterranean
civilization. In Calderón's day such commonplaces are also found in
moral treatises such as Baltasar Gracián's *Oráculo manual y arte de prudencia* and various emblem books, for instance the collections of Juan de
Borja, Don Juan Horozco y Covarrubias, and Sebastian de Covarrubias
Orozco. Furthermore, what the audience sees on stage in sets, costumes,
and properties reinforces not only the wisdom of the emblem books but
the very means by which they are embodied and set forth, while the
dialogue in the plays echoes the conventional maxims found in the collections of proverbs, *sententiae,* and handbooks of moral behavior. The

2. Lope de Vega, *El arte nuevo de hacer comedias* (Madrid, 1609), ll. 327–328.
The complete text is conveniently available in *Dramatic Theory in Spain,* ed. H. J.
Chaytor (Cambridge, Eng., 1925). There is a translation in Allen Gilbert, *Literary
Criticism: Plato to Dryden* (New York, 1940). The same lines are cited by C. A.
Jones in an inconclusive introduction to his edition of *El médico de su honra*
(Oxford, 1961), p. xiv.

topoi inform the tragic action and, as more than merely sententious maxims, become integral parts of Calderón's dramaturgy.

Calderón and his audience generally agreed about the basic meanings of honor in *siglo de oro* Spain: "reputation, manifested as keeping up appearances," and "intrinsic virtue and personal integrity." [3] The second definition describes what most concerns the hero of Calderón's honor tragedies. Baltasar Gracián, the moralist and critic, puts it succinctly: "Honor is the throne of integrity." [4] In fact, honor is tantamount to identity itself.[5] Calderón's *galanes* echo Shakespeare's hero in *Antony and Cleopatra* who says, "If I lose mine honour, I lose myself" (III.iv.22–23). When honor is felt to be sullied or lost, the hero's entire world is upset. The feeling that the world is out of balance is also felt by those around him; and the only way his world can regain its equilibrium is for the hero to regain his honor. Thus the *pundonor*—the point of honor—becomes the focal point of dramatic action.

No one can doubt the audience's knowledge of the honor code, even though at this time nothing like official statutes concerning honor exist for scholars and critics to examine.[6] Although the sources of the concept of honor are multiple and complex, its stipulations are simple and unequivocal.[7] The *afrenta* (affront), *injuria* (outrage), or *agravio* (insult) suffered by the Spanish hero is always personal, and the need to restore

3. R. D. F. Pring-Mill, *Lope de Vega (Five Plays)*, trans. Jill Booty (New York, 1961), p. xxxiv. For a compendious bibliography of studies of honor in the *siglo de oro*, see C. A. Jones, *The Code of Honor in the Spanish Golden Age Drama, with Special Reference to Calderón* (Ph.D. diss., Oxford University, 1955).

4. Baltasar Gracián, *The Oracle: A Manual of the Art of Discretion* (*Oráculo manual y arte de prudencia*), trans. L. B. Walton (London and New York, 1962), pp. 134–135.

5. For the background of the "soy quien soy" motif, see Leo Spitzer, "Soy Quien Soy," *Nueva Revista de Filología Hispánica*, I (1947), 113–127, and II (1948), 275.

6. See J. G. P. Peristiany, *Honour and Shame: The Values of Mediterranean Society* (Chicago and London, 1966), for a pertinent essay on the legal and cultural aspects of honor by Julio Carlo Baroja, "Honour and Shame: A Historical Account of Several Conflicts," pp. 81–137.

7. An accurate, concise, and clear summary of the tenets of the honor code as dramatized on the Spanish stage is found in George Tyler Northrup, *Three Plays of Calderón* (Boston, Mass., 1926), pp. xvi–xxiii. Longer studies are cited in the dissertation by C. A. Jones, *Code of Honor in the Spanish Golden Age Drama*.

his honor is truly demanding. His sense of injustice is less political than private; thus the dilemma is primarily psychological. Yet in each case justice is dispensed by the reigning monarch. Whether social or psychological, justice finds its incarnation in the King, who enters during the final moments of Calderón's honor tragedies to condone the acts of the hero and even praise him.

At the center of an honor tragedy is the seemingly unjust tenet of the honor code which stipulates that a man's honor depends on a woman's behavior. A Spaniard's psychology resembles that of Hamlet when he feels that his own honor has been affected by his mother's hasty and adulterous remarriage. But Hamlet's outcry, "Frailty, thy name is woman!" (I.ii.146), scarcely matches the complaint of the Calderón hero against both the rank injustice of the code itself and against the weakness of women who embody the code. Don Juan Roca, the hero of *El pintor de su deshonra* laments,

The tyrannical legislator who put my reputation into another's hands, and not my own, knew little of honor. That my honor be subjected to another, and that it be—oh unjust treacherous law!—that the insult over which I now weep I did not even commit!

(III. 491–496)

Don Lope, the hero of *Á secreto agravio,* also presents himself as a man unjustly accused by a harsh law as he complains:

Oh the world's insane legalities! That a man who has ever labored in the cause of honor cannot know if he has ever been insulted!

(III. 259–262)

And Don Gutierre, in *El médico de su honra,* makes the object of his complaint explicit: "You are in peril, honor. Each hour you live is so critical that you are already living in your tomb, because a woman guards your life . . ." (II. 643–647).

Once he feels that his honor is lost, the hero knows that he must follow the cruel tenets of the code to their bloody and tragic conclusion. Unfortunately, he cannot guard himself and the woman (in these cases, his wife) against what often initiates the fatal movement toward her death: the unexpected.

The event initiating the tragic action in *El médico de su honra,* while

unexpected, reveals more than Calderón's penchant for sensational the-
atrics:

> [*A sound of galloping, and* Prince Don
> Enrique *enters, as if falling, and after-
> wards* Don Arias *and* Don Diego *en-
> ter, and then lastly,* King Don Pedro.
> *All are dressed for traveling.*]

DON ENRIQUE

Christ save me!

[*He falls unconscious.*]

DON ARIAS

Heaven save you!

KING

What happened?

DON ARIAS

The horse fell and threw the Prince to the ground.

(I.1–4)

This whirlwind entrance echoes the image seen in Sebastian de Covarrubias Orozco's *Emblemas morales,* number 249. There a rearing horse
throws its rider, and the caption reads SOLUS NESCIT ADVLARI (see Plate 1).

The interpretation spells out the moral:

Carneades, the Cirenean Philosopher (according to Plutarch) says that the
sons of Princes and grandees did not learn anything more perfectly than riding a horse, managing him, and running him. For if they are not secure in
the saddle, without any respect to rank, one can be thrown from it. Likewise,
a person who does not know the difference between rich and poor, or between master and vassal, then any guide would deceive him; they would even
praise, at times, what they should berate and rebuke.[8]

8. Sebastian de Covarrubias Orozco, *Emblemas morales* (Madrid, 1610), no. 249.
Another emblem of a rearing horse throwing its rider is in Théodore de Bèzé,
Icones . . . (Geneva, 1580), no. x. The emblem, figuring uncontrolled passion,
probably derives from the *Phaedrus* (as well as from Plutarch's *Moralia,* "How to
Tell a Flatterer From a Friend," see the Loeb edition, I, 315 [58F]). For a similar
emblem see Pierre Costau (Petrus Costalius), *Petri Costallii Pegma, cum narration-
ibus philosophicis* (Lyons, 1555), no. LIII. The Bèzé and Costau emblems can be
seen in the useful reference book of Arthur Henkel and Albrecht Schöne, *Emblemata.* Handbuch zur Sinnbildkunst des XVI und XVII Jahrhunderts (Stuttgart,
1967), col. 1071.

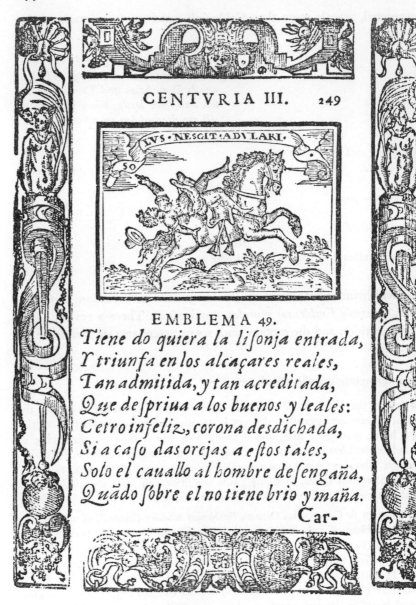

CENTVRIA III.   249

EMBLEMA 49.

Tiene do quiera la lisonja entrada,
Y triunfa en los alcaçares reales,
Tan admitida, y tan acreditada,
Que despriua a los buenos y leales:
Cetro infeliz, corona desdichada,
Si a caso das orejas a estos tales,
Solo el cauallo al hombre desengaña,
Quãdo sobre el no tiene brio y maña.

Car-

PLATE I. Sebastian de Covarrubias Orozco, *Emblemas morales* (Madrid, 1610), no. 249. Reproduced from the original with the permission of The Huntington Library, San Marino, California.

In citing this particular emblem in connection with Calderón's opening scene I am not arguing that the emblem is Calderón's source. Both the emblem and the entrance underline a moral commonplace—a topic, whose ramifications in one case are explicated by the accompanying verse and commentary and in the other are enacted through the remainder of the tragedy. What must be noted, however, is that in each case, whether with the reader of the book or the member of the theater audience, the author is intent upon catching the audience's eye first, for it is through the eye that we instantaneously apprehend the idea embodied in the image or picture.[9]

Calderón's stagecraft, then, needs to be examined in terms of his exceptional ability to visualize concepts that inform the action. This spectacular entrance foreshadows not only the bitter falling out between the Infante and his brother, the King, but the fatal situation that develops between Don Gutierre and his wife, Mencía, for it is Don Gutierre's home where the injured Infante is carried after the fall from his horse.

Prudence is the byword of the honor hero. His prudence (or discretion—the concept has a wide range of meaning) is by no means unheroic. As Gracián puts it, "Be bold, but discreetly so." [10] Since the hero in an honor tragedy is in constant danger, he must choose his course of action wisely. Prudent choice will make possible his revenge, whereas a foolish choice could mean his disgrace. The first part of his prudence will be a

9. For a discussion of the epistemological tradition behind this concept, see E. H. Gombrich, "*Icones Symbolicae*: The Visual Image in Neo-Platonic Thought," *JWCI*, XI (1948), 163–192; and the introduction by George Boas in *The Hieroglyphics of Horapollo*, trans. George Boas (New York, 1950), pp. 17–43. The studies relating this concept to Renaissance drama are few. A recent article by Dieter Mehl, "Emblems in English Renaissance Drama," *Ren D* N.S. II (1969), 39–57, does not mention the more useful discussions in Maurice Charney, *Shakespeare's Roman Plays: The Function of Imagery in the Drama* (Cambridge, Mass., 1961); Russell A. Fraser, *Shakespeare's Poetics in Relation to King Lear* (London, 1962); and Martha Hester (Golden) Fleischer, *The Iconography of the English History Play* (Ph.D. diss., Columbia University, 1964).

10. Gracián, *Oráculo* . . . , no. 54, pp. 88–89. Gracián's editor notes, "The whole point of the maxim . . . is intended to emphasize the contrast between courage and mere rashness" (p. 285). Gerald Brenan, *The Literature of the Spanish People*, 2d ed. (Cambridge, Eng., 1953; repr., 1947), p. 284, notes that "Calderón has drawn [Don Gutierre] in the mold of Gracián's *Discreto* . . ." but his interpretation of the play differs from mine considerably.

discreet silence. Gracián advises, "A discreet silence is the sanctuary of wisdom." [11]

Don Gutierre in *El médico de su honra* realizes the importance of silence:

... What the physician of his own honor prescribes for is this. First a diet of silence, which is to guard the mouth . . . [i.e., keep it closed].
(II. 656–660)

In *Á secreto agravio* we hear such phrases as "I will know how to proceed silently" (II. 335–336) a half-dozen times.[12] Calderón further dramatizes the importance of silence in a scene between the protagonist, Don Lope, and his friend Don Juan, who suspects that Don Lope's honor has been called into question because of the behavior of his wife. In order to broach this most delicate matter, Don Juan adopts the "I have a friend who has a problem . . ." strategy in approaching Don Lope. Don Lope's answer is harsh:

I'd say that if a friend, like you . . . came to tell me any such thing, assuming or imagining he could do so freely, he would be the first I would avenge myself upon. . . .
(III. 121–122; 124–128)

Fortunately for Don Juan, his ruse, although seen through by Don Lope, allows him to escape with his life while at the same time it enables him to tell his friend that Leonor, Don Lope's wife, is being unfaithful.

The importance of a discreet silence is also underscored in a number of emblems.[13] The commonplace, then, is widespread. Calderón's accom-

---

11. Gracián, *Oráculo* . . . , no. 3, pp. 50–51.

12. For other references see II.728–730 and 918–921, and at greater length, III.394–403, 757–759, and 803–805.

13. For the *topos* of silence, see Horozco's and Covarrubias' collection, *Emblemas morales* (Saragossa, 1604), bk. III, nos. 14, 41. Both are accompanied by nearly three pages of commentary referring the reader to numerous classical and biblical authorities, such as Matthew, Job, Pliny, Cicero, Isaiah, and Psalms. In the first emblem book of Alciati (Augsburg, 1531), A3 concerns silence. Almost every collection has at least one emblem recommending a prudent silence. A relevant discussion of silence and wisdom can be found in Edgar Wind, *Pagan Mysteries in the Renaissance,* 2d ed. (Baltimore, Md., 1967), index under "Mystic silence." See also Raymond B. Waddington, "The Iconography of Silence and Chapman's Hercules," *JWCI,* XXXIII (1970), forthcoming.

plishment is that of turning this *topos* into a facet of dramatic action that illuminates character, helps advance the plot, and focuses the audience's attention on a tragic action motivated by the loss of personal honor.

When the honor-bound hero begins to act, his first action is apt to be intrigue. He dissimulates by adopting a disguise, like Don Juan Roca in *El pintor de su deshonra,* spying or eavesdropping, like Don Gutierre, or by a combination of such strategies. Because such behavior may seem not only unethical but dishonorable, it is essential to understand not only what motivates these near desperate men but also that such connivances do not injure their reputation.

Gracián again provides some maxims which illuminate the action of the honor tragedy. In the hero's predicament, "The most practical kind of wisdom consists of dissimulation." [14] The idea of dissimulation is linked with craft, the practical wisdom applied by the hero which allows him to restore his own honor; and Calderón uses the hero's own intrigues and schemes as devices to advance his plot.

The practice of Calderón's hero necessarily extends to elaborate cunning: "Candor flourished in the Golden Age; in this Iron Age, cunning [guile, or dissembling] is supreme." [15] The hero of *El médico de su honra,* Don Gutierre, has seen the Infante carrying a sword adorned with a pattern identical to that on a dagger which he has found in his wife's room after she has had a mysterious visitor at night. Dissimulation is part of the medicine which he, the physician of his own honor, prescribes for himself:

Tonight I'll go back to my house in secret to prosecute a further diagnosis. And, till I find how far the ill has progressed, I shall dissimulate. . . .

(II. 671–674)

Don Gutierre enters his own garden not openly through the gate but "as if vaulting a low wall" (l. 844 s.d.). He awakens his sleeping wife, allowing her to think that he is the Infante. She warns him to be careful of her husband who will be returning soon. Beside himself with passion, he can hardly contain himself enough to exit and re-enter pretending that he, as Don Gutierre, has just arrived. He shouts a greeting to his wife, this time as her husband:

14. Gracián, *Oráculo* . . . , no. 98, pp. 120–121.
15. *Ibid.* no. 219, pp. 216–217.

DON GUTIERRE

Beautiful Mencía!

DOÑA MENCÍA

Oh my husband, my good and glorious husband.

DON GUTIERRE

([*Aside*] What extreme pretense! But heart and soul, we must dissimulate.)

(II.967–970)

He will dissimulate even further. Now he goes to the King, explaining that he suspects the Infante, the King's brother, of attempting to seduce his wife. He feigns belief in the honesty of Mencía, stressing that he has only suspicions. (Ironically he is right, but by this time he is so worked up that he cannot recognize the aptness of his own remark.) The King, cooperating with the intrigue, allows Don Gutierre to witness the testing of the Infante. From behind a screen, Don Gutierre hears what he takes to be an admission of adultery with Mencía.[16] His next move—and his last—will be the cunning vengeance on his wife.

What Don Gutierre witnesses is of first importance as an example of Calderón's dramaturgy. As the King offers the dagger brought by Don Gutierre as evidence to his brother, "It is a hieroglyph of your crime" (III. 210–211), the Infante reaches for it:

[*He gives him the dagger, and on taking it, the* Infante *distracted, cuts the* King *in the hand.*]

(l. 217 s.d.)

The King's immediate response to this "accident" is full of implication not only for the characters onstage but the members of the audience also. "What have you done, traitor? . . . Do you desire to kill me" (III. 218, 223)? Historically, King Don Pedro did not live long following this incident; and it was his half brother, the Infante, who was responsible for his death. All this was well known to the audience, for the dispute

16. For the screen business, there is a historical analogue to the secret room built by Philip II in the Escurial from where the monarch could observe inhabitants of the palace through a grating. This grave and prudent King might have been a good touchstone for *siglo de oro* audiences. Surely this kind of cunning was part of the Spanish conception of discretion. See Garrett Mattingly, *The Armada* (Boston, Mass., 1959), p. 73.

between the brothers was the subject of many popular ballads.[17] What occurs between the brothers with the dagger also reveals deep, traditional concerns well established in iconographical tradition. The dagger was a traditional weapon of Cain, the first murderer (whose victim was, of course, his brother); it later became an attribute of the figure of tragedy itself in one of the best known Renaissance handbooks of iconography, Cesare Ripa's *Iconologia*.[18] More relevant for a Spanish audience, however, was the dagger that appeared in Juan de Borja's collection, *Empresas morales*. Here the sheathed dagger lies on a table with an uncut loaf of bread, symbolizing the need for prudence and discretion (see Plate 2).

Part of the commentary reads:

The case in which prudence and discretion is more noticeable in a man is in seeing the friends he chooses . . . That is what Pythagoras mandates beneath the figure which says that the bread ought not to be broken, which is to be understood by the bread here and the dagger which is in the sheath, with the caption: NE FRANGITO. That is to say, in neither case should it be broken nor break friends apart.[19]

The sheathed dagger of the *impresa* contrasts with the drawn dagger in the tragedy, and the imprudence suggested by that unsheathed dagger reflects the imprudent action of the Infante himself as he pursues Mencía, another man's wife. As the dagger reminds us of tragedy, the final outcome of the incident is foreshadowed—not only in the matter of the two brothers, but in Gutierre's own case—as Calderón's drama moves forward.

Like Don Gutierre, Don Lope, in *A secreto agravio,* has been given cause to doubt his wife's honor, therefore his own. Suspicious of a fault, he has no proof; to reveal his suspicion would dishonor himself as well

17. For a reading of the play in terms of the falling out between the brothers, see A. Irvine Watson, "Peter the Cruel or Peter the Just," *Romanistisches Jahrbuch,* XIV (1963), 17–34.

18. For the association of the dagger with Cain, see the *Byzantine Guide to Painting,* in Alphonse Napoleon Didron, *Christian Iconography, or the History of Christian Art in the Middle Ages* (New York, 1907), II, 268. The representations in Ripa may be found in his *Iconologia* (1764–1767 ed.), II. 185, and V. 288. For a fuller discussion of the dagger as stage image, see Fleischer, *Iconography of the English History Play,* pp. 135 ff.

19. Juan de Borja, *Empresas morales* (Brussels, 1680), p. 303. An earlier 1581 edition may have been known to Calderón.

EMPRESAS MORALES. 303

PLATE 2. Juan de Borja, *Empresas morales* (Brussels, 1680), p. 303. Reproduced from the original with the permission of The Huntington Library, San Marino, California.

as Leonor. In one of the nighttime scenes which occur in nearly all of Calderón's plays,[20] Don Lope and Leonor search for a stranger rumored

20. In *El médico de su honra*, the nighttime scene occurs in Act II near the same place in the action as the scene in *Â secreto agravio*. The actors walk around the stage carrying candles; if a man has no candle he cannot see what takes place, or if his candle is extinguished he is "in the dark" metaphorically as well.

to be in their house. The audience by this time knows that Don Lope has every reason to be suspicious, since Don Luis is in the house and is dishonoring him by adultery with Leonor. But Don Lope does not know this. He does know that if such is the case, dissembling will help him in his revenge.

I must now act most cautiously, and if I find my honor stained, I'll be so cooly circumspect that only in my deepest silence will the world discover any hint of my revenge.

(II. 726–730)

Don Lope, like the other heroes in Calderón's honor tragedies, links together under the central *topos* of prudence, the notions of keeping silent and being cunning.[21]

In *El pintor de su deshonra,* Don Juan Roca dissimulates more than Don Lope or Don Gutierre. He disguises himself. In Act III a stage direction reads: *"Enter Don Juan dressed as a beggar . . ."* (l. 460 s.d.). He hires himself out to the Prince as a painter, and the Prince, unknowingly, aids Don Juan in carrying out his revenge.

The somber Spaniard in these plays will thus go to uncommon lengths in dissimulating and practicing what the *siglo de oro* understood by the word *discreto.* He is talented at maintaining a social pride and dignity of demeanor while plotting remarkable stratagems to bring about a most cunning vengeance without indicating any untoward behavior. But all this time the tension grows, and the suffering of the hero intensifies as it is prolonged. He bides his time, cautious, watchful, until that propitious moment arrives when he can act effectively. When the occasion is finally revealed, the hero makes the most of his opportunity.

Gracián once more offers advice by using a commonplace echoed by Calderón:

To know how to yield to the times is to surpass them; the man who gets his own way never loses his reputation; when you lack power use cunning; [get on] somehow or other, either by the highway of merit [fortitude] or by the byway of artifice. Craft has achieved more than power and the wise have overcome the brave more often than the brave the wise.[22]

21. Don Lope emphasizes the necessity to be circumspect elsewhere; see II.335–342 and III.381–417.

22. Gracián, *Oraculo* . . . , no. 220, pp. 216–217. See also no. 39, "Conocer las cosas en su punto, en su sazón, y saberlos lograr" ("Recognize the times and seasons in affairs and learn how to take advantage of them"), pp. 78–79.

We also have evidence from emblem books to illustrate the fact that to know the time is of utmost importance to the man of discretion. One of the emblems in Juan de Borja's collection, *Empresas morales,* reminds us that

There is nothing more important to a man in being discreet and prudent than to know the time, and to know how to use it so that it suits the purpose . . .[23]

while another called TEMPORIS MINISTER tells us

Then in the same manner, it suits us to serve the times.[24]

The corollary to waiting in order to serve the time properly is possessing the virtue of patience. For both "knowing the time" and being patient, Ecclesiastes 8:6 is pertinent: "Because to every purpose there is a time and judgment, therefore the misery of man is great upon him." His patience is, of course, part of his faith. As he waits, "ripening" as it were, he knows that God's justice itself works in its own slow time.

You must traverse the domains of time in order to reach the goal of opportunity. A prudent dilatoriness ripens one's aims and brings secret schemes to maturity. . . . God himself punishes at the proper time, not with the truncheon. . . . Fortune herself rewards those who wait with a magnificent prize.[25]

The hero knows that the mills of the gods grind slowly, but surely.[26]

As the hero waits, the expectation of the audience is alternately

23. Juan de Borja, *Empresas morales,* pp. 72–73.
24. *Ibid.,* pp. 258–259; see also the *empresa* DISCE TEMPUS, pp. 238–239.
25. Gracián, *Oraculo* . . . , no. 55, pp. 88–89.
26. The *topos* is, of course, commonplace. See S. F. Johnson, "The Spanish Tragedy, or Babylon Revisited," *Essays and Studies on Shakespeare and Elizabethan Drama,* ed. Richard Hosley (Columbia, Mo., 1962), p. 29, nn. 8, 9. A well-known instance in Spanish drama, but in another context, is the scene in *El burlador de Sevilla:*

> How long this vengeance seems to be in coming
> Especially if you are going to wreak it!
> You mustn't be so sleepy. . . .
>
> (III.466–468)

There Don Juan challenges the statue of the *comendador* to awaken and take his vengeance. The statue does come to life and revenges himself on Tirso's protagonist.

aroused and satisfied by means of swiftly moving episodes followed by slower paced soliloquies. They not only vary the tempo of the action; they serve to make clear the character of the hero. They also indicate subsequent action as they reveal the themes and *topoi* which are basic to Calderón's honor tragedy. For example, in *Á secreto agravio,* Don Lope's important soliloquy in Act III ends with his decision to leave his wife, join his King in battle, and return to take vengeance,

. . . when occasion beckons me I'll strike, and thereby bring about the world's most overt vengeance. The King, Don Juan, and everyone will know of it; . . .

(III. 289–293) [27]

Don Lope amends part of his plan, however, when his friend Don Juan reappears after having fought a second duel to save his honor. Although changing his intent from public vengeance to private and secret action, he still emphasizes the *topos* of occasion. He has learned from his friend's multiple misfortunes the importance of knowing the proper time to act:

Meanwhile, until that most secret of occasions beckons, oh injured heart, be strong in sufferance, silence, and dissimulation.

(III. 414–417)

Later, when Don Lope meets Don Luis, the man who has dishonored him with Leonor, he seizes this opportunity to take the first step in avenging himself by swamping the boat carrying both of them. Don Lope swims back to shore alone; Don Luis is dead—killed by the man whom he has insulted. Calderón's hero has fulfilled the first part of his task in an efficient and effective fashion.

In *El médico de su honra,* Don Gutierre hears enough evidence to be convinced that his wife is being unfaithful with the Infante, Enrique. He also prepares the audience for that moment when he will seize his opportunity to strike:

([*Aside*] Is there in the world anyone who could hear this and contain himself in patience? Yes, there is one such—if cautiously he measures the occasion for sudden vengeance.)

(II. 938–940)

27. For Don Lope's other uses of "occasion," see II.918–921; II.335–342; and III.498–507.

Don Gutierre seizes his opportunity at the end of the next act and has his wife bled to death.

The protagonist of *El médico de su honra* is literally a prisoner. Don Gutierre has been placed under arrest in Act I, but he persuades the jailer to allow him to visit his home at night. Don Gutierre regains his freedom only at the end of the action, after he has taken his fearful vengeance. In *El pintor de su deshonra,* Calderón presents the audience with a hero whom we see actually behind bars like Segismundo in *La vida es sueño.* At the beginning of Act II Don Juan Roca tosses away his brushes in disgust at being unable to complete a portrait of his wife, Serafina, giving up his occupation as painter. At the end of the act, Serafina is kidnapped by Don Álvaro, humiliating Don Juan so much that he disappears, dishonored and in disgrace. We do not see him for the first 460 lines of Act III. When he does appear, he is in disguise. He has, however, reassumed his occupation as a painter and accepts a mysterious commission from the Prince of Ursino.

The Prince demands secrecy concerning his commission, a request which Don Juan will comply with gladly. Abiding by the orders of the Prince and working behind a grating, his patience and readiness are rewarded when Serafina herself turns out to be the mysterious subject of Don Juan's portrait. Serafina sits with her back to the painter and falls asleep. Don Juan sees her face only after she turns toward him in her sleep. She then awakens from a frightening dream, Don Álvaro enters to comfort her, and Don Juan, at the moment when he appears to be most helpless, seizes the occasion to wreak his vengeance:

> [*He fires one pistol at him and the other at her; both fall, she in the arms* of Don Pedro, *and he in those of* Don Luis, *both of whom enter agitated by the noise, with* Porcia.]
>
> (III. 986 s.d.)

At the point in the action when the *topos* of occasion manifests itself, the hero has gained the audience's sympathy and understanding by his suffering as he has been waiting, while the playwright has gained its attention through careful, suspenseful plotting. When the time for action has arrived—the occasion the hero has been prudently awaiting—the audience is thoroughly prepared for what it expects but at the same time fears: the bloody spectacle of death.

If it is difficult for us to admire Calderón's hero in an honor tragedy, then we may be surprised to find that characters left alive to survey the results of his revenge look upon the hero's accomplishment with admiration. "Admiration" is the key word for understanding the effect in its literal meaning of "wonder." [28] *El médico de su honra* has perhaps the most famous (notorious might be the better word) finale in *siglo de oro* tragedy. Ludovico, a barber-surgeon, tells the King that he has just bled a woman to death. The King, investigating further, is told that he can recognize the house where Ludovico did his work by a bloodstained handprint on the door. As soon as the King sees the house, he knows that Don Gutierre is the man responsible for hiring the bleeder. The King is puzzled:

([*Aside.*] Then, last night, it was Gutierre, beyond doubt, who ruthlessly enacted the cruel deed of which the barber told me. I do not know how to act, so cunningly he settled his affront.)

(III. 741–745)

While the King is pondering his course of action, Doña Leonor enters on her way to mass. As they wait, Don Gutierre himself appears to tell the King

of the great misery, of the rarest tragedy, to speak of the wonder, which soars, astonishes and horrifies.

(III. 774–777)

28. J. V. Cunningham, "Woe or Wonder," in *Tradition and Poetic Structure* (Denver, 1960), p. 188. Cunningham's excellent study of Shakespearean tragedy traces the tradition of *admiratio* from antiquity to the Renaissance. In addition to the examples he adduces from several Italian and English sources, see Lopéz Pinciano, *Philosophia antigua poetica,* ed. Alfredo Carballo Picazo (Madrid, 1953), vol. III, index under *admiración;* E. C. Riley, "The Dramatic Theories of Don Jusepe Antonio González de Salas," *HR,* XIX (1951), 192; Bruce W. Wardropper, "Poetry and Drama in Calderón's *El médico de su honra,*" *RR,* XLIX (1958), 5; and Everett W. Hesse, *The Surgeon of His Honour,* trans. Roy Campbell (Madison, Wis., 1960), pp. xxii–xxiii. See also Bernard Weinberg, *A History of Literary Criticism in the Italian Renaissance,* 2 vols. (Chicago, 1961); Baxter Hathaway, *The Age of Criticism* (Ithaca, N. Y., 1962), and *Marvels and Commonplaces: Renaissance Literary Criticism* (New York, 1968).

Don Gutierre recounts to those present that the night before a great doctor prescribed bleeding for Doña Mencía and that this morning he discovered her dead body. By this time, the audience can identify "el médico de su honra," and the description of the bed, bathed in blood, supporting the body of Mencía, prepares us for a spectacle that Don Gutierre is about to present. "He discovers Doña Mencía on a bed, all bloody." The King responds:

What an amazing event! ([*Aside*] Here prudence is of the utmost importance. I must control my feelings. He took a most notable revenge.) Cover up that horror, the striking sight, that prodigy of sorrow and affright, that spectacle that astonishes, symbol of misfortune.

                                                              (III. 823–831)

Calderón's use of the conventional expectation in the last scene of an honor tragedy is explicit and pointed: the spectacle of the bloody corpse, however shocking, is a natural outcome since only blood can wash away the stain of dishonor. (Another emotion evoked by the catastrophe is sorrow, or pity for the victim. To the Middle Ages and the Renaissance, pity is one of the passions of the soul. A bloody and tragic spectacle such as the catastrophe of an honor tragedy is by nature full of pity. Thus it begets the same emotion in the spectator.) [29]

With this bloody spectacle as a backdrop, the King gives Doña Leonor to Don Gutierre in marriage, swiftly restoring her honor as he settles her suit against him who had insulted her long before.[30] Primarily, the effect depends upon superb plotting. The structure of Calderón's plays (indeed, the sense of structure enjoyed by most *siglo de oro* dramatists) has long been admired and is as traditional as it is admirable.[31] In *El médico de su honra,* the King's presence is prepared for by a previous scene referring to his roaming the streets (II.389 ff.). The King's role as justicer is emphasized early in Act I when Doña Leonor comes to him for justice and is reinforced in Act II when Don Gutierre approaches him for justice. As a result of Leonor's petition, Gutierre is placed under King's arrest

29. J. V. Cunningham, "Woe or Wonder," p. 148.

30. For this episode, see I.555–701.

31. The first part of the cogent study by Maurice Valency, *The Flower and the Castle* (New York, 1963), discusses the theory and practice of comedy and tragedy in antiquity and the Renaissance.

and it is expected that he will pronounce sentence in the unique situation presented in the final scene.[32]

Here his "character" becomes quite clear as his role in the action crystallizes at almost the same moment that the role of the "physician of his own honor" reaches its ultimate realization. In a single act of purification, the sacrificial death of Doña Mencía, Gutierre washes away the stain of dishonor and at the same time unwittingly prepares for another cure: the restoration of Doña Leonor's honor in marriage. Accordingly, the King releases Gutierre from arrest and commands the marriage. The three execute a rather grisly trio signifying both the redemption of Don Gutierre's honor (as he declares himself to continue to be his own physician) and the King's approval of his "profession" as he joins the hands of Doña Leonor and Don Gutierre.

KING

Give it [his hand] to Leonor. For I know that your glory deserves her.

DON GUTIERRE

Yes, I give it. But mark well, Leonor, that this hand is stained with blood.

DOÑA LEONOR

That does not matter. It means nothing to me and neither can surprise nor frighten me.

DON GUTIERRE

You see that I have been the physician of my honor. It is a science I do not forget, an art I have not lost.

DOÑA LEONOR

Then cure my life when it is in need of it.

DON GUTIERRE

On that condition then, Leonor, I give you this hand.

(III. 893–903)

Don Gutierre's threat is central to another effect besides that of *admiración*, however, for Calderón's tableau is meant to cause a *turbación* of the spirit in his audience. This *turbación* (sometimes *perturbación*) or "perturbation" is discussed by González de Salas in his *Nueva idea de la tragedia antigua,* published in 1633.

32. The quality of the King's justice has been questioned by critics, but if we attend to the scenes with Coquín earlier in the play we should be prepared for his harshness. From the first scene we know his reputation, and any member of the audience would recognize him as Don Pedro, called *el cruel* and *el justiciero.*

Two substantial parts, says the Philosopher, *of the Compound Plot* are the Changes in fortune and the *Recognitions,* and then a third, which is *the Perturbation* or *Passion* which is caused in the spirits of the audience.[33]

The effect is magnified by Calderón's strong visual sense. We see a bloodstained handprint on the door of Don Gutierre's house. Not only do we hear repeated references to it, but the finale is played with that handprint—the bloody symbol of Gutierre's vengeance—before us. Not only is it pertinent to the action (it reminds us of the King's hand which was bloodied in the encounter with the Infante earlier in the play), it is reminiscent of both the image and the moral of an *impresa* found in Borja's *Empresas morales.* The impresa is of an open palm captioned VITA BREVIS (see Plate 3). Part of the commentary reads:

. . . what is meant by this impresa of an open hand, measuring one *palmo* with the caption that says: VITA BREVIS, that is to say, life is short. And all things considered . . . That is reason enough for us to live prudently.[34]

The theme that life is short, thus it should be lived prudently, is surely commonplace; what attracts attention is not the moral, then, but the awesome and troubling way in which Calderón drives the idea home. Calderón draws on an unambiguous and traditional commonplace, but in dramatizing it seeks to arouse feelings both of tragic wonder and perturbation in his audience.

In *Á secreto agravio,* we also see the King condoning, even praising, a horrible vengeance while dramatizing a common image from the emblem tradition. At the beginning of Act III, Don Lope, convinced of his wife's infidelity and the necessity of taking vengeance, sees himself as perhaps a "phoenix of . . . misfortunes" (III. 219).[35] Having already disposed of Don Luis, Don Lope now plans to murder his wife and

33. Gonzáles de Salas, *Nueva idea de la tragedia antigua* (Madrid, 1778), p. 56. These lines are quoted by Eric Bentley, *The Life of the Drama* (New York, 1964), p. 290. See also Raymond R. MacCurdy, *Francisco Rojas Zorrilla and the Tragedy* (Albuquerque, N. M., 1958), pp. 129 ff. For another use of *turbación,* see Bruce W. Wardropper, "The Unconscious Mind in Calderón's *El pintor de su deshonra,*" *HR,* XVIII (1950), 285–301. See also López Pinciano, *Philosophia antigua poetica,* ed. Alfredo Carballo Picazo (Madrid, 1953), II, 39, 55.

34. Juan de Borja, *Empresas morales,* pp. 38–39.

35. Emblems of the phoenix are ubiquitous in collections. Knowledge of the legendary Arabian bird was, of course, widespread. Calderón often uses the phoenix in his plays, but not so strikingly as here.

EMPRESAS MORALES. 39

VITA BREVIS

PLATE 3. Juan de Borja, *Empresas morales* (Brussels, 1680), p. 39. Reproduced from the original by permission of The Huntington Library, San Marino, California.

burn his house down, using the destruction of the house to cover the murder.[36]

36. Don Lope's revenge suggests that of Cinthio's Moor in the story that may have been Shakespeare's direct source for *Othello*. In the novella, the ensign and the Moor pull the ceiling down on Disdemona in order to disguise the murder of

. . . now [I] entrust to earth and fire the other half of my sorrow. Tonight I must boldly burn my own house down; . . . from that blaze I'll snatch up again the honor of my former high renown, purified of the alloy basely dulling it. By experiment in such crucible, one extracts the gold to which the lowly metal clung that dimmed its glow and purity. . . . The earth must turn away from it, and fire reduce it all to ashes. This indeed is the fate of every mortal breath which dares becloud the sun; by water cleansed, by earth interred, by wind borne off, by fire totally consumed.

(III. 808–811, 818–827, 832–837)

By evoking the four elements and their participation in his revenge, Don Lope becomes (poetically) a participant in the cosmos itself, as he bodies forth his cause in the imagery that informs his world.[37] As part of his cause they will act in accord with him, leading to a scene in which that rarity of nature—the phoenix—comes alive in the last moments of the play.

The process of Don Lope's revenge is expressed in images of the fire of refinement and purification. The pure gold of his honor, dulled by alloy of base metal, has been refined by burning away the impurities. Doña Leonor has attracted the base alloy, Don Luis. She must be purified because the sullied honor of Doña Leonor reflects upon that of Don Lope. Her husband's honor will be purified by the same flames which refine her own. Thus, after the house burns down, Don Lope can snatch up his wife's body and present it, pure and innocent now, as proof of his own honor and identity: *"Enter* Don Lope, *half naked, and carrying* Doña Leonor, *dead, in his arms"* (l. 920 s.d.).

KING

Is this Don Lope?

DON LOPE

I am, sir, . . . now my heart and soul, plunged in this hideous catastrophe, this horror, this tragedy, lying smoldering in white ashes.

(III. 924–926, 928–932)

---

the Moor's wife. Like Cinthio's Moor, who crushed Disdemona's skull with a stocking full of sand, Don Lope first executes his wife, then destroys his house.

37. For Calderón's use of the elements in his imagery see Edward M. Wilson, "The Four Elements in the Imagery of Calderón," *MLR,* XXXI (1936), 34–47, and "La discreción de Don Lope de Almeida," *Clavileño,* II (1951), no. 19, pp. 1–10. Professor Wilson's interpretation differs from the one presented here.

The phoenix—the legendary bird who is reborn from the ashes of his own funeral pyre—stands before us. The revenge complete, he has regained his identity. He had lost his name and honor through the dishonoring of his wife, but he has reclaimed both through a catastrophe that partakes of the wind and water for his revenge on Don Luis, his adversary (see above p. 253); and the other two elements were complicit in his wondrous but disquieting revenge on Doña Leonor. The fact that his honor has been recovered permits Don Lope to live again; now he will join the King as a soldier in his army as the monarch declares his approval:

> In this most notable of cases antiquity has known, we have seen how secret insult most requires secret vengeance.
>
> (III. 982–985)

In *El pintor de su deshonra,* the hero is also absolved of a double murder. We have seen Don Juan, like a prisoner, shoot his wife and her lover from behind a cage. Don Gutierre, another prisoner, becomes the physician of his own honor to free himself, and Don Juan becomes the painter of his own dishonor as he completes the commission offered by the Prince of Ursino.

Calderón's final scene makes a striking tableau: the lovers lie dead. Witnesses have appeared onstage—their entrance cued by the resounding gunshots—while Don Juan stands behind the grating. Among the witnesses, Porcia expresses a sense of wonder over the dead bodies of Don Álvaro and Serafina: "Heavens, who has seen so great a tragedy?" (III.997–998) The Prince of Ursino, the highest ranking official in the play, condones Don Juan's murder of his wife and her lover, as do Álvaro's father, the governor of Naples, and Don Pedro, Serafina's father.

> PRINCE
>
> Let no one have intent to harm him, because I am pledged to defend him. These doors shall be opened. . . .
>
> DON PEDRO
>
> As for me, even though my blood be spilled, more than being offended, I am obligated to let him go and to protect him now.
>
> DON LUIS
>
> I say the same thing, even though my son be killed, he who avenges his own honor does not offend.
>
> (III. 1020–1022, 1025–1034)

The Prince's command, "The doors shall be opened," allows "el pintor de su deshonra" out of his "cage." By this single command, Don Juan is freed of his obligation, his disguise, and his dishonor. Thus, the unwitting agent who made possible the revenge is the same man who wonders at the way the hero has completed his commission. The Prince of Ursino does so not in his words alone but in significant action: freeing Don Juan from his "imprisonment," and sending him off without punishment.

At the end of Calderón's honor tragedies, the audience's lack of tranquility is mixed with tragic wonder. For instance, in *El médico de su honra,* the possibility of another tragedy is made clear in Don Gutierre's last lines. Judged by the King and allowed to go free, he threatens his bride-to-be with his determination to continue to be the physician of his own honor. The audience, too, is threatened by these lines, for they reflect the obligation to the unrelenting laws of the honor code as Don Gutierre survives as the agent who embodies its precepts.

The code by which these heroes live is not easy to uphold. Moreover, it is extremely unjust. To live by that code means that the hero must keep silent under painful circumstances, live by deceit and dissimulation, and suffer while patiently waiting for the propitious moment to act in order to regain his honor. That act itself will be the most difficult part, for it means the murder of his own wife. Yet the hero will live after he has achieved his vengeance. He lives because the King, who is the final judge (since as monarch he constitutes all virtue of authority), approves the murder. But because Calderón's monarch condones the hero's acts, it would be a mistake to take this as Calderón's own position about wife murderers. That is not why we are gripped by a strong feeling of uneasiness. Instead, Calderón intends us to feel a *turbación* of the spirit because his hero who kills successfully in the name of honor is a vivid example and embodiment of an obligation that his audience fears and upholds at once—the honor code itself.

A Cambridge Playhouse of 1638

D. F. McKENZIE

Early in 1638 Queens' College, Cambridge had a building erected especially for the performance of plays. It was in Queens' Lane, almost directly opposite the main gate of the college, and throughout the seventeenth century it was known simply as "the stage house." The original plan does not seem to have survived, but there are extant two plans of the building as it was in the early nineteenth century. At least twice in its history modifications had been made to it, first in the 1690's when it was refurbished to serve as a printing house, and next in 1734–1735 when it was altered for use by the professors of chemistry and anatomy. The extant plans indicate certain features, however, which are not likely to have been changed. From these I think it is possible to deduce the general characteristics of the 1638 building and of its stage. The fresh evidence, if it is accepted, seems to support comments recently made by Professor Richard Hosley about tiring-house doors and inner stage and to supplement usefully Professor Glynne Wickham's new account of the Cockpit-in-Court.[1]

1. Richard Hosley, "The Origins of the So-called Elizabethan Multiple Stage," *TDR*, XII (1968), 28–50; Glynne Wickham, "The Cockpit Reconstructed," *New*

The primary documentation is in the muniments of Queens' College:[2]

Magnum Journale (1637–8), f. 77: "February. To Booth for 2 da: worke at 16d & his lab: 2 at 10d ye day to mend ye Acting-Chamb: Chimny 0.4.0." f. 77: "March It. to him [i.e., 'Jo: Ruddock'] more for 7000. tile for ye new Stagehouse 4.14.6." f.77^v: [March] "To ye 2. Carpenters for framing ye timber-worke about ye Stage-house 1.2.0." f. 77^v: "April 5 To Mr. Killingworth by bill for 11. lo: of lime for ye Stage-house 4.8.0." f. 77^v: [April] "14 To Jo: Harrow by bill for brick & sand for ye Stage-house 18.13.0." f. 77^v: [April 14] "It to him [i.e., 'Fra: Wright'] for a peck ½ of tilepins for ye Stage-house 0.0.8." f. 77^v: [April] "28 To M. Booth for Stagehouse brick-worke at a penny ye foot, & tiling 6s.8d. ye Pole, meas: by mr Pick: 6.13.7"

Magnum Journale (1640–1), f. 93^v: [October, 1640] "To mr Ward for a press for ye Acting cloaths 0.7.8." f. 97: [August, 1641] "For mending ye walls over ye Acting Chamber 0.5.10."

By 1696 the playhouse was derelict, but the university as part of its plan to establish a press undertook to "repair and build up" the old theater; in 1696 Queens' received from the university £1 10s. in rent for the "Stage-house," and in 1697 a further £1 10s. "Of the Vicechancellr for ye University for the new printing-house formerly ye Stage house."[3] The renovations were extensive, but since the carpenter in 1696 claimed only "A Day of 2 men about pulling downe the Old House" and the brick-layer produced only ten loads of rubbish, the likelihood is that they *were* only renovations and that the basic structure remained fairly intact. So too the subsequent (and evidently minor) alteration of the building for use as an anatomy theater suggests that it had retained its essential characteristics of stage and auditorium.

Theatre Magazine, VII (1966–1967), 26–36, reprinted in *Shakespeare's Dramatic Heritage* (London, 1969), pp. 151–162.

2. Extracts from these accounts were published by R. Willis and J. W. Clark, *The Architectural History of the University of Cambridge,* 4 vols. (Cambridge, Eng., 1886), II, 54–55; fuller extracts appear in "The Academic Drama at Cambridge: Extracts from College Records," by G. C. Moore Smith, in Malone Society *Collections,* vol. II, pt. ii (1923), pp. 182–204, 229–230. I very gratefully acknowledge the kindness of Dr. Mary Chan in rechecking the original entries for me.

3. Cf. my book *The Cambridge University Press, 1696–1712: A Bibliographical Study,* 2 vols. (Cambridge, Eng., 1966), I, 16–35, and the primary documents transcribed in II, 73–77. That the stage house was in use again after the Restoration is suggested by an entry of May, 1665, in the Magnum Journale: "To ye glasier for worke in ye Acting Chamber 0.5.0."

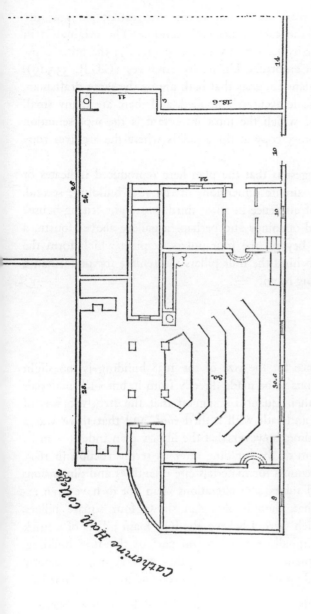

Plan of a building originally erected in 1638 as a playhouse by Queens' College, Cambridge. It was converted for use as a printing house in 1696 and again altered during the eighteenth century to serve as an anatomy theater. The plan dates from ca. 1828 (Cambridge University Library: Views aa.53 91.2 [79]). Reproduced by kind permission of the Cambridge University Library.

The accompanying plate shows one of the two extant plans of the building as it was in the early nineteenth century. The original is in the Cambridge University Library (Views aa.53.91.2 [79]); the other copy, dated 1828, is in the Cambridge University Archives (C.U.R. 33.5.19). The lettering on the plans suggests that both are by the same draftsman, but in neither is the scale accurately applied, and there are many small differences in detail of which the most important is the representation of windows in the library copy at three points where the archives copy shows doors.[4]

What I wish to suggest is that the plan here reproduced indicates or implies first, the approximate dimensions of the 1638 building; second, a similar disposition of audience in 1638; third, a straight "tiring-house" wall with three arched openings and perhaps a gallery above; fourth, a short stage projection beyond the four pillars or piers which form the arches; fifth, an area behind the four pillars too remote for performance but ideal as a small tiring room.

I

The primary evidence for the size of the 1638 building is too slight for any useful deductions to be made directly from it, but such materials as are recorded and their quantities suggest that the structure was of brick, timber, plaster and lath with a tiled roof, and that there was a fireplace. We may assume, however, that the library plan indicates, in its main outlines, the form of the building after its reconstruction in 1696, for the tradesmen's accounts for materials cite quantities and dimensions consistent with it, and subsequent alterations seem not to have been extensive. More than that, though, the plan shows four square pillars, probably of brick, which were, I believe, the four main pillars of a brick arcade constructed originally as an integral part of the 1638 building. Despite some inconvenience to the printers, they were kept for structural reasons when the building was renovated in 1696 and an upper floor laid.

4. A reproduction of the archives copy forms Plate II in the first volume of *Cambridge University Press*. I am grateful to the Cambridge University Archivist, Miss H. E. Peek, and to the Syndics of the Cambridge University Press for permission to reproduce the figures accompanying this article.

In Figure 1 the area covered by the arcade is marked B2; the areas to either side of it (B1 and B3) would also have been part of the original structure and have served at ground level as passages or small rooms (one of them beneath a staircase) with entries from the arcade. The area marked A served later as a composing room, but it is unlikely to have been specially designed as such and therefore almost certainly

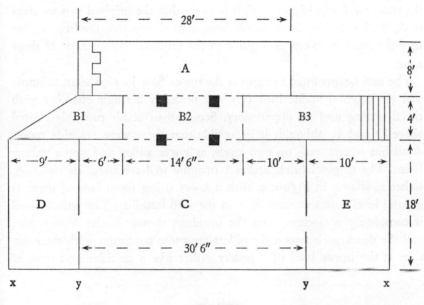

Figure 1.

formed part of the original 1638 complex of stage area, arcade or tiring-house wall and gallery, and greenroom complete with fireplace.

If the area in front of the four pillars originally formed an auditorium and its adjacent rooms, it would probably have had to be built up in 1696 to the level of the existing stage and tiring room, and this seems to have been what happened. For in 1696 the amounts supplied for flooring were: "9 Square and A halfe of Timber worke of the lower Floore" and "5 Score & 13 Boards for the upper Floore 10 & 11 foote Deales." These figures give 950 and 904 square feet respectively. And a claim like "For the Lintells makeing ready of the old Timber ouer the Windowes to bear the Gysts for the [upper] Floore" makes it pretty clear that the new upper floor was being fitted into the old shell. Now the areas (in square feet) for each of the sections marked in Figure 1 are: A, 224; B1, 38; B2, 58; B3, 82; C, 549; D, 162; E, 180. The pillars were probably about 15 inches square with a central arch of six feet and two side arches of three feet each. The areas forward of the pillars total 891 square feet (i.e., C + D + E); the grand total is 1293 square feet. I suggest that since the figure of 891 square feet is not much less than that accounted for by each of the two new floors laid in 1696, it is likely that the original surface areas of A, B1, B2, and B3 have simply been re-used, and that the library plan may therefore be taken as a guide to the original arrangement of those areas.

The new beams fitted to support the upper floor in 1696 seem to imply that the original auditorium (C) was probably a single chamber with tiered seating and no upper story. Second-floor levels probably existed above D and E, although it is possible that these were not side rooms at all but served, each on two levels, as lower galley and upper gallery boxes. The original brick arches I imagine to have been, in elevation, rather as shown in Figure 2, with a lower tiring room behind them at ground level corresponding to A in the 1696 building. The gallery itself is completely conjectural, but the openings shown in the library plan and the distances between the pillars are quite consistent with the existence at the upper level of a gallery rather like a corridor and open at

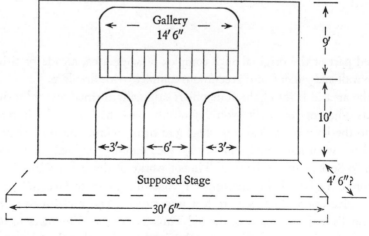

Figure 2.

either side. The façade itself was probably ornamented, but the only indication of its shaping is the slight forward projection of the two foremost pillars.

Some further support for the idea of a brick arcade, as inferred from the library plan, is given by the 1696 accounts for timber for the upper floor and for the roof. The upper story was probably supported by "4 Beames . . . 4 Score foote in length," but as there are no 20-foot spaces to be spanned they cannot have been of equal length. If two were 18 feet each, spanning either end of the building (from the points marked x in Figure 1), the remaining two could have run (from the points marked y on the wall fronting Queens' Lane) to the far side of the brick arcade and have been firmly supported by it. This distance is 22 feet, so that the total length of the four beams at these points would have been 80 feet.

The original roof probably extended over an upper tiring room, but this portion of the upper roof structure and the upper tiring room itself did not survive the alterations of 1696. The new roof, however, seems to have been designed to fit in with a pre-existing wall at a point in line with the far side of the brick arcade posited at B1, B2, and B3. It required "4 paire of Principall [trusses]" measuring in all 190 feet, each pair consisting of two principal rafters and a tie beam. There were "4 Coller Beames in all 36 foote in length." If the main roof covering had a span of 22 feet (extending to the far side of the brick arcade), and if the 9-foot collar beams were placed at a height of 4 feet above the tie beams, the truss would have been in the form of an isosceles triangle with a base of 22 feet and sides of about 13 feet. There were also four hip rafters to slope the roof down to the four main corners of the building. That the upper story was roughly equal to the perimeter of the large rectangle formed by the main walls at ground level is further suggested by the figure of "7 Score foote of the waiseings [i.e., wallings or wall plates] for the Roofe 6 and 8 Square of Oake." If one can trust the few nineteenth-century engravings which show a portion of the building as it was then, the distance from ground to eaves was about 19 or 20 feet.

One final piece of evidence, a mason's list of "Prises for Building ye Printing House," refers to "all Brick arches of ye Cellars." Its date is uncertain, nor is it clear whether the quotation is merely for making good an existing structure or for building a new one; but if one treats it in the same way as the carpenters' and bricklayers' accounts, it must be assumed to refer to a combination of refurbishing and new work. It is consistent with the suggestion of a brick structure at B1, B2, and B3 and heightens the possibility of a cellar area below the stage and tiring room in the 1638 building. Presumably there was a short stage projection beyond the brick arcade (perhaps about 4½ feet deep, as in the Cockpit-in-Court), but there is nothing at all to show it.[5]

We must again remark that, while none of this evidence is conclusive, the arrangement shown in the library plan and designated by the areas B1, B2, and B3 in Figure 1, would have been quite inappropriate for a printing house. It was not so inconvenient, however, that it could not be kept to give important structural support at the first-floor and roof levels. And if the arrangement *is* vestigial, it bears a remarkable similarity to certain features of the Cockpit-in-Court.

II

Moore Smith has noted that by 1640 "Trinity and Queens' seem to have been the only colleges left in which plays were still performed with distinction. Queens' was . . . especially active in the thirties when it had Peter Hausted to set against Tom Randolph of Trinity."[6] Hausted, who matriculated as a sizar from Queens' in 1620, had acted in a college production of Robert Ward's *Fucus Histriomastix* in 1622–1623; his own play, *Senile Odium,* was performed at Queens', possibly in 1631; and his *Rivall Friends* was played before the King and Queen, though little to their liking, on 19 March 1632. But Hausted appears to have left Cambridge for a curacy in Uppingham, Rutland, in 1634, and the subsequent promotion of the stage house, if indeed Hausted initiated it, must have

5. In his notes in Malone Society *Collections,* Moore Smith reprints, under the heading "The Colledge Stage" and dated "Feb. 18. 1639," detailed directions for the erection of a stage structure. No dimensions are given, but it is clear from the orientation of the structure that it was intended for erection at the north end of the college hall and has no relevance to the stage house; reconstruction of this stage, however, with its "Vpper scaffold," "first gallery," "2d gallery," "Drs Gallery," "trapdore," "stage Frame," "East Tyring house," and "West Tyring-house," would doubtless be most informative.

6. *College Plays Performed in the University of Cambridge* (Cambridge, Eng., 1923), p. 10.

been the work of other Queens' men. Chief among them were undoubtedly Thomas Pestell, author of the lost play *Versipellis,* probably performed by members of the college early in 1632; William Johnson, author of *Valetudinarium,* performed on 6 February 1638, also by members of Queens'; and those actors who played together with Pestell and Johnson in both their plays—William Wells, Michael Frear, and Samuel Rogers.[7] The Queens' College stage house, although still incomplete, may have been used for the first time on 6 February 1638 for the performance of Johnson's *Valetudinarium.*

The Cockpit-in-Court, as remodeled by Inigo Jones, opened around October, 1630, and there can be little doubt that it was used frequently in the years immediately after.[8] Jones's amalgamation of "the proscenium and orchestra of the Teatro Olimpico into a single stage and forestage of ample dimensions, with access to it from five doors instead of two or three," [9] was not copied at Cambridge where the more traditional straight tiring-house wall was retained. Nevertheless, in their general dimensions the two theaters were not unlike. At the Cockpit the depth of the tiring rooms was 11 feet (at Queens' it was 8); the combined heights of the lower and upper tiring rooms were 20 feet (at Queens', from ground level to eaves, it was 19–20); the width of the front stage or apron was 35 feet (that of Queens' is indeterminate, but the full width of C was 30 feet 6 inches, and the distance spanned by the three arches 14 feet 6 inches); the distance from the stage rail to the rear wall of the auditorium was 31 feet (at Queens' the distance from the front of the brick arcade to the rear wall of the auditorium was 18); the width of the auditorium, including boxes, was 58 feet (at Queens', including the two side rooms, it was 49 feet 6 inches); the width of the pit was 36 feet (at Queens' it was 30 feet 6 inches).

To sum up: I cannot pretend that either the plan or the deductions made from it and from the accounts of 1696 tell us *anything* certain

7. The cast lists of *Versipellis* and *Valetudinarium* are given by Moore Smith, *ibid.,* pp. 85–86, 88. Information about Hausted, Johnson, and Pestell will be found most readily in G. E. Bentley, *The Jacobean and Caroline Stage,* 7 vols. (Oxford, 1941–1968), IV, 532–537, 600–602, 952–955.

8. Wickham, *Shakespeare's Dramatic Heritage,* p. 155; and Bentley, *Jacobean and Caroline Stage,* I, 28–29.

9. Wickham, *Shakespeare's Dramatic Heritage,* pp. 161–162.

about the 1638 playhouse; but I find it interesting that the plan shares
many general features with that of the Cockpit-in-Court, that the tiring-
house façade corresponds much more closely to the straight wall, with
doors, shown in De Witt's drawing of the Swan theater, and that no
provision was made for an inner stage. So much can be deduced from
the plan; it offers no direct evidence at all about the upper sections of
the tiring-house façade, but, if the lower part was of the kind described,
it could certainly have supported a gallery, and the areas B1 and B3 in
Figure 1 are hard to explain unless they can be assumed to have given
access at an upper level. We are not, I think, so well furnished with information about the structure of Elizabethan and Jacobean theaters that
we can afford to overlook the evidence of these Cambridge documents,
inconclusive though it be.

Reviews

BEVINGTON, DAVID. *Tudor Drama and Politics.* Cambridge, Massachusetts: Harvard University Press, 1968. Pp. 360. $10.00.

SANDERS, WILBUR. *The Dramatist and the Received Idea: Studies in the Plays of Marlowe and Shakespeare.* Cambridge, England: Cambridge University Press, 1968. Pp. xi + 391. $9.50.

WINNY, JAMES. *The Player King: A Theme of Shakespeare's Histories.* London: Chatto and Windus, Ltd., 1968; New York: Barnes and Noble, Inc., 1968. Pp. viii + 219. $4.00 (Barnes and Noble).

THREE BOOKS ON TUDOR DRAMA published in 1968 follow radically different paths in reacting against criticism limited either to the Elizabethan "historical world picture" or to dramatic structure and the uses of convention. One sees the drama as a direct outgrowth of Tudor political and social controversy, while the second sees it as dependent on a highly complex set of interreactions between the author and the ideas provided him by his culture. The third, disdaining contemporary political and intellectual influences, sees Shakespearean drama as a reflection, through the "poetic imagination," of the author's personal moral outlook on the "conflicting passions" of men. While only one author limits his discussion to the history play, the other two treat it at some length. They all find it less concerned with promulgating orthodox Tudor doctrine than with exploring the right of subjects to rebel "for conscience' sake."

David Bevington says that drama throughout the sixteenth century reflected political and social division. He sees Shakespeare as one of several playwrights in whose works this tendency culminates. In reviving topical interpretation of these plays, Bevington is careful to disclaim any attempt to identify dramatic characters with specific people; he is interested rather in the ideas for which they stand. Obviously, royal figures must be an exception, but the author shows that allusions to living kings in plays "pertain to the office instead of the man."

Drama in the late fifteenth century, says Bevington, moved from concern with church-related politics (never doctrine) to more exclusively secular controversy. He discusses the plays in categories representing controversies or sides in a particular controversy. The moralities (*Everyman* and *Wisdom*) focused on corruption and reform in the priesthood, while Henry Medwall, an adherent of the *status quo* in *Fulgens and Lucrece,* regretfully represents the defeat of the old aristocracy by the new "active politician" of the Tudors. John Skelton in *Magnificence* surrounds the king (almost certainly Henry VIII) with "traditional moderates" as wise counselors and "new men" as the seven deadly sins. John Heywood followed a middle course between old and new aristocracy, while John Rastell focused attention on the common man, attacking the "aristocratic idleness" of the wealthy. Henry VIII's break with Rome brought on a rash of plays with moderate to extreme Protestant implications, most notably the explosively antipapal *King John* by John Bale. Mary's Catholic reign prompted plays like *Respublica,* which made an appeal for reconciliation and religious unity.

Because Elizabeth forbade plays containing political or religious controversy, her accession forced playwrights to seek more indirect ways of providing vent for popular sentiment, the most common being exploitation of antiforeign (Spanish and French) feeling—always a sure-fire theme. But despite her rigorous prohibitions, Elizabeth got unwelcome advice on the need for a successor in *Gorboduc* and on what to do with Mary of Scotland in *Horestes*. Plays highly devoted to Elizabeth and most directly subject to topical interpretation flourished at court, of course, where the talents of John Lyly excelled. More political were the increasingly jingoistic, Protestant, in many cases antiaristocratic, plays which followed defeat of the Spanish Armada. In this light Bevington reviews, among others, Robert Wilson's *The Cobbler's Prophecy,* Greene's *Friar Bacon,* and his *George a Greene.* (Dekker's *The Shoemakers' Holiday,* which clearly belongs here, is treated under a different category.) In order to avoid direct concern with contemporary topics, the author of *The Famous Victories, The Troublesome Reign, Edward I,* and *Edward III* turned to Holinshed, but these plays too represented contemporary issues. Into the related category of anti-Catholic, antiaristocratic plays, Bevington also places Marlowe's *Massacre at Paris, Tamburlaine,* and *The Jew of Malta.* Marlowe and Peele go still further, says Bevington, and investigate the faults of royalty itself in *Edward II* and *David and Bethsabe.*

Support in the drama for "new social groups previously accustomed to servitude" naturally prompted an "orthodox reply." Lodge's *The Wounds of Civil War* and the anonymous *Life and Death of Jack Strawe* enunciate conservative positions. Bevington places Shakespeare in this category but sees him as a moderate from the start. The malicious violence of Wat Tyler's revolt in *Jack Strawe* makes Jack Cade's revolt in *2 Henry VI* tame by comparison. In *King John* Shakespeare favors order and points out the folly of rebellion, even against a tyrant; but Bevington's discussion stresses Shakespeare's ambivalence toward John more than his support for order. Ambivalence toward the monarch is emphasized in *Richard II* and carries over to the *Henry IV* plays and even *Julius Caesar.* In the anonymous but Shakespeare-oriented *Thomas of Woodstock,* says Bevington, it becomes an irresolvable dilemma. That play stops short of counseling regicide, but the orthodox reply ends in considerable uncertainty. (And no mention is made anywhere of Divine Providence.)

Bevington's book continues with a discussion of Jonson, Chapman, and other playwrights who were then or later to be associated with private companies. Fundamentally satirical, these playwrights see law and authority in unsympathetic terms. Generally speaking, they address youthful aristocratic attitudes less respectful of minor public officialdom than was customary in popular drama in the 1590's. The place of this chapter among the categories previously established is puzzling. The pro-aristocratic tendency of these playwrights would seem to suggest orthodoxy, yet they are anything but orthodox. Jonson goes farther than any in questioning the obligation of the well-born to submit to the authority of inferiors. Not only the aristocrat but the artist, he implies in *Cynthia's Revels,* may be a law unto himself; and the latter may even be a fitting adjudicator among others. The complex implications of this chapter and its obvious connection with Jacobean rather than Tudor attitudes suggest that it might more suitably open a similar (and much needed) study of drama and politics from James's accession to 1642 than conclude one of Tudor drama and politics.

On the whole, the clarity and coherence of Bevington's book are outstanding, especially when one considers the large number of plays covered. In pointing out their political meaning, Bevington has left intact sharp-edged impressions of many earlier plays that have previously been tapped for character types or uses of dramatic convention and then been thrust aside. When he gets to the more crowded 1590's, his categories run the danger of being oversimplifications, but he successfully counters this by showing Shakespeare as a defender of orthodoxy persistently and increasingly pulled toward a questioning, ambivalent attitude.

Wilbur Sanders in *The Dramatist and the Received Idea* shares with Bevington the view that plays reflect political and intellectual issues, but their books are very different from each other. Sanders is far more concerned with philosophical issues than Bevington and focuses on only a few selected plays of Marlowe and Shakespeare. The "received idea" may be used superficially by one artist and deeply by another. Sanders intersperses his critical chapters with discussions, really as he says "notes," on the philosophical or political context of the plays he is examining. He is close to Bevington when he calls *Richard II* a "critique of Elizabethan policy" (*pace* L. B. Campbell); but normally what he says about the "received idea" is much more far-reaching. One chapter shows the different ways in which Marlowe and Shakespeare see and use Machiavellianism; another relates the basic problems posed by Calvinism to *Dr. Faustus;* a third discards the medieval theological problem of evil discussed by Augustine, Aquinas, and Hooker as a dominant influence on the vision of evil in *Macbeth.* But Sanders is also concerned with the ideas of later thinkers. Blake and Nietzsche are as important in his approach to the Renaissance dramatist as Machiavelli and Calvin.

Sanders alternately discusses the plays of Marlowe and Shakespeare, regularly demonstrating how the latter succeed where the former do not. Following the "journalistic bombast" of Marlowe's *Massacre at Paris* and the superficial irony of *The Jew of Malta,* Shakespeare's *Richard III* successfully evokes the deepest ironies of sixteenth-century Machiavellianism. Marlowe is concerned with a stage Machiavel, says Sanders—be he Jew Barrabas or Christian Ferneze or Guise. *Richard III* makes a far more penetrating analysis by revealing the workings of conscience in a world where instinctive morality can never be permanently pushed aside by the gross inhuman appeal of power acquisition. Sanders finds that the language in which the overt "Divine Providence" theme is presented (largely through Richmond) "lacks conviction." The true "providential element," he says, emanates from within, not from without.

Next, Sanders finds *Edward II* surprisingly insensitive to "received ideas."

> The weak homosexual king, the sensational violence of his death, the Machiavellian ambition of Mortimer . . . take charge of Marlowe's pen; and when their momentum is spent, he is obliged to trace meaningless patterns . . . until the fit seizes him again.
>
> (p. 125)

Richard II, on the other hand, contains a meaningful pattern deriving directly from contemporary political controversy. Like Bevington, Sanders feels that Shakespeare "voices the dialogue" between orthodox Tudor policy and the theory that permitted rebellion against a tyrant but that he does not seek to adjudicate "between the two sides." Richard's role implies a "severe critique" of divine right theory, but his "culpability" cannot excuse Bolingbroke's "aggression." Nevertheless, says Sanders, Shakespeare includes an "incipiently tragic" awareness of the "historical necessity" for Bolingbroke.

In considering *Dr. Faustus* and *Macbeth,* Sanders leaves political controversy for the realm of theological and moral debate. Continuing to denigrate Marlowe, Sanders feels *Faustus* reveals the author's "unresolved" conflicts about whether evil is still to be represented in medieval terms—the objective and tangible presence of devils—or in new, widely discussed subjective terms. Marlowe intellectually leans toward the latter but seems still tormented by childhood terrors. The play, Sanders suggests, may be successful for a sixteenth-century mind, but we today are well beyond its problems. It is now clear that Sanders is seeking a critical approach in which important elements of "contemporary culture" are explored with broad scholarship, but in which the subjective responses of the critic are the ultimate measure of a play's effectiveness.

The limits of this approach are perhaps revealed in his extended discussion of *Macbeth*. He acknowledges the possibility to begin with:

> In approaching a work as manifold and inexhaustible as *Macbeth*, there is considerable danger of losing one's way in the very richness of the play, leaving the reader with a lapful of oddments and annotations, and no coherent image of the whole.
>
> (p. 253)

Sanders seeks to give us an image of the whole; some may question the clarity of the result. In succession, he reviews the "individualized" image of virtue murdered in Duncan; Malcolm's callowness and distrust which can bode no renewal of Duncan's saintly spirit; and the "grace" which is variously figured in the play as "that dynamic moral order" which "will have blood," the "naked new-born babe," and the compassion Lady Macbeth feels she must violently destroy in herself. Finally, he discusses the "primacy of evil" which is the "superior actuality" in the play. This "actuality of evil"—emerging in many combinations of action, scene, rhythm, intonation, syntactical arrangement, and image—is strangely freeing to Macbeth, freeing in "beyond good-and-evil" terms. Late in his analysis, Sanders turns frequently to Nietzsche to make clear his responses. Evil is not victorious in the play, but neither is good—certainly not in the figure of a triumphant Malcolm. "We are left," he concludes,

> with an awed sense of the overwhelming potency and vitality of evil, and with a subdued question about this concealed intention of nature. It is not a resolution, but a tremulous equilibrium between affirmation and despair, in which we submit ourselves to an unknown fear.
>
> (p. 307)

It should be added that Sanders' response to the language of individual passages is unusually sensitive. He notices such things as the "gestural" quality of Marlowe's verbs and the "trust incarnate" implicit in Duncan's syntax. Sanders' critiques should be read for his ability to relate poetic effect to meaning in individual plays.

James Winny, whose *The Player King* focuses on the second tetralogy, sharply defends the honor of imaginative poetry against what he considers the onslaught of E. M. W. Tillyard. The history play, an accident of the first folio, says Winny, has little or nothing to do with contemporary politics. In his introduction, Winny cites several passages from *The Rape of Lucrece* to show that "the characteristic imaginative outlook . . . of the young Shakespeare" is seen in the detailed imagery of horror associated with violence, and this carries over to the history plays. His province, he says however, will be the imagery of royalty, "the attempts of . . . Richard II, Henry Bolingbroke, and Henry V . . . to assume the royal identity."

In *Richard II,* says Winny, "verbal ingenuity" and superficial ceremony reveal Richard's futile search for his royal identity, whereas Bolingbroke's actions, rather than his words, reveal a moral concern not apparent in Richard. The play is held together by a prodigality pattern in which sons disappoint their fathers' expectations: Gaunt-Bolingbroke, York-Aumerle, Bolingbroke-Hal. The chief issues of the play are seen ironically in Bolingbroke's praise of York for betraying his own son, who has been guilty of precisely the crimes Bolingbroke committed in obtaining the throne. "Want of self-awareness," says Winny, prevents any character from being tragic. Basing his argument on Shakespeare's modifications of Holinshed, Winny finds the Bolingbroke in *Henry IV* debased into a "shifty, hypocritical figure" who provokes the Percies' revolt to prevent his former supporters from becoming too powerful. Falstaff is a parodist who mimes the actions of the royal thief; and Hal is a confused youth growing to manhood with full knowledge of his father's culpability and deeply desirous of correcting his crimes and abuses, something he can never do because of the political system of which he must be a part. Winny finds *Henry V* a contradictory play in which Hal's nature is "deeply divided" between ruthless Lancastrian administrator-warlord and introspective critic of that royal identity he alone has been successful in symbolizing.

Winny uses no scholarly apparatus, and he never precisely defines his critical approach, other than to suggest a highly subjective examination of what seem to be patterns of image in word and action within a play. His insights are intriguing, but he occasionally goes too far, as when he claims that the appearance of others in the King's dress during battle indicates Bolingbroke's cowardice. What Winny calls Shakespeare's "creative energy" seems, if anything, directed at this point toward Henry's true honor in battle despite earlier crimes. In addition, Winny's heavy insistence that Shakespeare's primary interest was "literary" and not "political" seems unnecessary. Clearly the plays are a literary treatment of political issues. Winny may question Tillyard's divine providence theme and the relevance of contemporary political controversy to the plays, but he is obviously concerned with politics in a larger sense when he says that "a history-play . . . is concerned to show the underlying irony of historical political event" and when he speaks with reference to *Henry V* of "the point where uncertainty over established values tries to obtrude on Shakespeare's interest in man's political identity."

What we have learned about the inconsistency of characterization in Elizabethan drama has been largely ignored or submerged in these books. All take even a minor character's speech in one scene or situation as representative of that character's personality and position throughout the play. Sanders takes pains to show how the attractive Young Mortimer early in *Edward II* is consistent with that ruthless Machiavel late in the play, and Winny is angered by the shiftings of York in *Richard II*. Bevington correctly speaks of a "pattern of transferred sympathies" in *Richard II* "by which the barons are largely in the right until they reach the point of open defiance," but he does little more with this idea. The linking of political and intellectual debate to these plays has been immensely needed, but the direct leap to character or situation is questionable. More remains to be done in relating context and form in the drama of the period.

MICHAEL MANHEIM

The Elizabethan Theatre, ed. David Galloway. Toronto: Macmillan of Canada, 1969. Pp. xiv + 130. $5.50.

THIS BOOK celebrates a memorable event: the first International Conference on Elizabethan Theatre, held at the University of Waterloo, Ontario, in July, 1968, and under the gracious chairmanship of David Galloway. The essays in *The Elizabethan Theatre* were originally papers presented at the conference, but it is a pity that some of the questions and answers from the discussion period were not also included, as they were in the volumes of the earlier *Stratford Papers on Shakespeare*.

The Elizabethan Theatre concentrates on stage architecture and theatrical management. In this area, Herbert Berry's account of the tangled affairs of the playhouse in the Boar's Head Inn, Whitechapel, is the most characteristic essay in the collection. It is based on transcripts of law suits in the Public Record Office, and we see the Boar's Head Inn chiefly from the point of view of the unscrupulous moneylenders who controlled the destiny of its theater. Francis Langley, the former owner of the Swan and a notable dealer in cloudy titles, emerges as the villain of the piece and proves that a playwright did not need to look outside his own theater for griping usurers like Sir Giles Overreach. Berry's essay is leisurely and full, with each point carefully documented, but one detail seems tantalizingly undeveloped: "The playhouse in the Boar's Head, then, was probably rectangular, and its stage was on one of the long sides, the west. The arrangement is quite unusual in scholarly speculation about Elizabethan theatres, but apparently sensible enough from a theatrical point of view" (pp. 53–54). I am not convinced.

Richard Hosley's "A Reconstruction of the Second Blackfriars" deals almost exclusively with architectural matters, and it is supported by nine excellent line drawings by Richard Southern. This brief, speculative essay is a bravura performance in the art of analogical reasoning. Each step in the argument is taken on the basis of some known piece of evidence: for example, "In seeking to arrive at likely dimensions of the Blackfriars tiring-house we are aided by the analogue of the Fortune tiring-house" (p. 78); "The height of the Blackfriars stage may be set at 4 ft. 6 in. on the analogy of the stage at the Cockpit-in-Court (1630)" (p. 78); "A likely depth for the Blackfriars galleries can be established by the analogue available in Inigo Jones's plan of the scenic stage in the Great Hall at Whitehall in 1635" (pp. 82–83). The tightness and lucidity of the discussion conceal the fact that it is highly conjectural, but it is also highly imaginative and without the analogies there could be only the most meager reconstruction.

Also in the area of imaginative interpretation, Glynne Wickham's reading of the Privy Council order of 1597 for the destruction of all London's theaters shows that the implications of that document are almost the reverse of its literal meaning. Expropriation of theaters without compensation to the owners is almost unthinkable. After all, the Privy Council was no Latin American junta, and the rights of property owners in 1597 still prevailed over mere ideology. Once we grant Wickham's view of the Privy Council order, some of his wider generalizations are puzzling, especially within the compass of a short essay. I do not see how the 1597 edict in itself "spelt the end of a predominantly amateur and casual theatre and the start of the strictly professional and commercial theatre that we know" (p. 21). Or why are there "very strong reasons for supposing that after 1597 any playhouse licensed and built for 'public playing' must have borne a close relationship in its stage and scenic devices to conditions of performance normal at court" (p. 44)? Can this be supported, for example, in plays presented both at court and in a public theater, or is the opposite true?

D. F. Rowan's discussion of the Cockpit-in-Court does much to sustain the professional tone of this volume. The presentation assumes a wide knowledge of the subject, so that special questions about the existence of an inner or upper stage may be broached without any preliminaries. I am disappointed that Rowan did not pursue further his startling observations about Inigo Jones's drawings for the Cockpit-in-Court. Apparently, despite the classical façade, it "was not, as had been generally believed, a classical, 'coterie' theatre for elegant amateurs, but was, in fact, a traditional, 'popular' theatre for experienced professionals, which only happened to be located at Court" (p. 96). I would have been delighted to see these points developed in the context of other Elizabethan and Renaissance theaters.

I admire Clifford Leech's learned and original essay, "The Function of Locality in the Plays of Shakespeare and His Contemporaries," but it doesn't seem relevant to the topic of the conference in the same way that the contributions of Berry, Hosley, Wickham, and Rowan are. Despite Leech's strong protest against the scene-heading places of eighteenth-century editors, he too seems to be thinking of locality as an actual scene rather than as a setting in the mind's eye. In *Antony and Cleopatra,* for example, Leech argues that Shakespeare avoids alternating the action between Alexandria and Rome "by giving us scenes at Misenum, on Pompey's galley, at Athens, on a plain in Asia Minor . . . , and at Actium" (p. 110). But the scenes supposed to be set near Misenum

(II.vi,vii) and Athens (III.iv,v) say not one word at all about either of these places; the location has been inferred by editors from the relevant passages in Plutarch. One may also protest that the scenes near Actium convey no feeling at all that one may visualize the promontory in Acarnania on the west coast of Greece to the south of the Bay of Previsa (39° north latitude, 21° east longitude). Some of Granville-Barker's strictures on Chambers are relevant here (see "A Note upon Chapters XX. and XXI. of *The Elizabethan Stage*," *RES*, I [1925], 67–71).

The same problem is raised by Leech's comment on *Hamlet:* "We have seen that we are at Elsinore throughout the play, almost always within the castle walls, but here if ever we have a play for which a modern edition ought to include a map of Europe" (p. 113). This may be a useful scholarly tool, but what has this kind of localization to do with the Elizabethan theater? In what sense could the staging demonstrate that we are "almost always within the castle walls"? I must confess, therefore, that I don't see much theatrical value in the full tabulation of localities in Elizabethan plays (with supplementary maps) that Leech calls for at the end of his essay. This endeavor puts an undue emphasis on locality as a tangible, geographical entity apart from the limitations of playhouse performance.

I have left for last the papers of T. J. B. Spencer and Terence Hawkes, since they both serve the self-conscious function of introduction and postscript. Spencer offers a witty, urbane, and perceptive consideration of "Shakespeare: The Elizabethan Theatre-Poet," with apt supporting passages. Shakespeare is seen in the perspective of Shakespearean criticism, which becomes part of a larger cultural history. Spencer also raises interesting questions about the drama as a genre with its own special requirements. When Shakespeare writes poems for his characters, he "shows exceptional skill in giving them, not good poems, but perfectly appropriate poems" (p. 9). This functionalism raises one of the central difficulties for literary criticism in dealing with a "Theatre-Poet."

Terence Hawkes's postscript, "Theatre Against Shakespeare?" was first presented as an after-dinner speech, but its bantering tone should not conceal its messianic impulse to revitalize the Shakespearean theater. As Hawkes also noted in his controversial BBC talk, "Stamp out Live Theatre," modern productions of Shakespeare tend to be the repository of " 'official' or 'formal,' and certainly 'literary,' middle-class culture in our society." "In these circumstances, the play *Hamlet* becomes, as it were, a dramatization of the book" (p. 123). Hawkes's essay is adventurous but tentative. Only "live theatre," he says, can rescue Shakespeare from the stranglehold of the Establishment and assert his connection with a popular, oral tradition, but it is difficult to know what sort of "live theatre" Hawkes has in mind, or whether it has actually come alive yet.

As a participant at the second International Conference on Elizabethan Theatre in July of 1969, I can attest to the ceremonial nature of the occasion, which can only be imperfectly conveyed in a book of collected papers. Under the clear blue skies of Ontario at the height of the cherry harvest, the conferees were made to feel a New World expansiveness about their proceedings. In many subtle ways, the context contributed to the content. The University of Waterloo proudly displayed its new, pagoda-like library open twenty-four hours a day (and thus, like a hospital, able to provide emergency service); a student activities building really run by students and dispensing to all uninterrupted music and an unlimited supply of birth control handbooks; and a parking lot in which the highest administrative officers of the university had only recently removed their name-plates from their no longer reserved parking places. This heady atmosphere and the proximity to the Shakespeare Theatre at Stratford (as well as to the historic Blue Moon Inn in Petersburg) helped to give the conference a sense of intellectual euphoria. We look forward to a long series of these festival celebrations, with their accompanying volumes of essays.

MAURICE CHARNEY

Notes on Contributors

N. W. BAWCUTT teaches at the University of Liverpool and has recently
published articles on Marlowe, Foxe, and Chapman. He has edited
Middleton and Rowley's *The Changeling, The Shorter Poems and
Translations of Sir Richard Fanshawe,* and John Ford's *'Tis Pity She's
a Whore.*

LIENHARD BERGEL, of the City University of New York, is the author of a
recent survey report on "The State of Comparative Literature in the
United States." He has contributed previously to *Renaissance Drama.*

MAURICE CHARNEY has written *Shakespeare's Roman Plays* and *Style in
Hamlet.* He is Professor of English at Rutgers University.

BRUCE GOLDEN teaches in the English Department at California State
College, San Bernardino. He is currently preparing a study of tragedy
in England and Spain during the Renaissance.

MICHAEL HATTAWAY, of the University of Kent at Canterbury, has written
on "Marlowe and Brecht."

ROBERT JORDAN is a Senior Lecturer in English at the University of
Queensland, Australia. He is currently co-editing the works of Thomas
Southerne for the Clarendon Press.

JOEL H. KAPLAN teaches at Ithaca College and has published articles on Medieval and Renaissance drama, including "Virtue's Holiday: Thomas Dekker and Simon Eyre," in *Renaissance Drama,* N.S. II, (1969). He is currently working on a book on Jacobean comedy.

R. J. KAUFMANN, of the University of Texas, is the author of *Richard Brome, Caroline Playwright.* He has edited collections of essays on the Elizabethan drama and on G. B. Shaw.

MICHAEL MANHEIM, Professor of English at the University of Toledo, has written on the English history play in *Renaissance Drama,* N.S. II, (1969).

D. F. McKENZIE is Professor of English at Victoria University of Wellington, New Zealand. He is the author of *The Cambridge University Press, 1696–1712.* His "Printers of the Mind: Some Notes on Bibliographical Theories and Printing-House Practices" appeared recently in *Studies in Bibliography.*

MICHAEL NEILL is a member of the English Department at the University of Auckland, New Zealand, and has written on "Ford and Gainsford."

CLAUS UHLIG, Lecturer in English at the University of Hamburg, has published articles on Shakespeare and Spenser, and is the author of *Traditionelle Denkformen in Shakespeares tragischer Kunst.*

ANN WIERUM is attached to the Humanities Library at Washington State University.

Books Received

BARTHOLOMEUSZ, DENNIS. *Macbeth and the Players*. Cambridge, Eng.: Cambridge University Press, 1969. Pp. xv + 302. $10.50.

BEAUMONT, FRANCIS, and FLETCHER, JOHN. *The Maid's Tragedy*, ed. HOWARD B. NORLAND. Regents Renaissance Drama. Lincoln: University of Nebraska Press, 1968. Pp. xxviii + 136. $1.65 (paper).

————. *The Maid's Tragedy*, ed. ANDREW GURR. Fountainwell Drama Texts. Berkeley: University of California Press, 1969. Pp. 123. $1.65 (paper).

BRADBROOK, M. C. *Elizabethan Stage Conditions: A Study of Their Place in the Interpretation of Shakespeare's Plays*. Cambridge, Eng.: Cambridge University Press, 1968. Pp. ix + 149. $4.95 (paper, $1.65). (Originally published 1932.)

CHARNEY, MAURICE. *Style in* Hamlet. Princeton: Princeton University Press, 1969. Pp. xxii + 333. $9.00.

The Drama of the Renaissance: Essays for Leicester Bradner, ed. ELMER M. BLISTEIN. Providence: Brown University Press, 1970. Pp. xiii + 199. $7.00.

FITCH, ROBERT E. *Shakespeare: The Perspective of Value*. Philadelphia: The Westminster Press, 1969. Pp. 304. $3.50 (paper).

HABICHT, WERNER. *Studien zur Dramenform vor Shakespeare*. Anglistische Forschungen, Heft 96. Heidelberg: Carl Winter, Universitätsverlag, 1968. Pp. 259. DM 36 (paper).

JONDORF, GILLIAN. *Robert Garnier and the Themes of Political Tragedy in the Sixteenth Century.* Cambridge, Eng.: Cambridge University Press, 1969. Pp. viii + 162. $6.00.

LEVIN, HARRY. *The Myth of the Golden Age in the Renaissance.* Bloomington: University of Indiana Press, 1969. Pp. xxiv + 231. $6.95.

LODGE, THOMAS. *The Wounds of Civil War,* ed. JOSEPH W. HOUPPERT. Regents Renaissance Drama. Lincoln: University of Nebraska Press, 1969. Pp. xxi + 115. $4.75 (paper, $1.65).

LYLY, JOHN. *Gallathea* and *Midas,* ed. ANNE BEGOR LANCASHIRE. Regents Renaissance Drama. Lincoln: University of Nebraska Press, 1969. Pp. xxxi + 174. $1.65 (paper).

McMANAWAY, JAMES G. *Studies in Shakespeare, Bibliography, and Theater,* ed. RICHARD HOSLEY, ARTHUR C. KIRSCH, and JOHN W. VELZ. New York: The Shakespeare Association of America, 1969. Pp. xvi + 417.

MARKELS, JULIAN. *The Pillar of the World.* Antony and Cleopatra *in Shakespeare's Development.* Columbus: Ohio State University Press, 1968. Pp. 191. $6.00.

MARSH, D. R. C. *The Recurring Miracle: A Study of* Cymbeline *and the Last Plays.* Lincoln: University of Nebraska Press, 1969. Pp. 197. $1.95 (paper). (Originally published 1962.)

MASSINGER, PHILIP, and FIELD, NATHAN. *The Fatal Dowry,* ed. T. A. DUNN. Fountainwell Drama Texts. Berkeley: University of California Press, 1969. Pp. 115. $1.65 (paper).

MIDDLETON, THOMAS. *A Chaste Maid in Cheapside,* ed. CHARLES BARBER. Fountainwell Drama Texts. Berkeley: University of California Press, 1969. Pp. 115. $1.65 (paper).

————. *Women Beware Women,* ed. CHARLES BARBER. Fountainwell Drama Texts. Berkeley: University of California Press, 1969. Pp. 136. $1.80 (paper).

RADCLIFF-UMSTEAD, DOUGLAS. *The Birth of Modern Comedy in Renaissance Italy.* Chicago: University of Chicago Press, 1969. Pp. ix + 285. $12.50.

SACCIO, PETER. *The Court Comedies of John Lyly: A Study in Allegorical Dramaturgy.* Princeton: Princeton University Press, 1969. Pp. vii + 233. $6.95.

The Seventeenth-Century Stage: A Collection of Critical Essays, ed. GERALD EADES BENTLEY. Chicago: University of Chicago Press, 1968. Pp. xvi + 287. $9.75 (paper, $3.45).

SHAKESPEARE, WILLIAM. *The Complete Works,* ed. ALFRED HARBAGE. The Pelican Text Revised. Baltimore: Penguin Books, 1969. Pp. xxx + 1481. $15.00.

————. *Antony and Cleopatra,* ed. C. J. GIANAKARIS. The Blackfriars Shakespeare. Dubuque: Wm. C. Brown Company, 1969. Pp. xvi + 89. $1.25 (paper).

Shakespeare's Contemporaries, ed. MAX BLUESTONE and NORMAN RABKIN. Second edition. Modern Studies in English Renaissance Drama. Englewood Cliffs: Prentice-Hall, Inc., 1970. Pp. xx + 411. $6.95 (paper, $4.95).

Shakespeare Survey 21: Othello. *With a Comprehensive General Index to Surveys 11–20,* ed. KENNETH MUIR. Cambridge, Eng.: Cambridge University Press. Pp. ix + 219. $7.50.

SHIRE, HELENA MENNIE. *Song, Dance and Poetry of the Court of Scotland under King James VI.* Cambridge, Eng.: Cambridge University Press, 1969. Pp. xi + 285. $18.50.

STUBBINGS, HILDA U. *Renaissance Spain in its Literary Relations with England and France: A Critical Bibliography.* Nashville: Vanderbilt University Press, 1969. Pp. xv + 138. $6.00.

SWINBURNE, ALGERNON CHARLES. *A Study of Ben Jonson,* ed. HOWARD B. NORLAND. Lincoln: University of Nebraska Press, 1969. Pp. xxxi + 212. $2.25 (paper).

TIRSO DE MOLINA. *La Venganza de Tamar,* ed. A. K. G. PATERSON. Cambridge, Eng.: Cambridge University Press, 1969. Pp. vii + 150. $3.75.